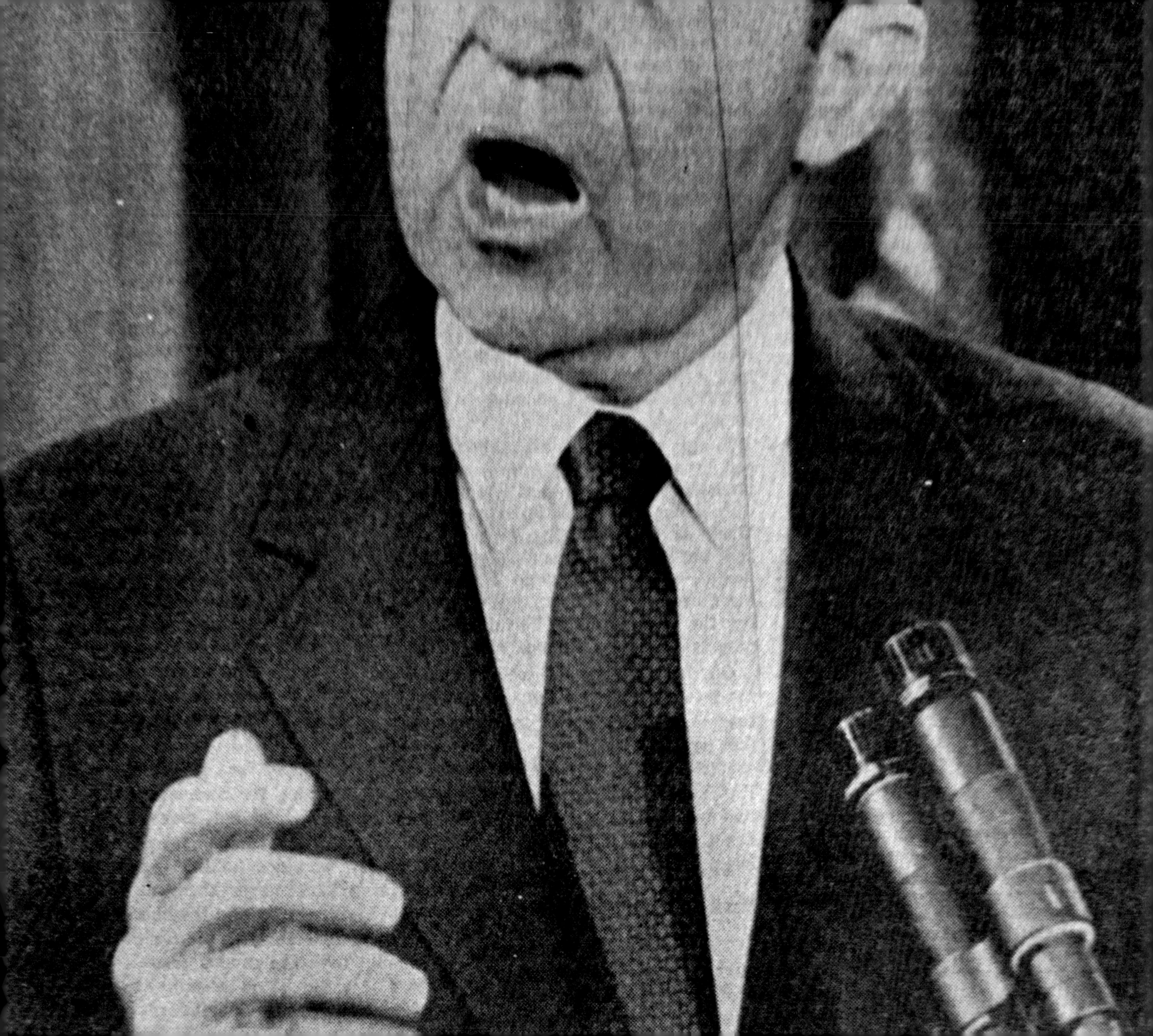

WORDS AND IMAGES FROM THE AMERICAN MEDIA

DONALD BLUMBERG

With an introduction by Jock Reynolds

Yale University Art Gallery
New Haven

Distributed by Yale University Press
New Haven and London

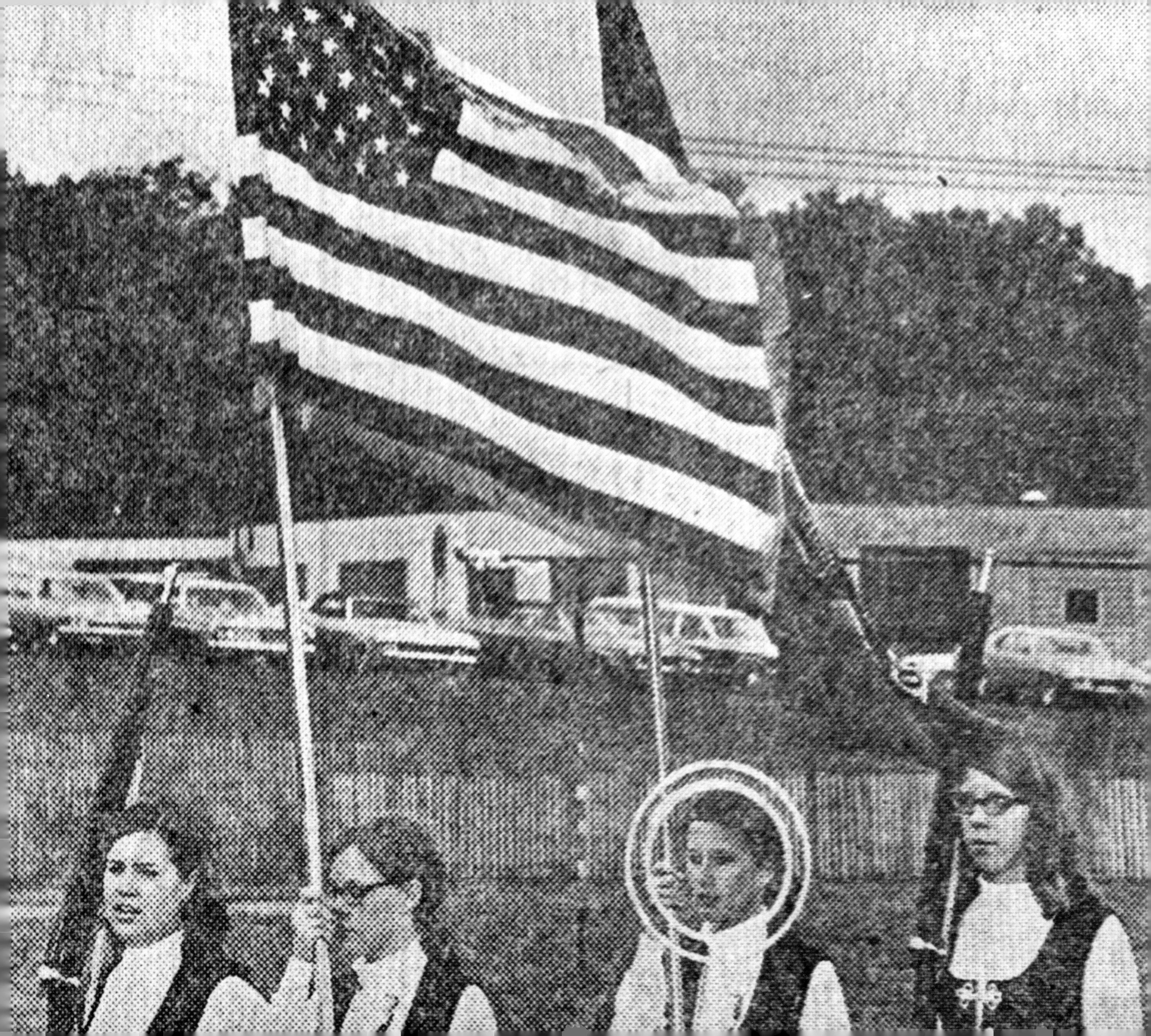

INTRODUCTION
Jock Reynolds

Over the last few years, photographer Donald Blumberg's master sets have come to reside at the Yale University Art Gallery, where curators, faculty members, and students have begun to engage this very large and diverse body of work that was created over some fifty-five years. Now, the Gallery presents a major exhibition of Blumberg's photographs and two accompanying publications: the present volume and *In Front of Saint Patrick's Cathedral: A New Edition*, a revised edition of the long-out-of-print 1973 artist's book through which Blumberg's art—its conceptual rigor, serial poetic logic, and visual beauty—first captured attention.

This new book, *Words and Images from the American Media*, presents a very different body of work than *Saint Patrick's*. The array of projects included here were created during two very distinct periods of time—the late 1960s and the second decade of the twenty-first century—and while some of the photographs are well known, others have never before been published or exhibited. Taken together, they illustrate Blumberg's sustained interest in how words and images can be combined via the medium of black-and-white photography to offer an arresting portrait of American culture—one that is at times highly humorous and darkly satirical, and deeply poignant.

Blumberg was born in 1935, when radio stations and daily newspapers were the dominant form of mass-media communication. The Great Depression–era broadcasts of Franklin D. Roosevelt's "fireside chats" remain memorable in this respect, as do the leading radio commenters and newspaper columnists of that time, such as Edward R. Murrow. But televisions would soon become ubiquitous: it was just one year before Blumberg was born, in 1934, that electronic television sets with cathode-ray tubes were first manufactured. Two years later, in 1936—on the tenth anniversary of the National Broadcasting System (NBC)—the electronics company RCA held a press conference in New York to make its first public demonstration of what was considered at the time to be a high-definition TV: the 343-line television. Meanwhile, as film companies and magazines also began their ascendancy, Henry Luce stepped forward to claim that the use of photography in his new *Life* magazine would allow its readers "to see life, to see the world; to eyewitness great events . . . to see and be amazed." He backed up this assertion by hiring some of the greatest photographers then at work in America.

Although World War II caused a rupture in the development of commercial television, by the time Blumberg was twelve years old, in 1947, RCA had placed some ten thousand of its new black-and-white television sets in American homes. That year, Harry S. Truman became the first president to address the nation via television from the White House, the nationally broadcast television news program *Meet the Press* debuted, and the *Howdy Doody* show began to air on weekday afternoons to entertain American children at the end of their school days. Only a year later, four television networks were broadcasting nationally via twenty-seven stations located in eighteen cities, and by 1950, there were almost ten million TVs in American homes.

Once the technology was in place, the popularity and frequency of television broadcasts skyrocketed. By the time Blumberg reached adulthood, having completed two years of study at Hunter College before volunteering to join the U.S. Army in 1955, the Army–McCarthy Congressional hearings held in the U.S. Senate—investigating Senator Joseph McCarthy's now-fabled Communist witch hunt—were presented in a live national television broadcast that was viewed by millions of Americans. In 1961, when President John F. Kennedy held his first live televised news conference, some sixty-eight million television sets tuned in from American homes and businesses. Yet as rapidly as television consumed American culture, it was not always embraced with open arms. Then-chairman of the Federal Communications Commission Newton Minow claimed that television was nothing but a "vast wasteland," and in a good number of American homes, parents began exercising strict limits on their children's television viewing, dubbing the new focal point of their living and family rooms the "idiot box."

This is the era in which Blumberg came of age. By 1968–70, the years during which Blumberg hit his stride as a mature young artist, the political career of President Lyndon B. Johnson was in tatters, the Vietnam War was raging, and the civil rights movement was surging. The assassinations of Martin Luther King, Jr., and Senator Robert F. Kennedy had traumatized the nation, and Richard Nixon was elected president. These events and more are reflected in the series of black-and-white photographs that Blumberg began making directly from television screens and daily newspapers for his projects *Television Abstractions* (1968–69), *Television Political Mosaics* (1968–69), and *Daily Photographs* (1969–70). The resulting photographs—which, in the case of *Television Political Mosaics*, he sometimes printed in the form of composite prints with many images merged to create a single work—beckon viewers to sustain a closer and longer look at some of the most consequential content being broadcast on TV and printed in newspapers at the time. Although Blumberg clearly loves his country deeply, as a vigilant and concerned citizen he has always been willing to critique it as well—its politics, its excessive consumerism, and some of its citizens' questionable cultural values. The *Daily Photographs* series, for example, includes newspaper stories dealing with the highly charged political, social, religious, and commercial agendas surrounding the Vietnam War. The photographs, which he also published in the form of an inexpensive broadside in 1971, were all derived from major newspapers in Buffalo or New York City. They present especially poignant images, such as a group of schoolchildren saluting the American flag, four mothers visiting the White House whose sons were killed in the war, and missing or deceased servicemen.

Blumberg recognized that a good deal of this important visual and textual content often evaporates once a broadcast concludes for the night or a newspaper ends up wrapping fish or lining a trash can. The photographs Blumberg created for these projects offer an opportunity to slow down and carefully examine how the media communicates with us, through an ever-expanding daily feed. The content that these outlets produce constitutes, in some respect, our complex communal sense of reality, one that can either be pondered passively or with some degree of critical attention.

Almost fifty years later, in the second decade of the twenty-first century, Blumberg once again, in the span of a few short years, intensively focused his creative attention on the American media's use of language and images. From the late 1960s to today, television programming has grown exponentially. No longer are there just a handful of networks and channels to view; instead, hundreds of them beckon for attention twenty-four hours a day. Gone is the late-night "snow" that once appeared on television screens when the first commercial stations went off the air during nighttime hours. Today, television viewers need not even rise from a couch or bed to change the channel but instead can simply push a button on the now-ubiquitous remote control to instantly surf a vast array of programming. All kinds of interests, beliefs, and desires have been carefully organized into individual networks, with political, social, religious, and commercial content viewable at any moment in time according to individual tastes.

But how are any of us making sense of the vast barrage of words and images? And how is this roiling surge of content affecting our minds, values, and lives? It is questions such as these that have prompted Blumberg to create the later photographic projects in this book: *In Their Own Words* (2011–12), *Newtown School Massacre* (2012), *Before and After* (2013), *I Have to Have It* (2013), and *UFC Fighting Television Images* (2014). Interestingly, in almost all of these photographs he has included the closed-captioning texts that accompany the programs, language that anyone can summon on their television screens via the use of a remote control. Blumberg photographs his screen directly at "decisive moments"—selecting these moments when the words and images, taken out of context, are especially unnerving or revelatory, then asking his viewers to quietly contemplate multiple possible narratives of contemporary American culture.

Blumberg's keen interest in including language in his photographic images actually hearkens back to some of the earliest photographs he made on the streets of New York between 1961 and 1965 (see, for example, the illustrations that follow this essay). It was images such as these that first began to convey the artist's interest in how a well-trained eye directing a camera could, with caring discernment, focus attention on conditions of urban poverty, the early advertising campaigns of Madison Avenue, strained labor relations, the burgeoning American civil rights movement, and the onset and escalation of the Vietnam War. Blumberg's essay in this publication, edited from a much larger memoir he is currently working on with his wife of over fifty-five years, Grace, discusses his early experiences with these topics and how he became a photographer. His creative work continues well into its sixth decade, produced with great thoughtfulness and visual clarity, and here at the Gallery, his master sets will continue to be made available for further exhibition and publication, his inquisitive eye inspiring generations to come.

New York City, 1961-63

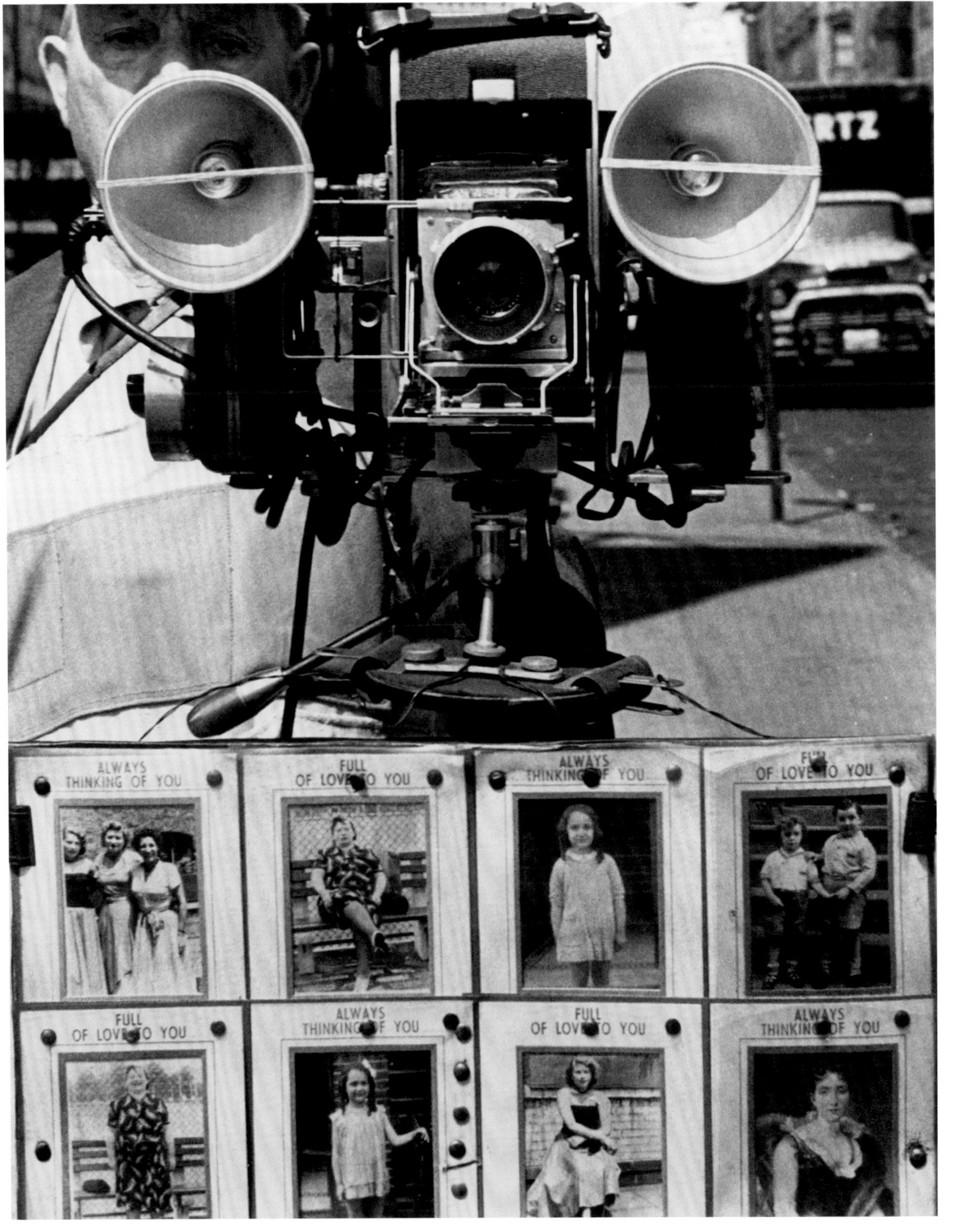
ALWAYS
THINKING OF YOU
FULL
OF LOVE TO YOU
ALWAYS
THINKING OF YOU
FULL
OF LOVE TO YOU
FULL
OF LOVE TO YOU
ALWAYS
THINKING OF YOU
FULL
OF LOVE TO YOU
ALWAYS
THINKING OF YOU

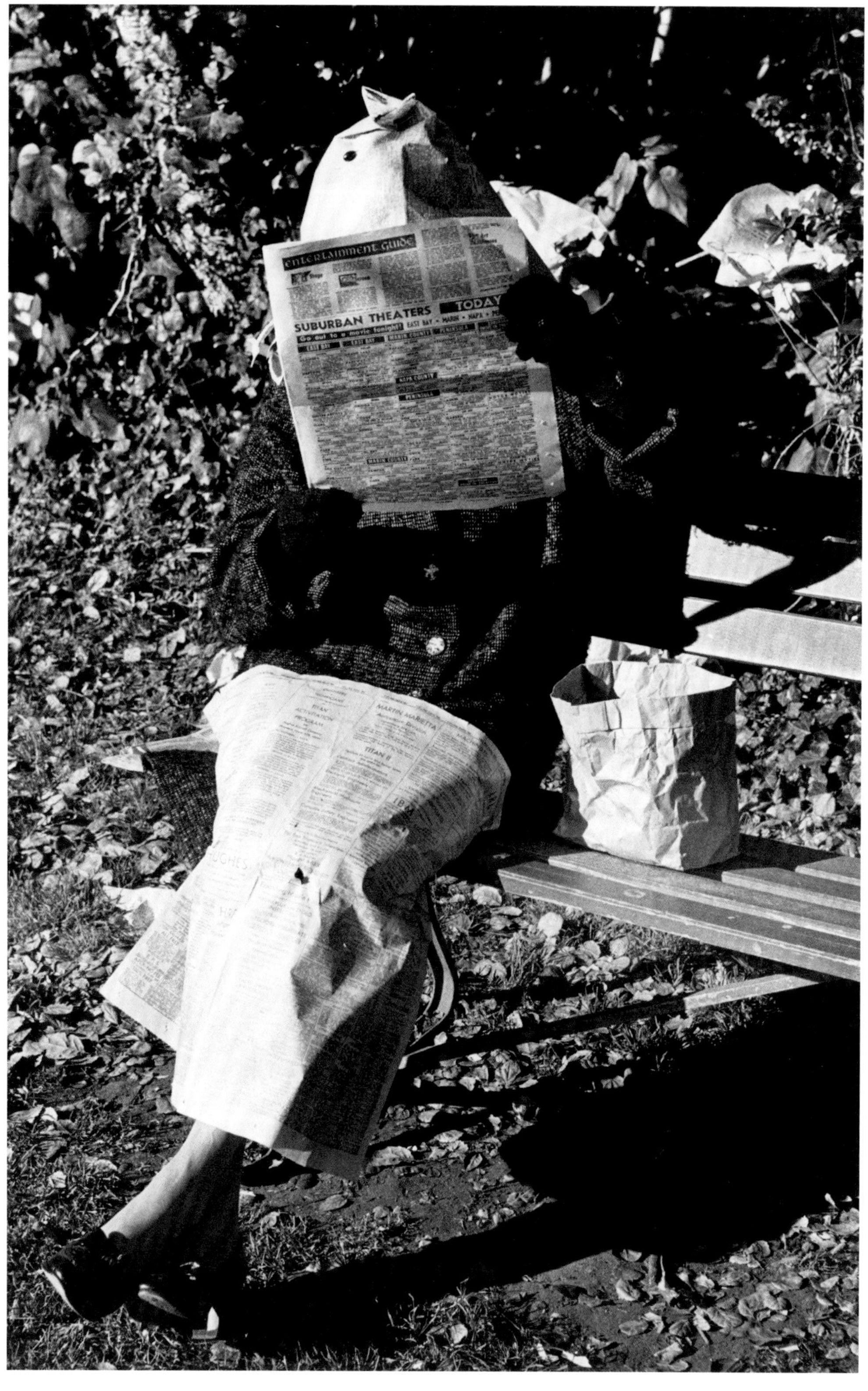

entertainment guide
SUBURBAN THEATERS
TODAY

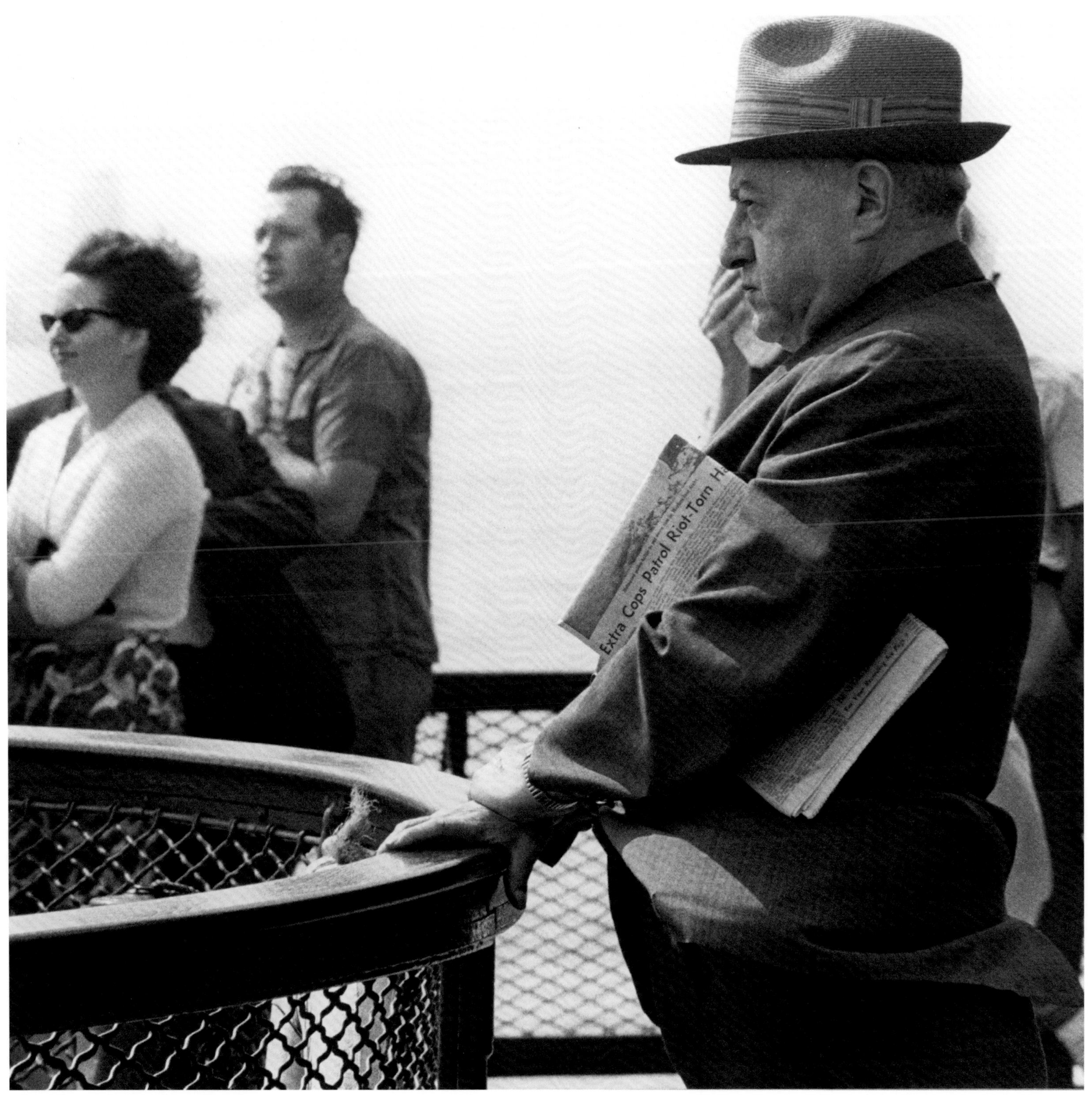
Extra Cops Patrol Riot-Torn H

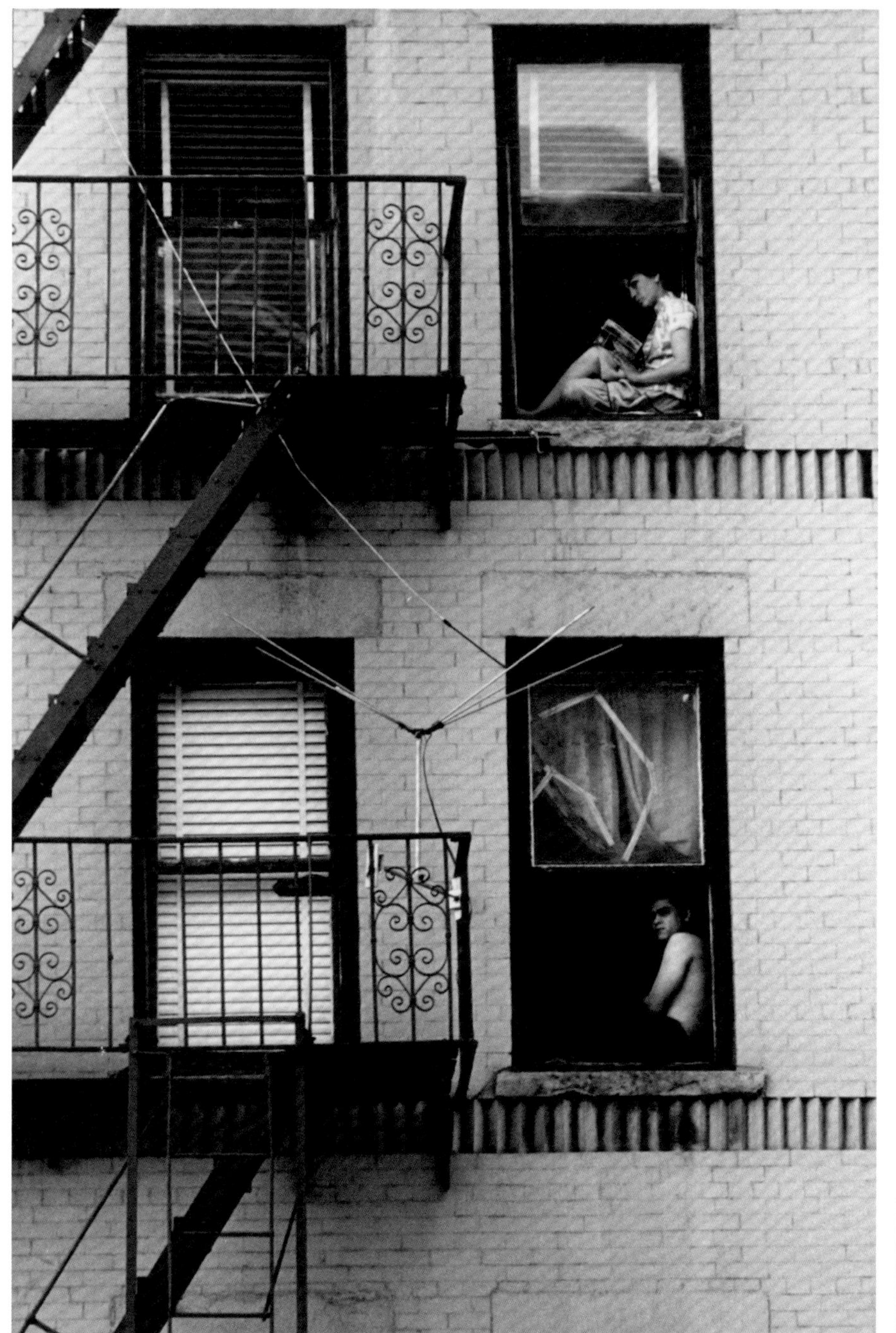
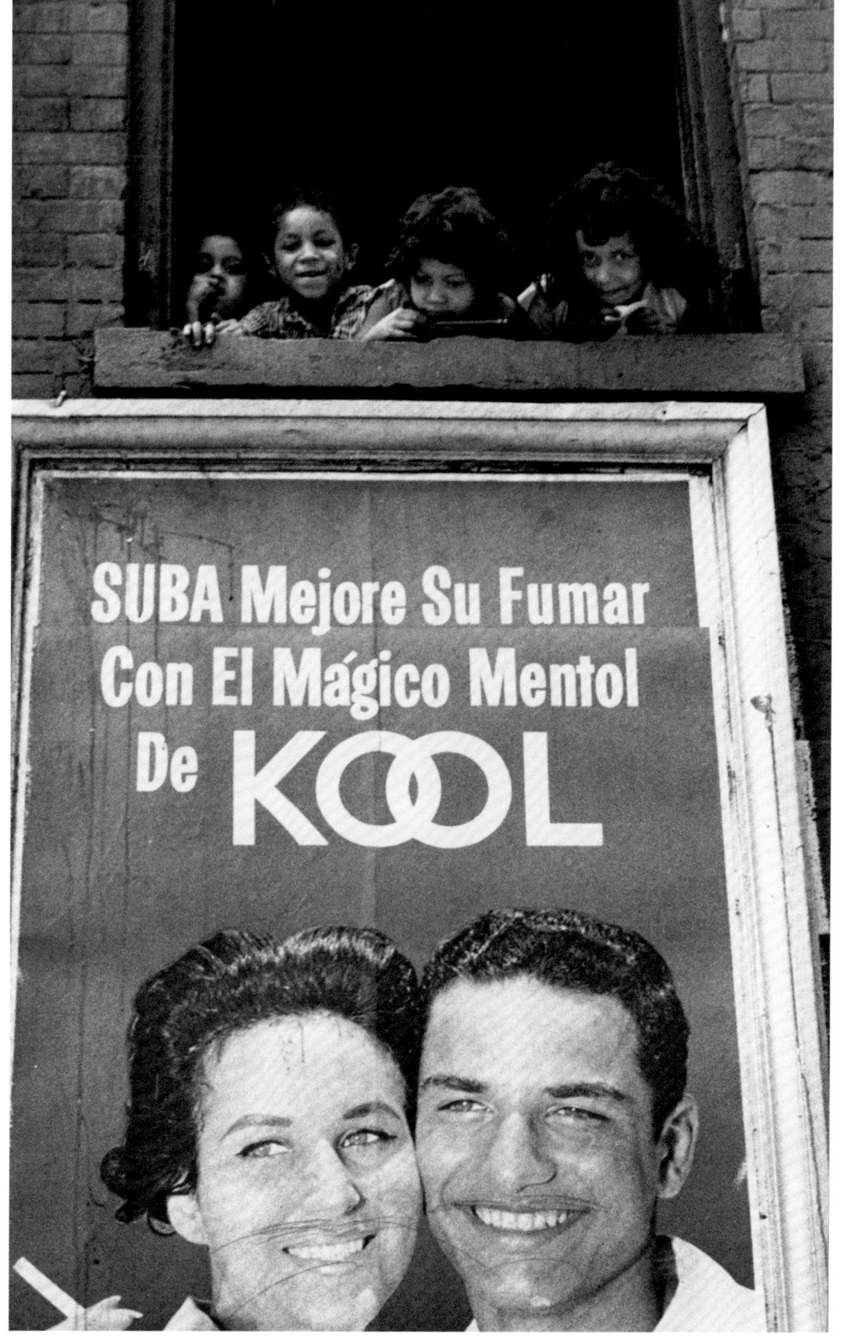

SUBA Mejore Su Fumar
Con El Mágico Mentol
De KOOL

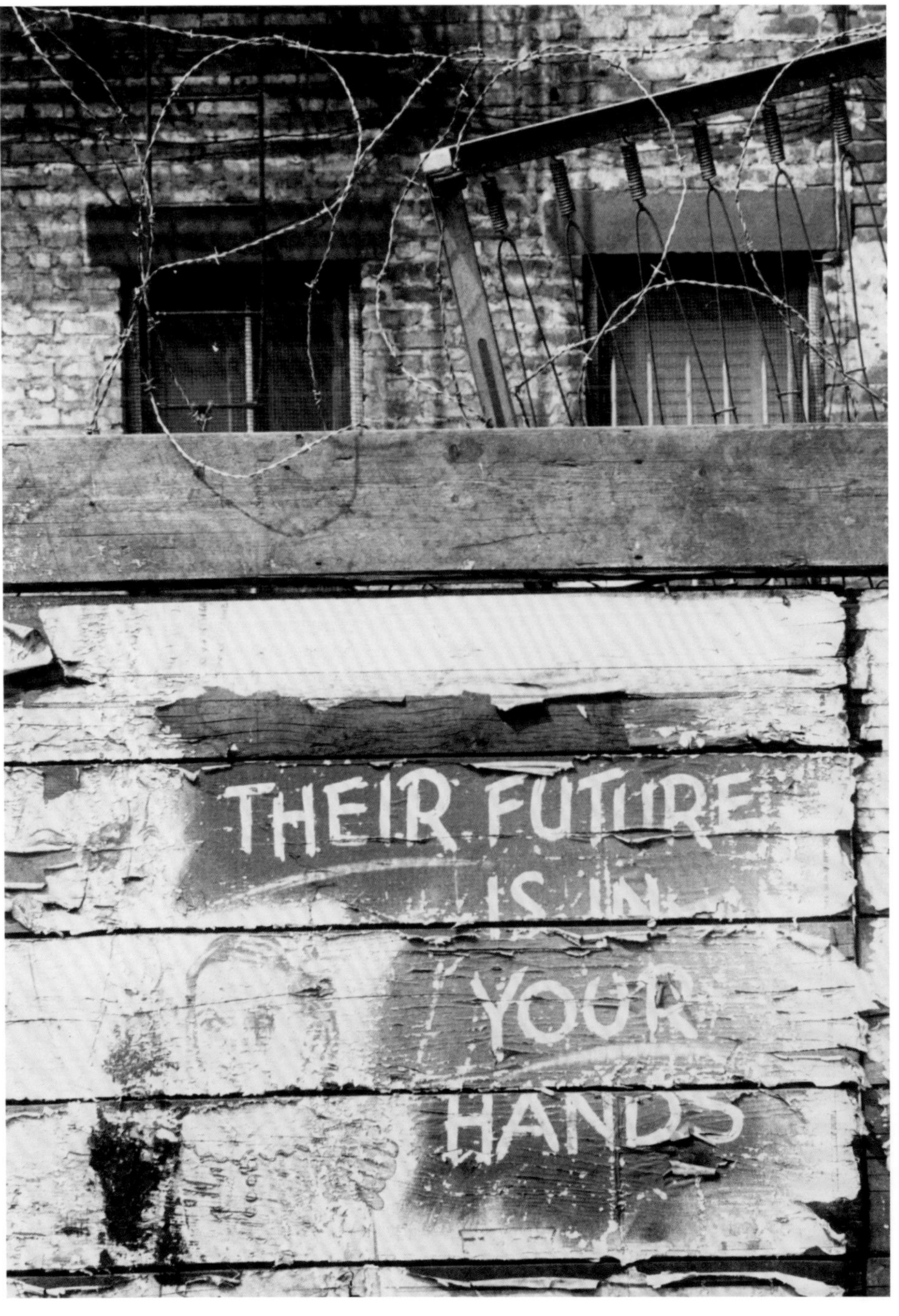

THEIR FUTURE
IS IN
YOUR
HANDS

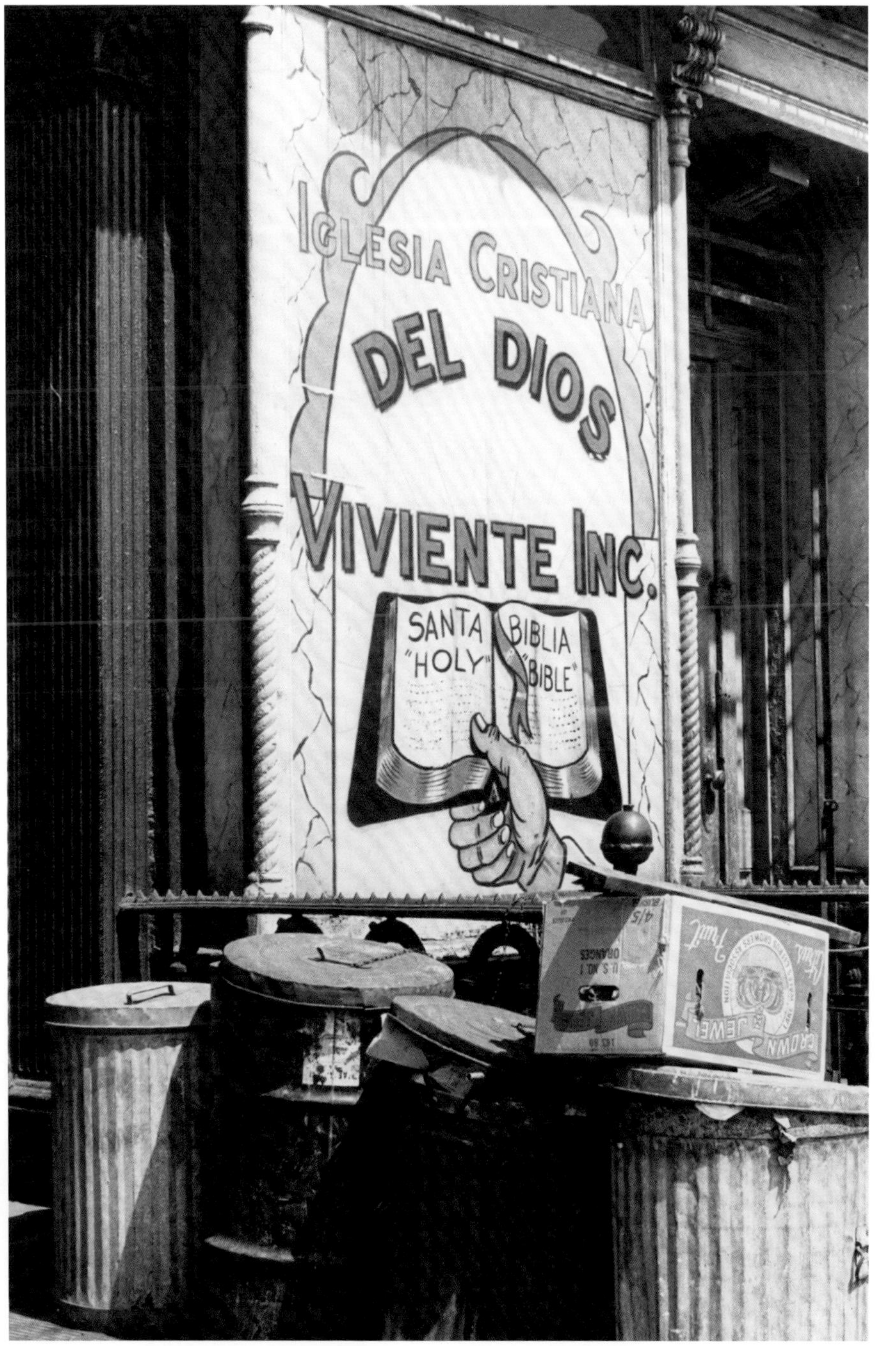

IGLESIA CRISTIANA
DEL DIOS
VIVIENTE Inc.
SANTA
"HOLY"
BIBLIA
"BIBLE"

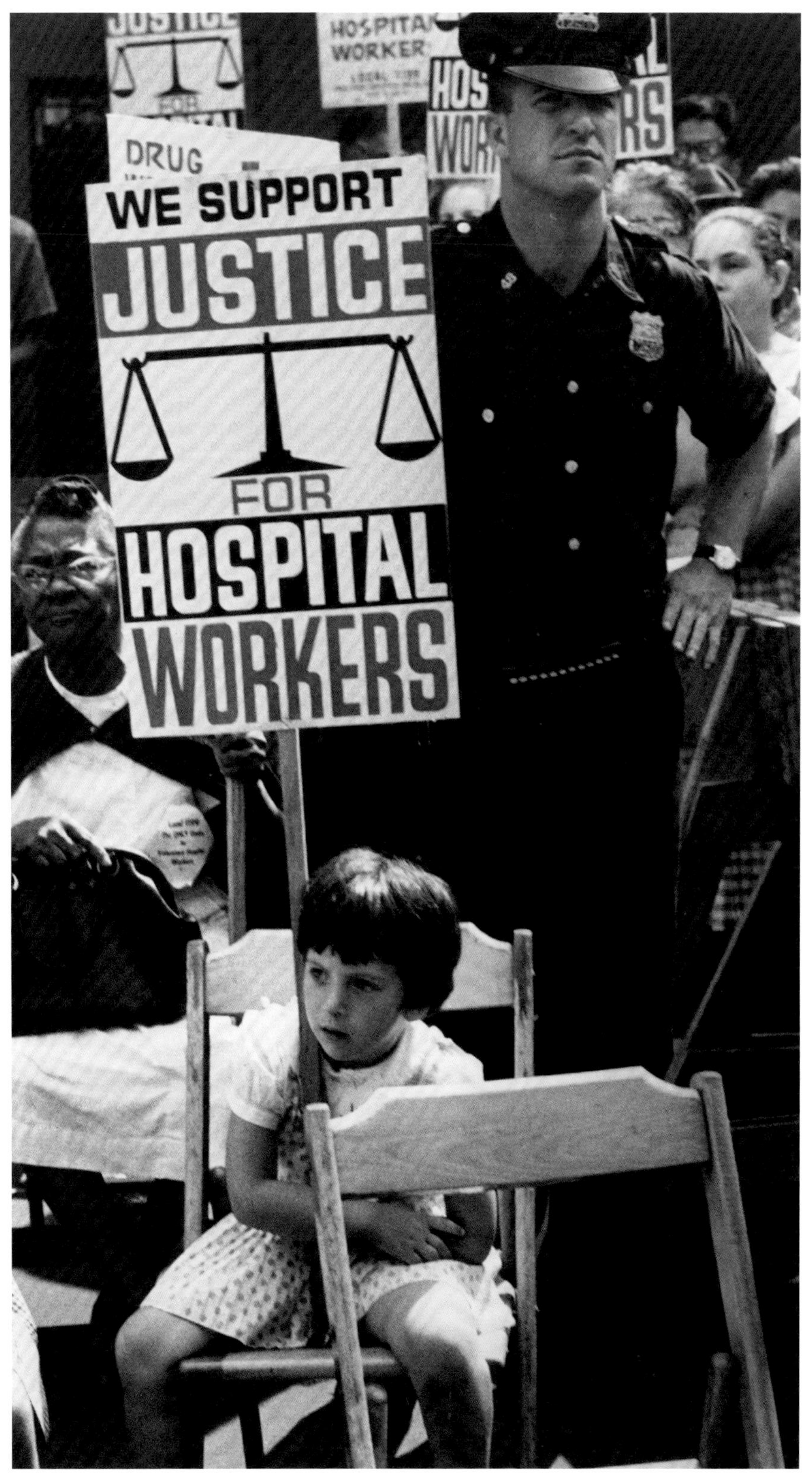

WE SUPPORT
JUSTICE
FOR
HOSPITAL
WORKERS
DRUG
JUSTICE
HOSPITAL
WORKER
LOCAL

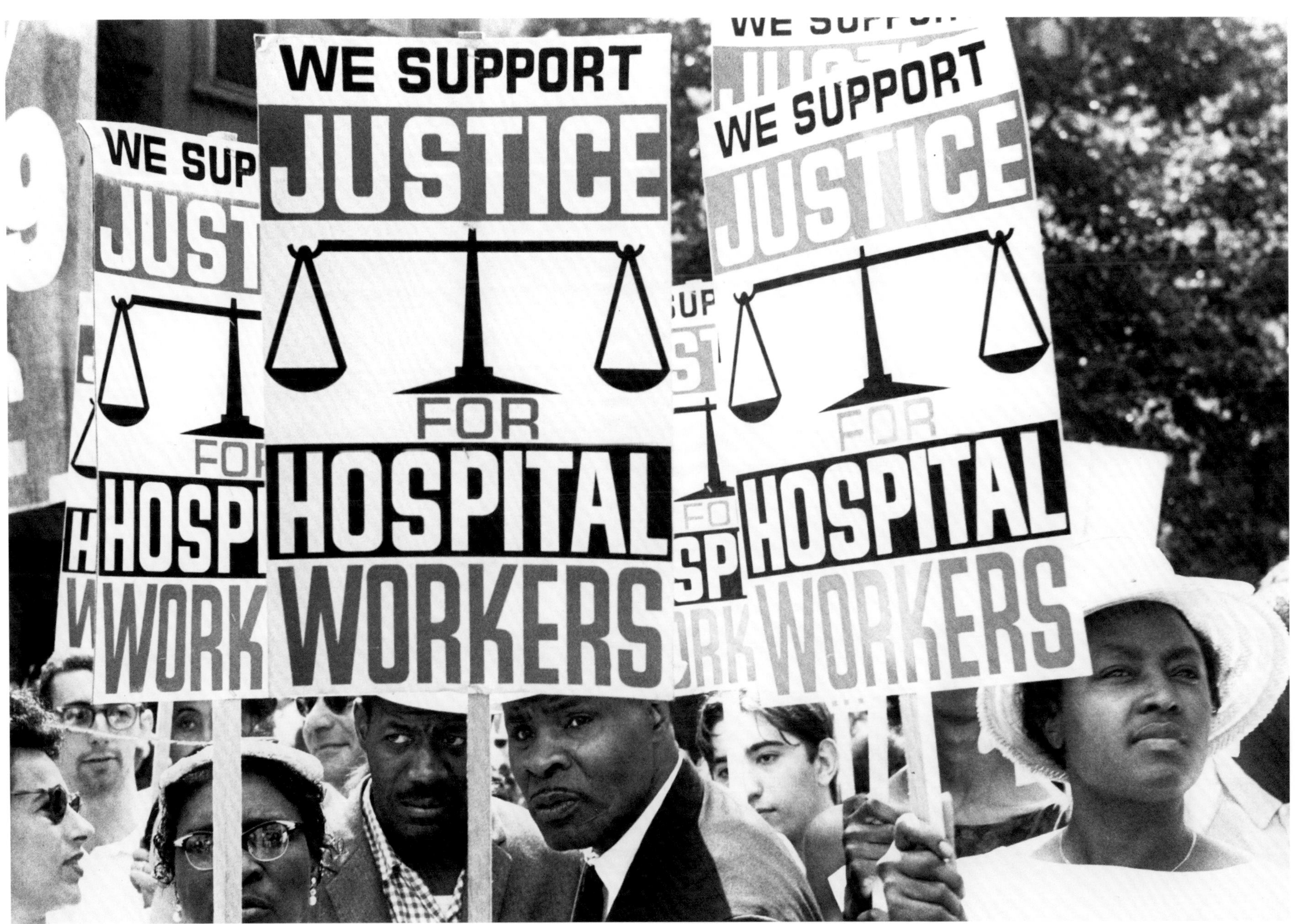
WE SUPPORT
JUSTICE
FOR
HOSPITAL
WORKERS

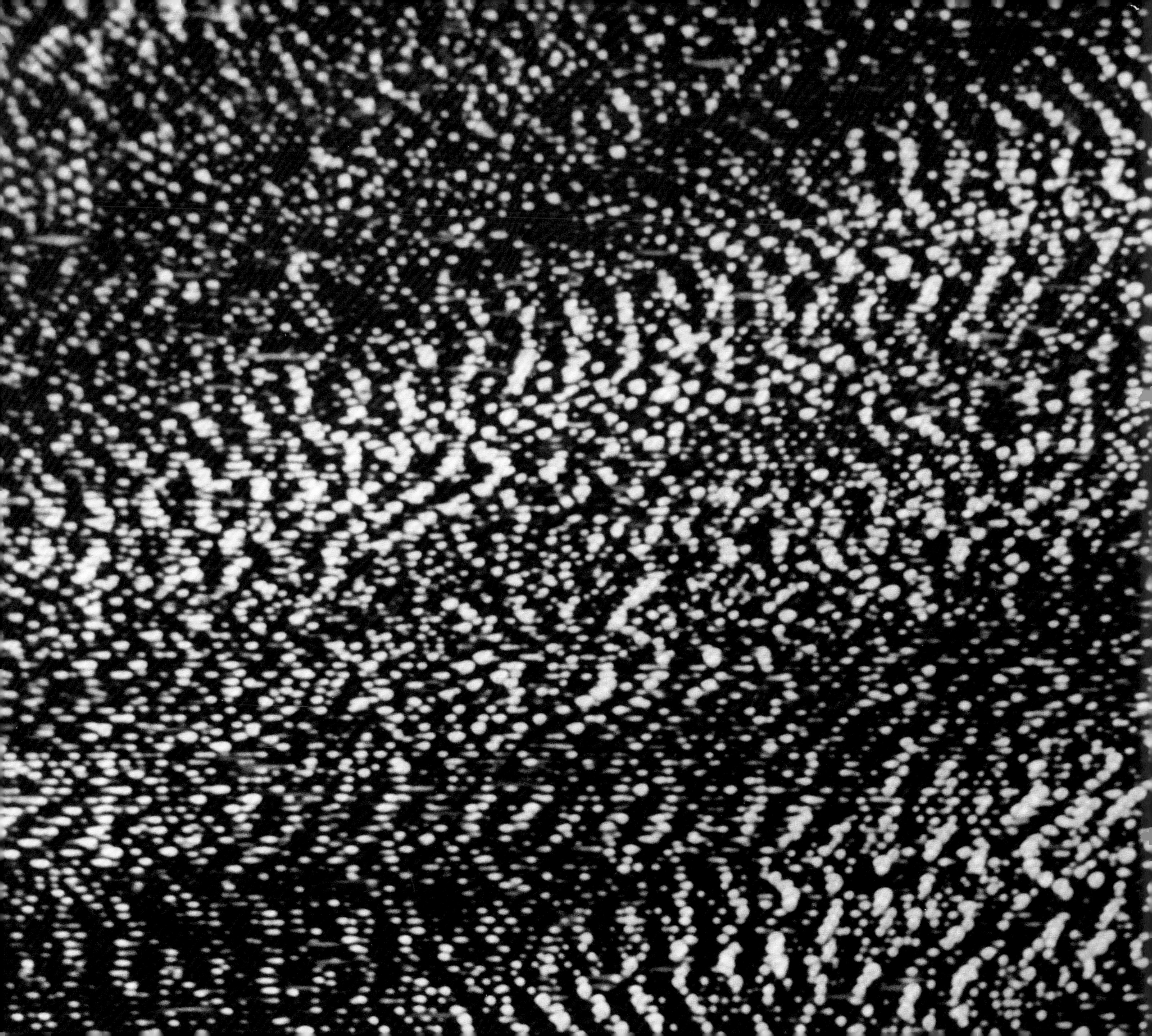

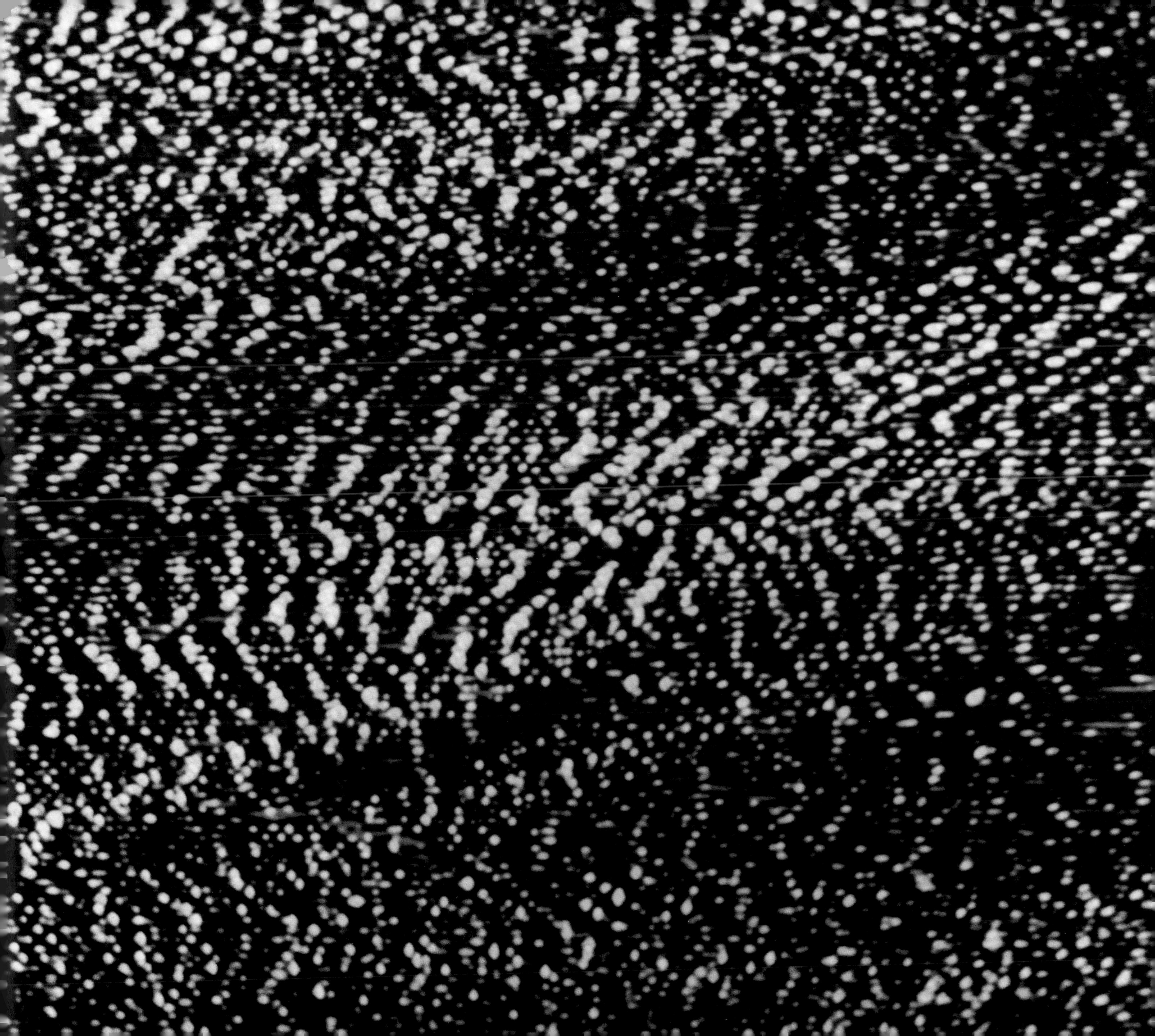

Television Abstractions and *Television Political Mosaics*, 1968-69

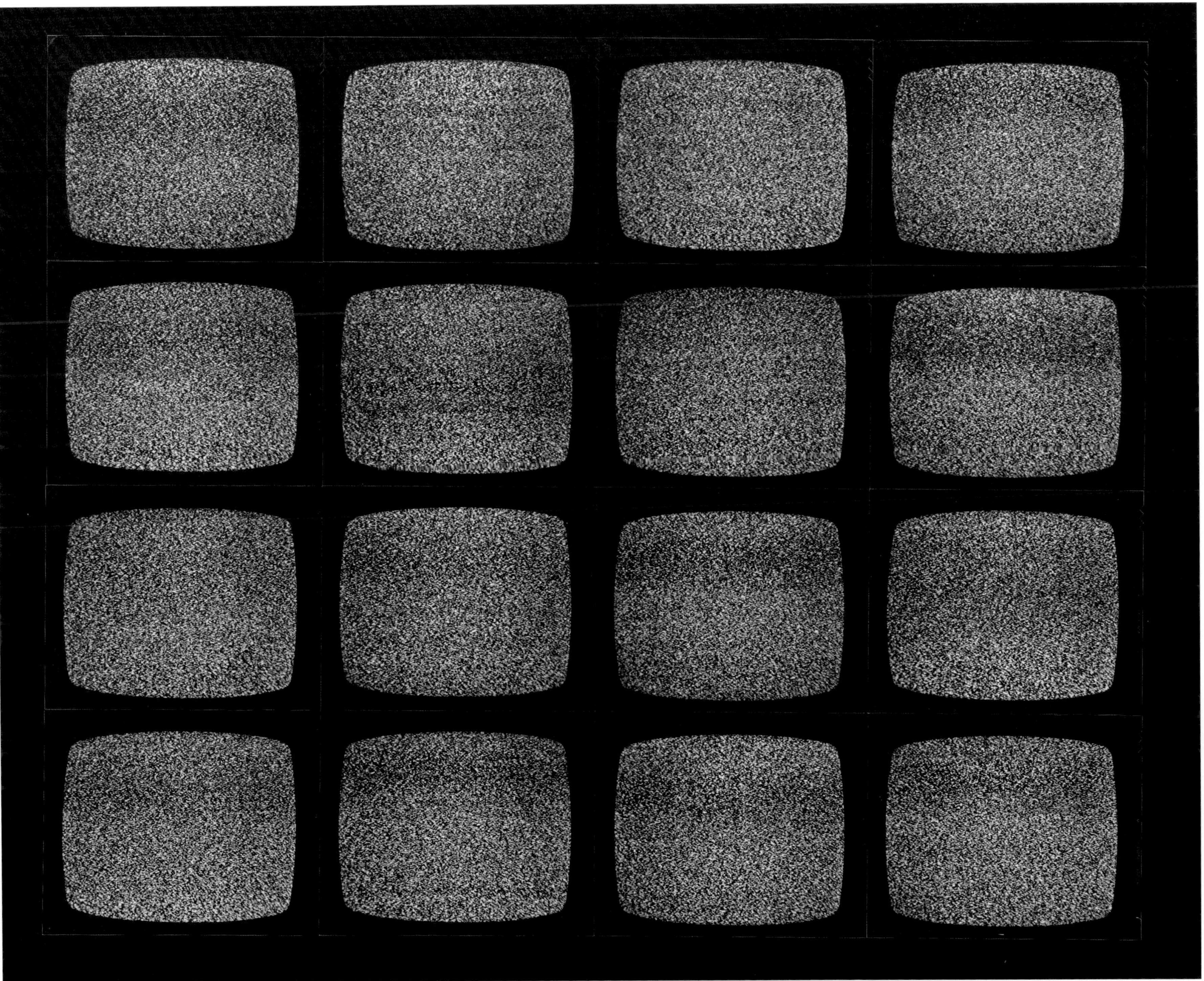

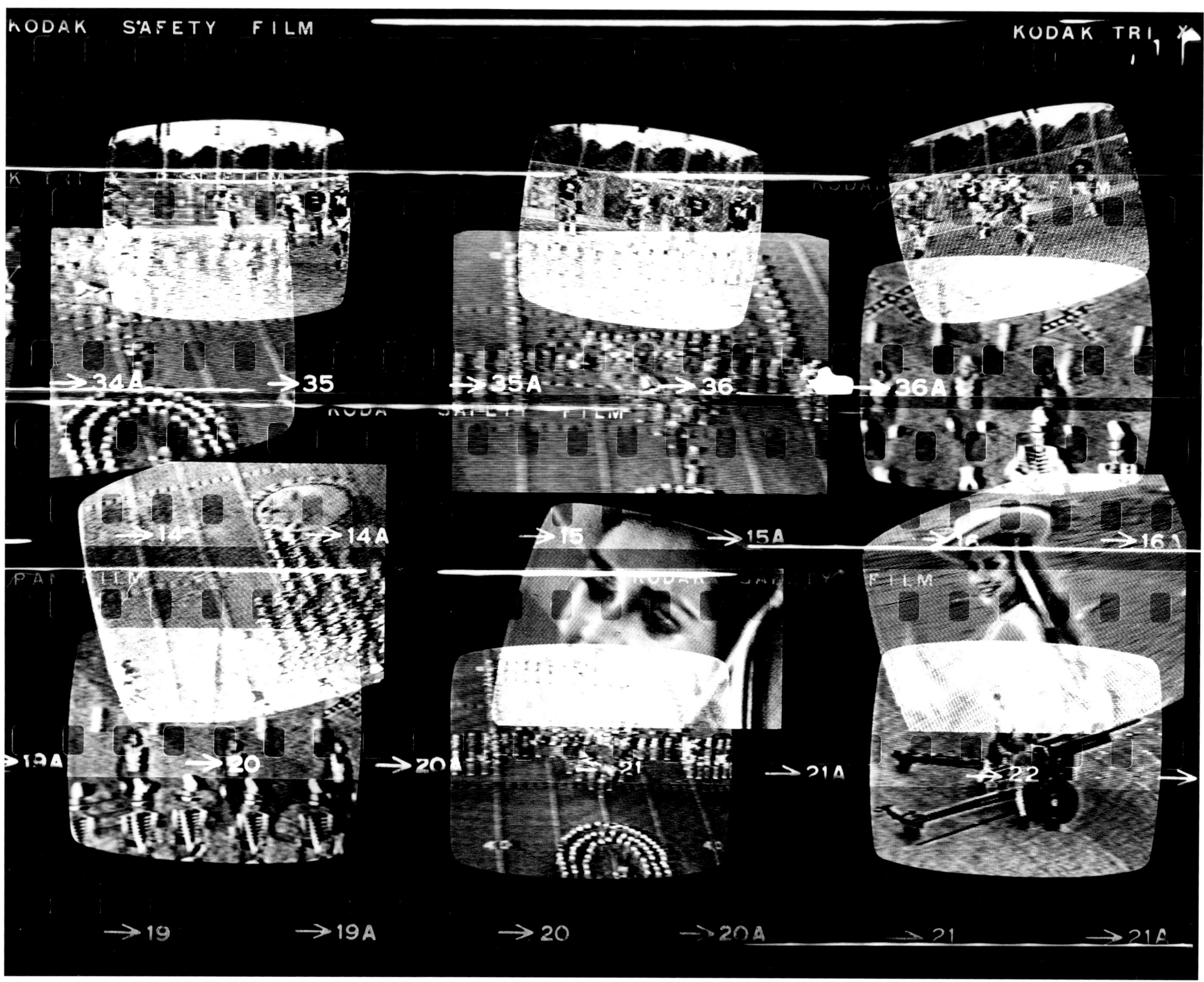

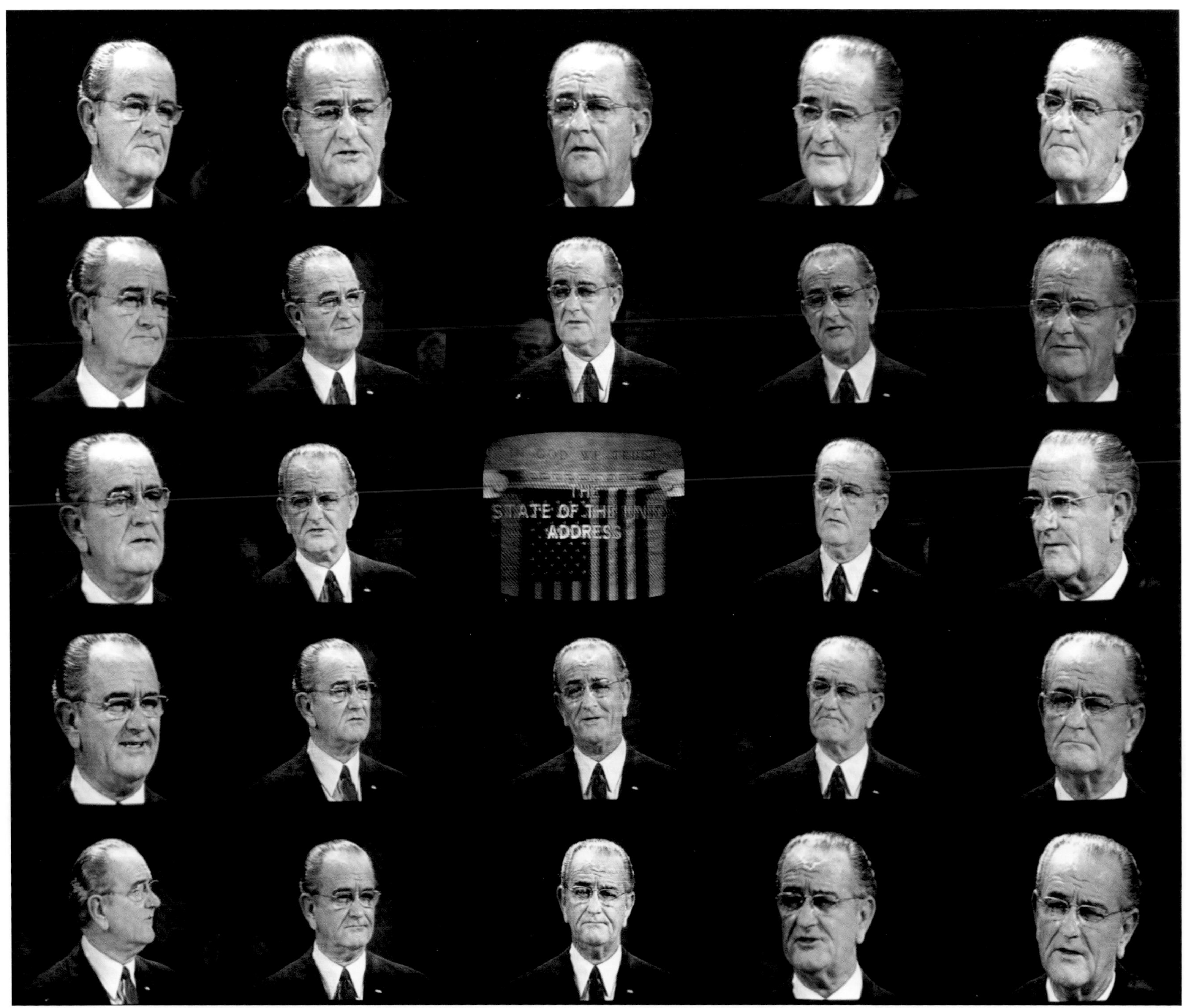
IN GOD WE TRUST
THE
STATE OF THE UNION
ADDRESS

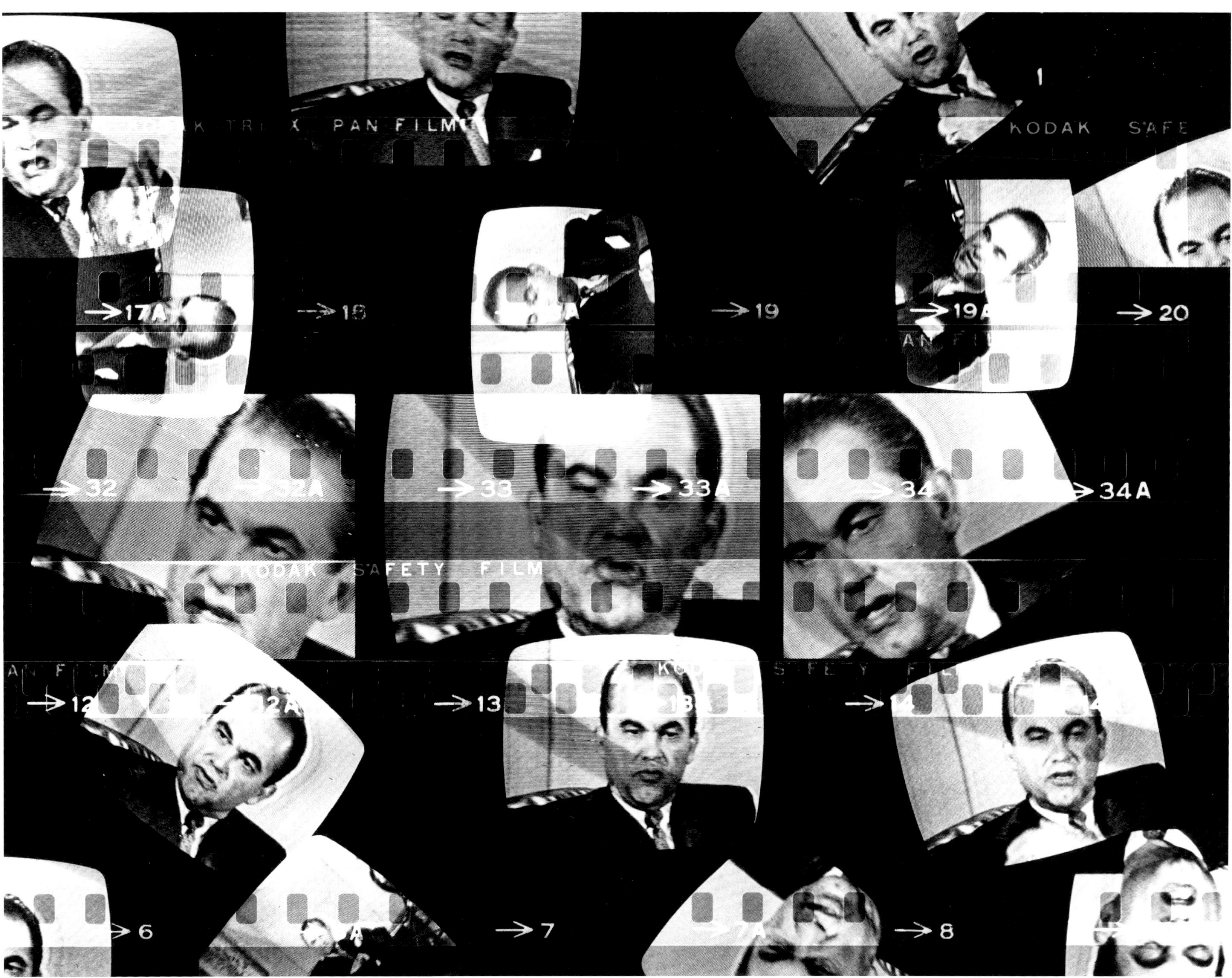

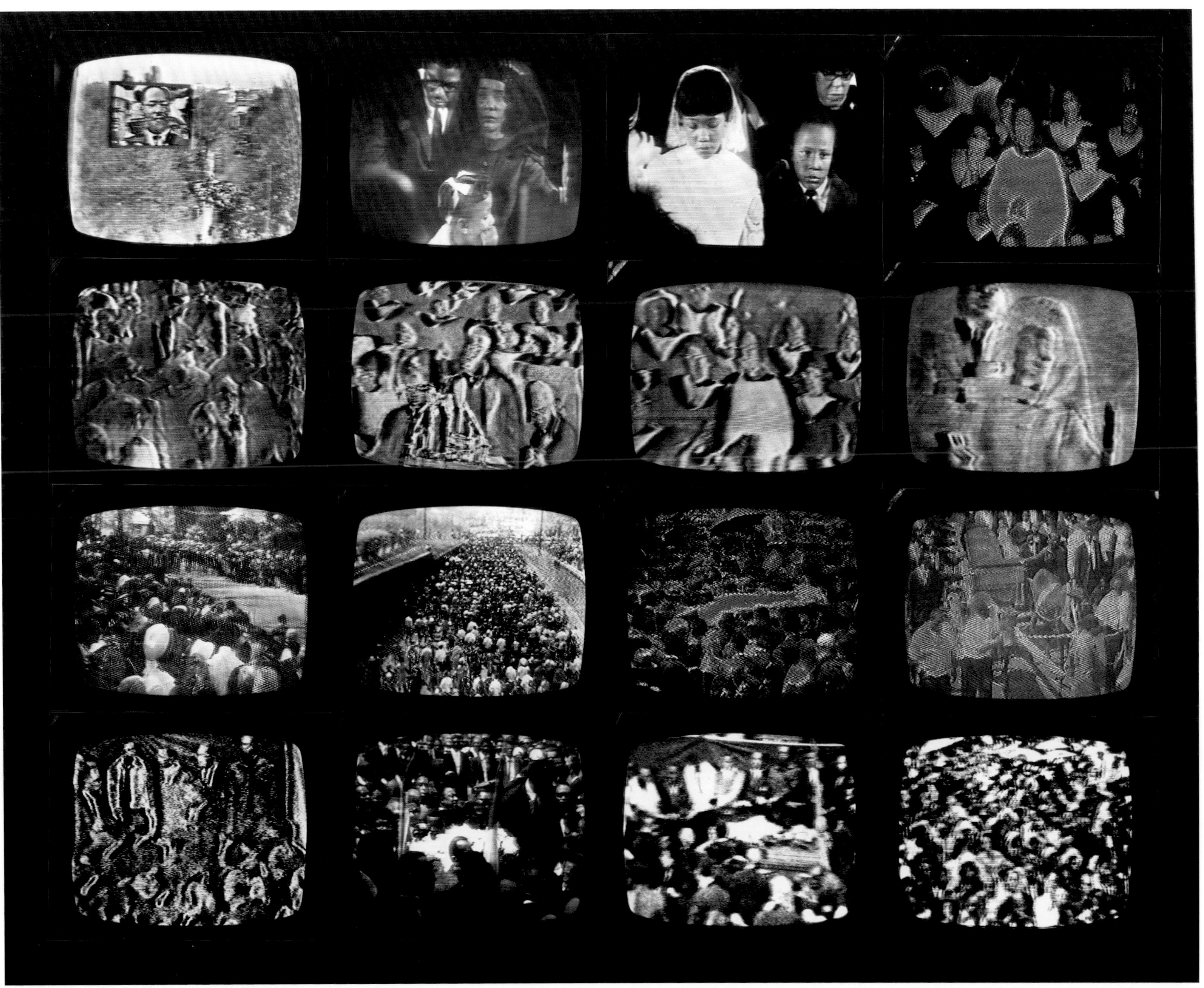

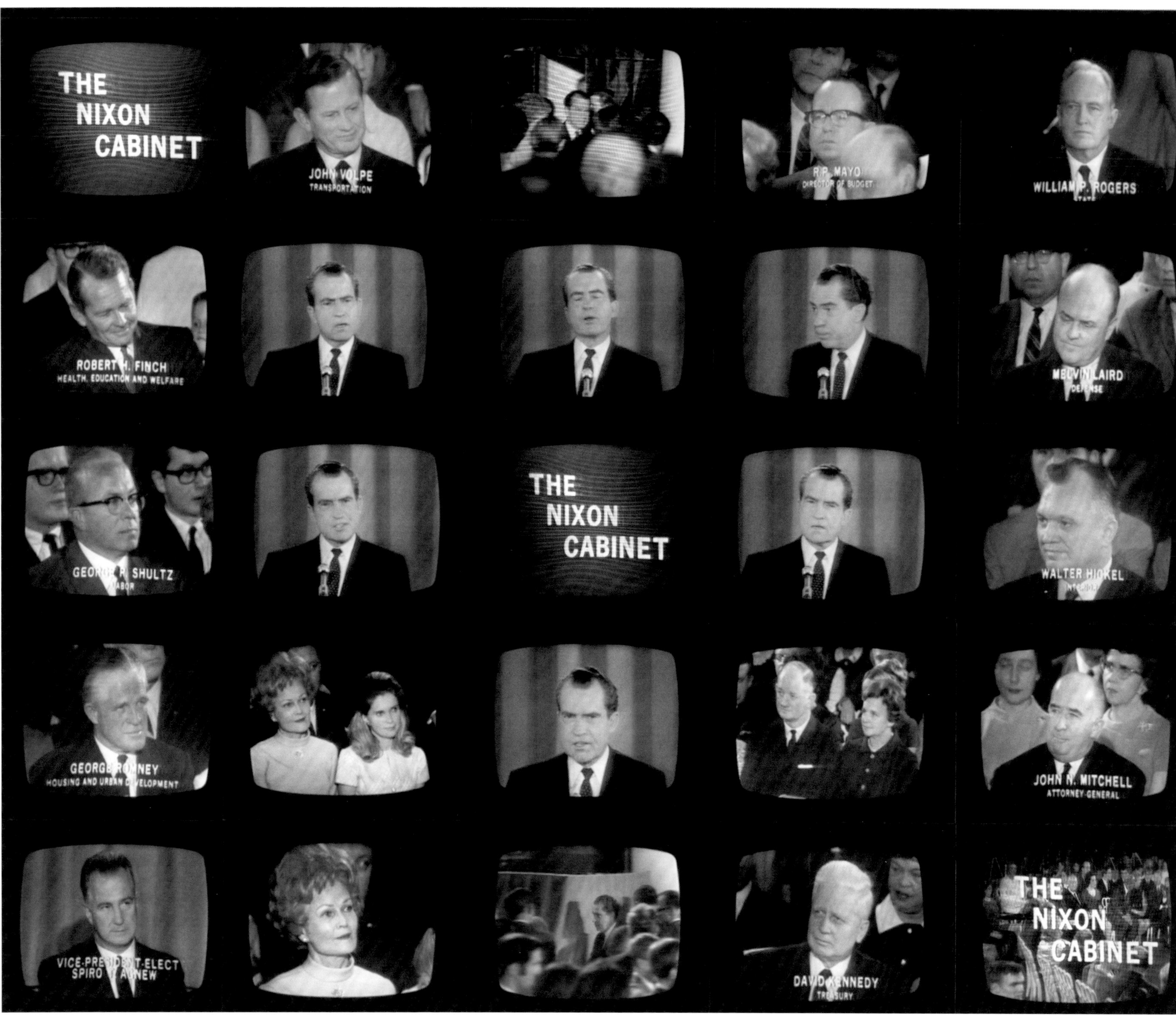
THE
NIXON
CABINET

JOHN VOLPE
TRANSPORTATION

R.P. MAYO
DIRECTOR OF BUDGET

WILLIAM P. ROGERS
STATE

ROBERT H. FINCH
HEALTH, EDUCATION AND WELFARE

MELVIN LAIRD
DEFENSE

GEORGE P. SHULTZ
LABOR

THE
NIXON
CABINET

WALTER HICKEL
INTERIOR

GEORGE ROMNEY
HOUSING AND URBAN DEVELOPMENT

JOHN N. MITCHELL
ATTORNEY-GENERAL

VICE-PRESIDENT-ELECT
SPIRO T. AGNEW

DAVID KENNEDY
TREASURY

THE
NIXON
CABINET

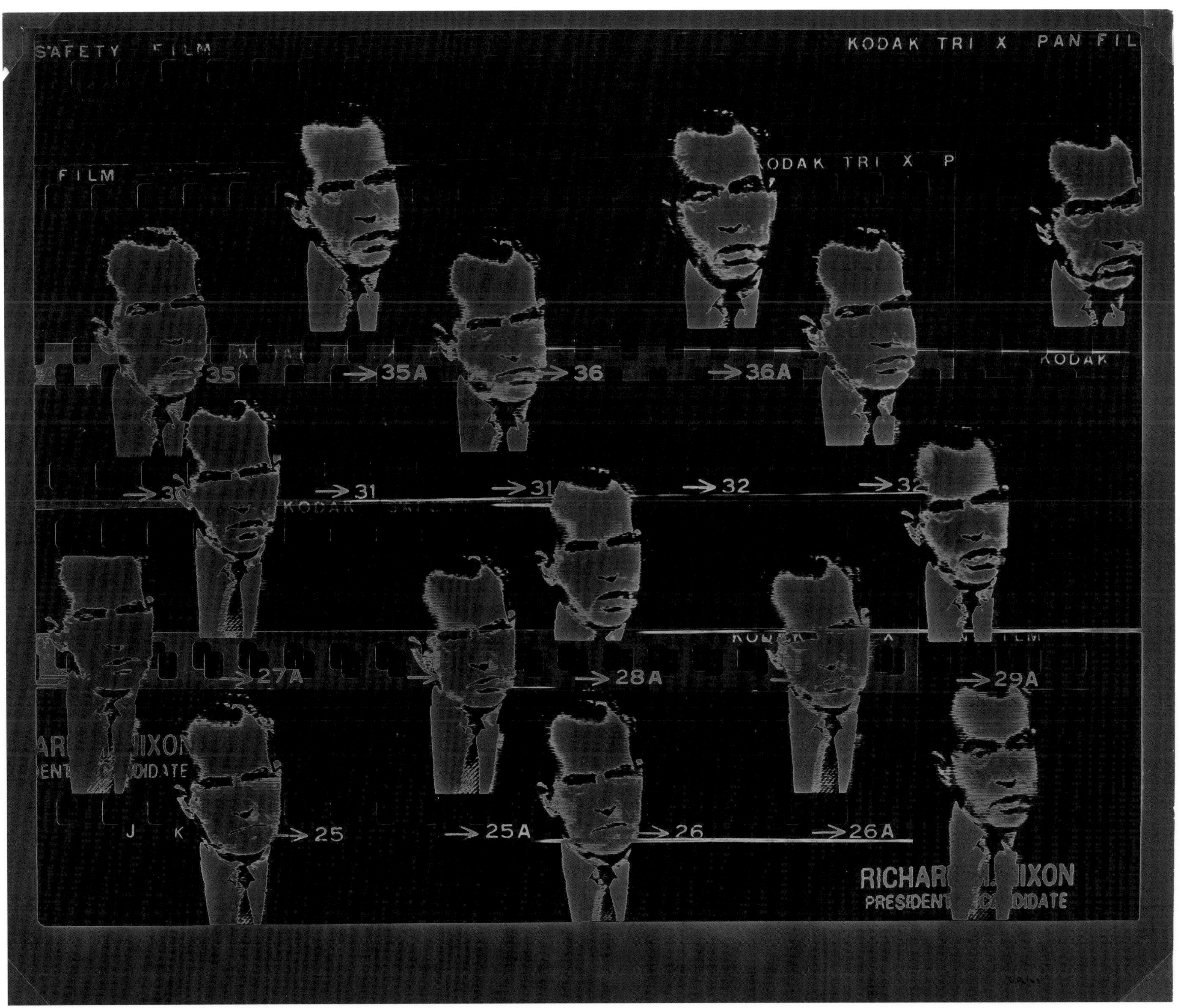
SAFETY FILM
KODAK TRI X PAN FIL
FILM
KODAK TRI X P
35 35A 36 36A
30 31 31 32 32
27A 28A 29A
J K 25 25A 26 26A
RICHARD M. NIXON
PRESIDENTIAL CANDIDATE

Daily Photographs, 1969-70

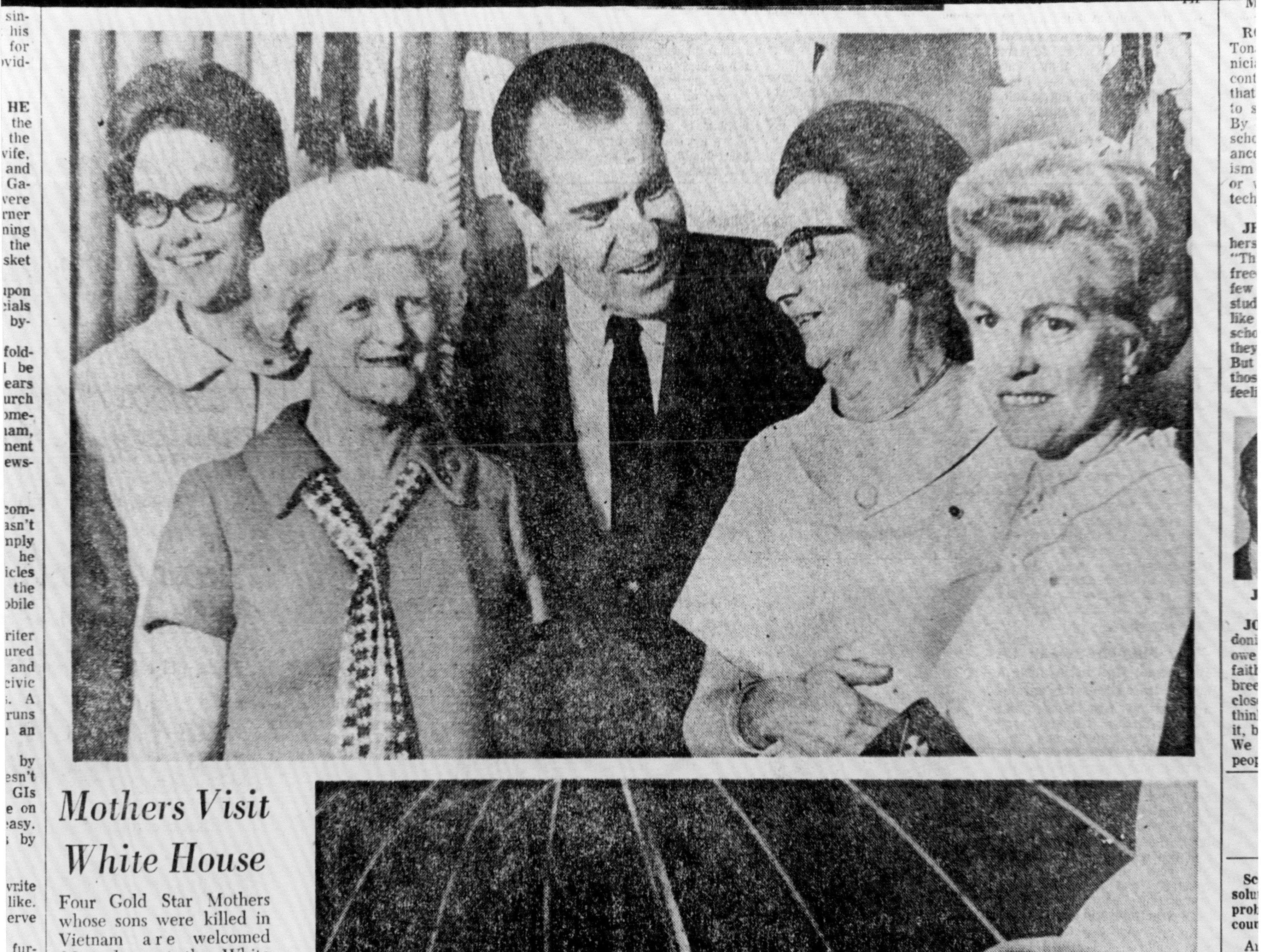

Mothers Visit White House

Four Gold Star Mothers whose sons were killed in Vietnam are welcomed Monday at the White

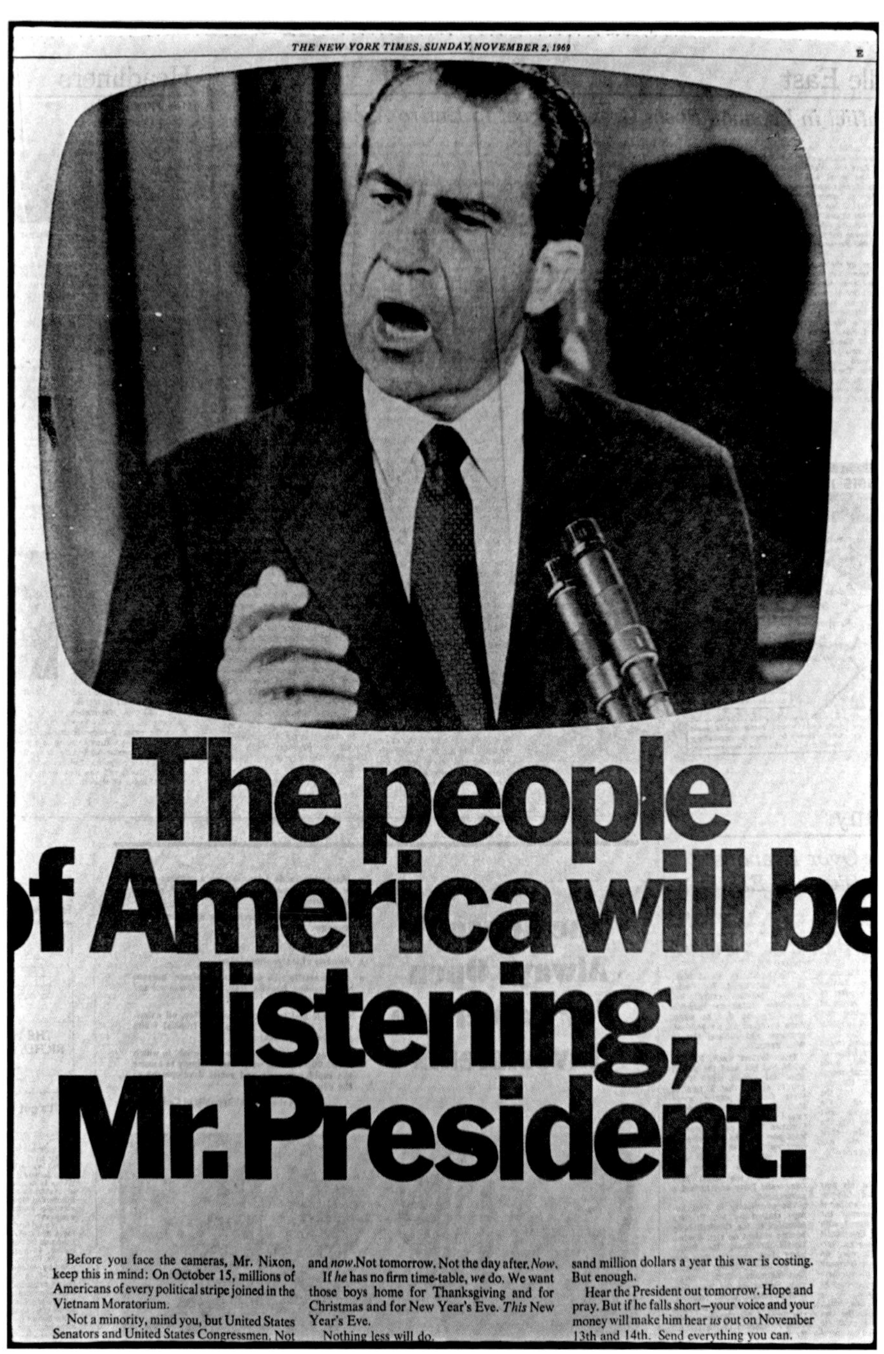

The people of America will be listening, Mr. President.

Before you face the cameras, Mr. Nixon, keep this in mind: On October 15, millions of Americans of every political stripe joined in the Vietnam Moratorium.

Not a minority, mind you, but United States Senators and United States Congressmen. Not

and *now*. Not tomorrow. Not the day after. *Now*.

If *he* has no firm time-table, *we* do. We want those boys home for Thanksgiving and for Christmas and for New Year's Eve. *This* New Year's Eve.

Nothing less will do.

sand million dollars a year this war is costing. But enough.

Hear the President out tomorrow. Hope and pray. But if he falls short—your voice and your money will make him hear *us* out on November 13th and 14th. Send everything you can.

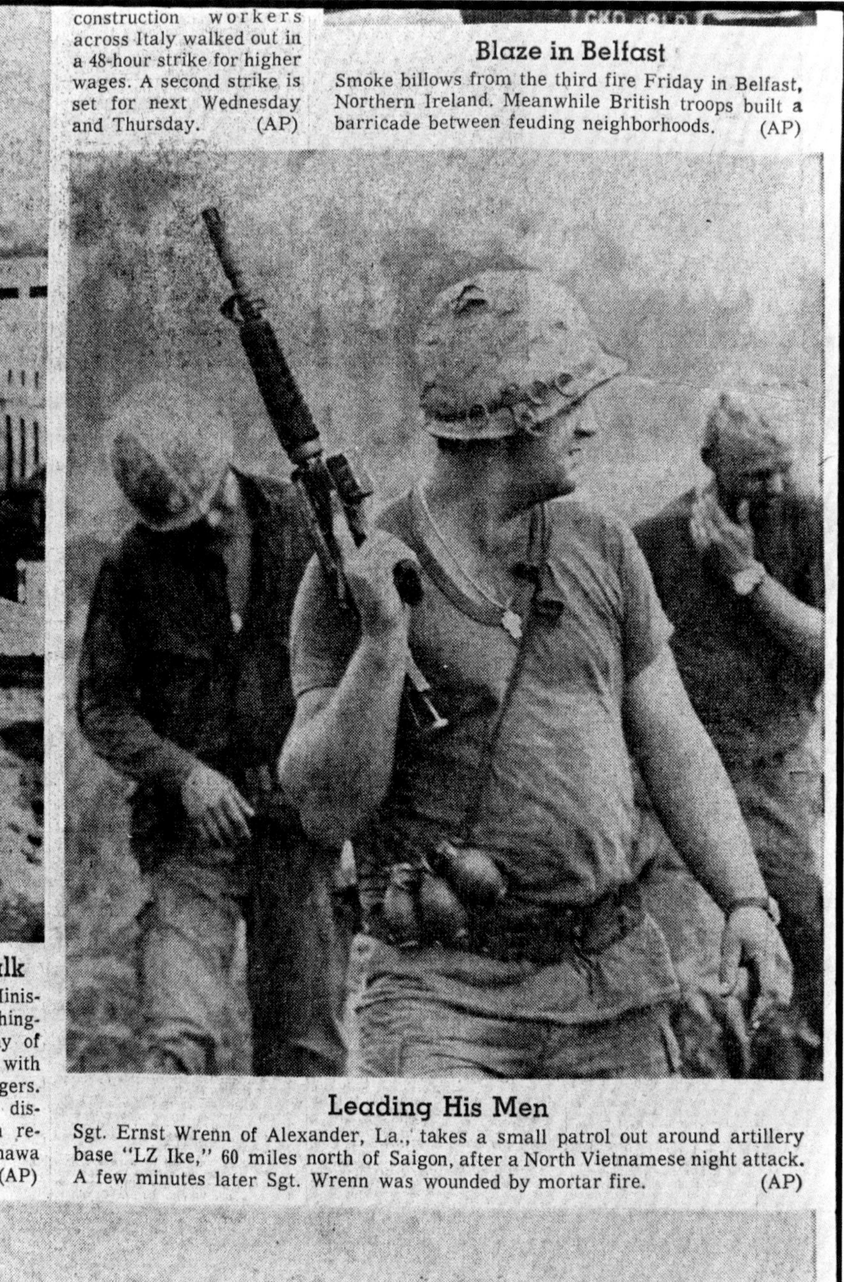

construction workers across Italy walked out in a 48-hour strike for higher wages. A second strike is set for next Wednesday and Thursday. (AP)

Blaze in Belfast
Smoke billows from the third fire Friday in Belfast, Northern Ireland. Meanwhile British troops built a barricade between feuding neighborhoods. (AP)

Leading His Men
Sgt. Ernst Wrenn of Alexander, La., takes a small patrol out around artillery base "LZ Ike," 60 miles north of Saigon, after a North Vietnamese night attack. A few minutes later Sgt. Wrenn was wounded by mortar fire. (AP)

Courier

Wes

—No. 143 ****. Published Daily at
787 Main St., Buffalo, N.Y. 14240   BUFFALO, N.Y

Rages
xon
Award

olice
Scores

K (P)—While
War demon-
paged outdoor
dorf Astoria
ent Nixon
Gold Medal
he National
ndation.

No. 1 football
nention of the
ling, window-
strators outside
were more than

orf, the major-
eats and stars
and hollered

steered clear
olitics and con-
football and
him.

rit

this country,
young people,
, but not just
n with the idea
lence."

e Texas beat
spirit, he said,

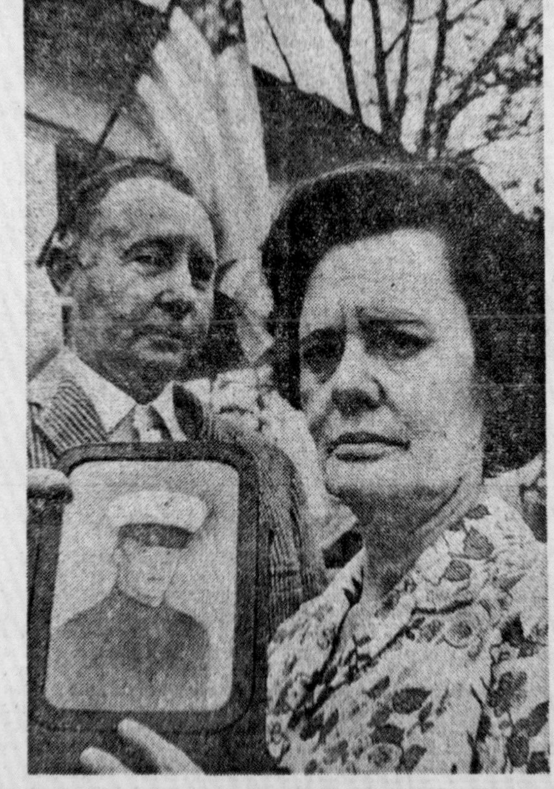

SEEK INFORMATION — Mr. and Mrs. James W. Jackson Sr. of Alpharetta, Ga., show a portrait of their son, Marine Lance Cpl. James W. Jackson Jr., 21, who is missing in Vietnam. They say he stepped from a helicopter near a field hospital Sept. 21 after being injured in a "non-hostile" ordnance explosion and no one, including the Marines, seems to know what happened to him. An intense search is underway, the Marines claim.   AP

S. Vi
Is St
Pane

Laire
Prais

WASHI
— Secret
William
the Com
negotiate
they knew
for them
until gr
Vietnam
power o
Hanoi's po

Rogers and
Melvin R.
sional testimo
day, said
armed force
stronger eve
new "Vietnam
If the Com
gotiate now,
Senate Forei
mittee, they
shake at prov
litical strengt
"If on the
gram—the V
gram for lack
—continues t
to this point

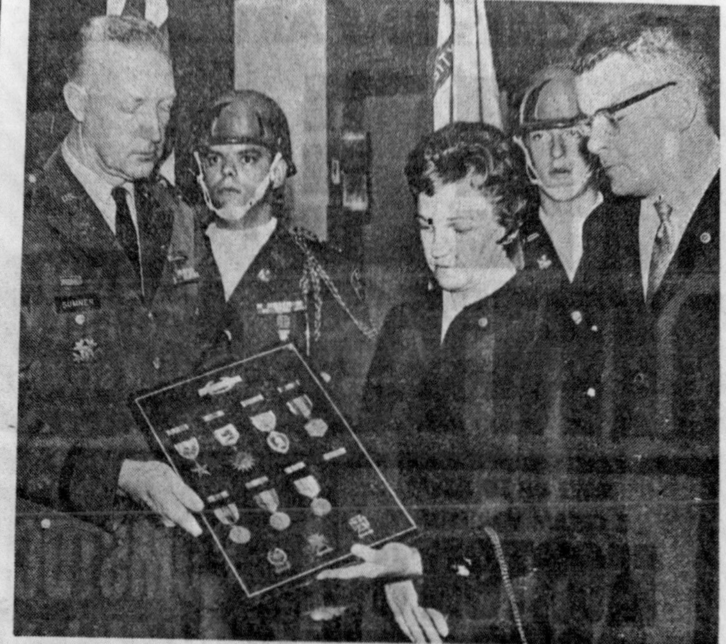

Col. Robert S. Sumner   Mrs. Albert W. Dalke   Albert W. Dalke

Military science professor presents case full of medals to parents of soldier

Parents Given Slain Hero's Medals

Courier-Express Niagara Falls Bureau

NIAGARA FALLS—The parents of a Tonawanda man killed in combat in Vietnam last May 6 received posthumous medals Tuesday afternoon in O'Shea Hall at Niagara University.

The medals were presented to Mr. and Mrs. Albert W. Dalke, of 95 Wheeler St., by Col. Robert S. Sumner, professor of military science at the university.

Their son, Spec. 4 Burton W. Dalke, 20, an Army infantryman, was killed in fighting in the Mekong Delta while serving with the 9th Infantry Division.

The awards included three Bronze Star medals for heroism and service, the Purple Heart, the Army Commendation Medal for "meritorious achievement," and the Air Medal for his participation in "sustained aerial flight in support of ground forces."

The citations listed two specific combat incidents in which Spec. Dalke distinguished himself "in the highest tradition of the military."

Aids Wounded

One was on March 19, 1969 when Spec. Dalke, a radio-telephone operator, was on a reconnaissance mission with Company D. The company encountered intense enemy fire and Dalke, "disregarding his own safety," braved enemy fire to aid his wounded comrades.

He then "took up an exposed position to return fire" and moved across an open terrain to destroy an enemy bunker with hand grenades.

The other action took place May 6, when he was killed. The company was again on reconnaissance and encountered heavy enemy fire. Spec. Dalkes moved across "hazardous terrain" to aid two wounded comrades, then was returning to his squad to organize an evacuation team when he was mortally wounded by an enemy explosive trap.

Obituaries

JOSEPH A. ZYNCZAK

Mrs. Nowak
Dies: Owner

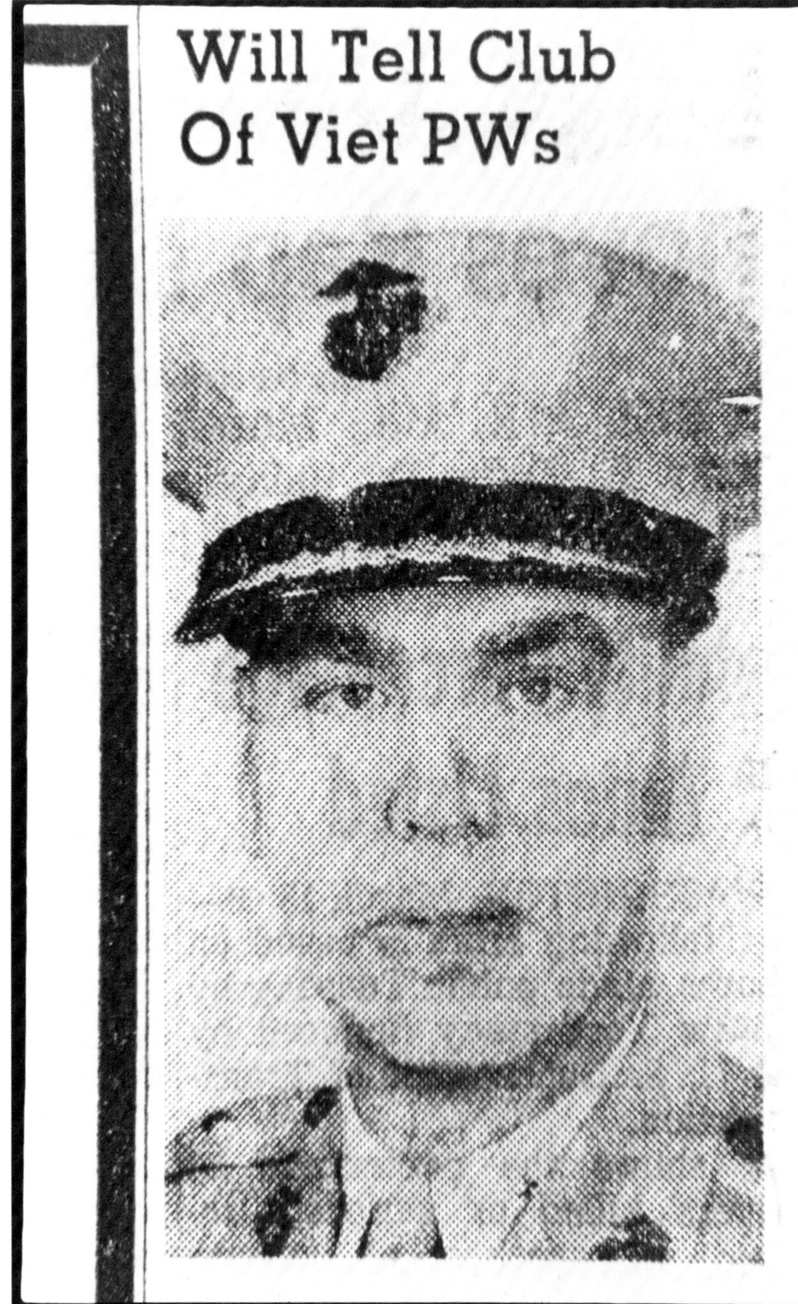

Will Tell Club
Of Viet PWs

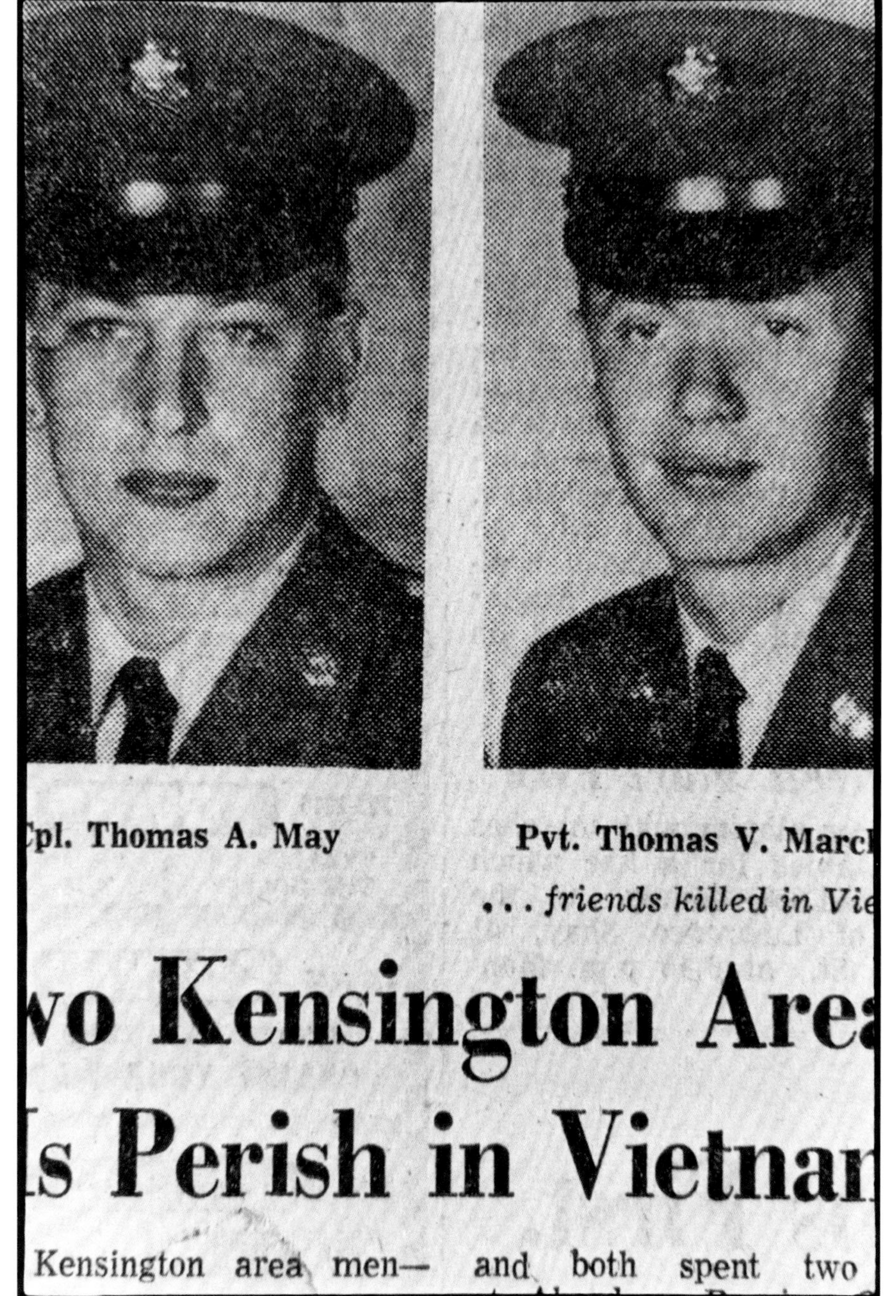

Cpl. Thomas A. May   Pvt. Thomas V. Marc[h]

... friends killed in Vie[t]

wo Kensington Area
s Perish in Vietnan

Kensington area men— and both spent two

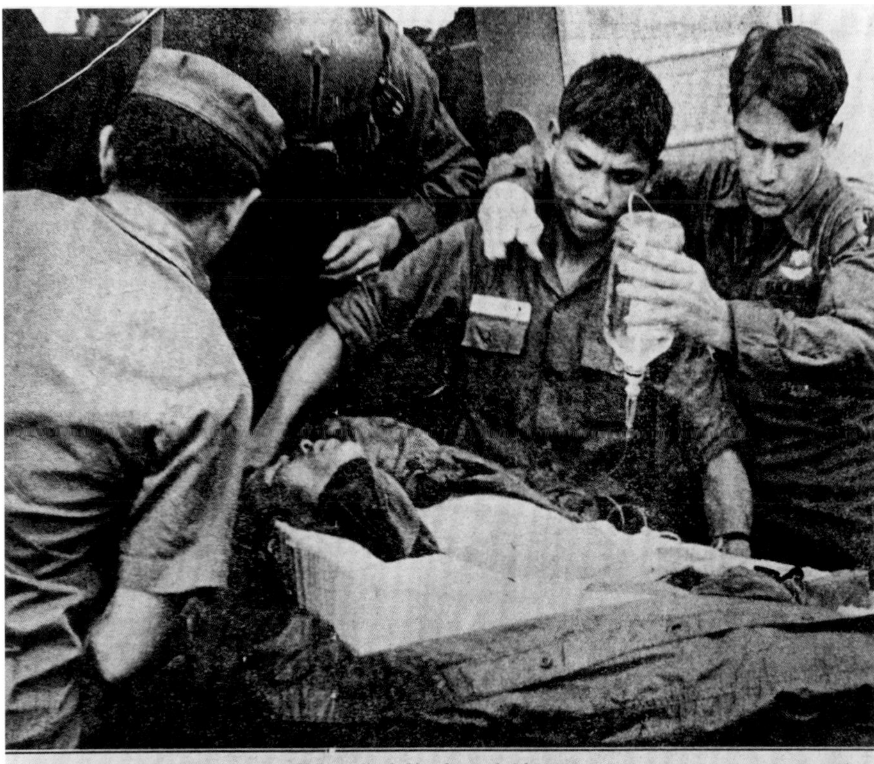

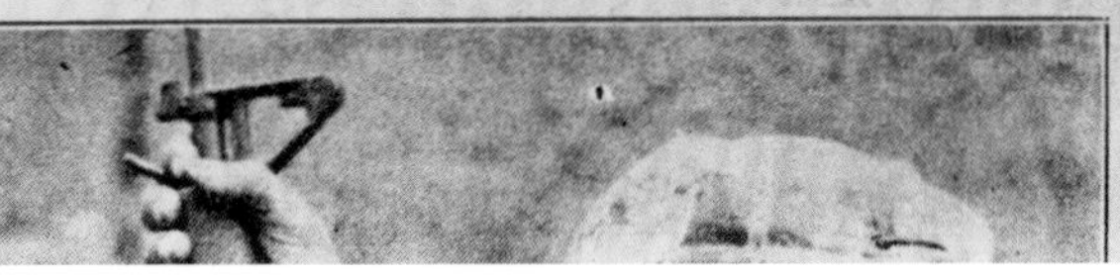

War Times

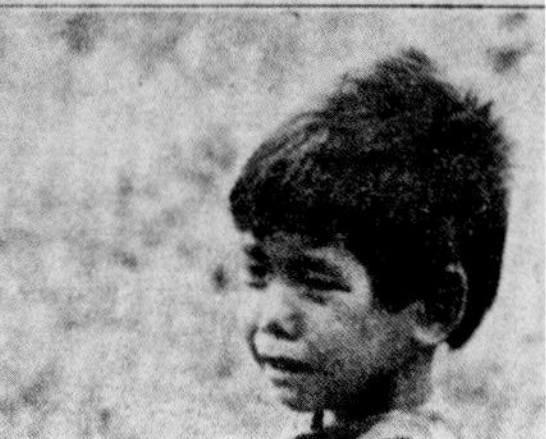

UPI photo

U.S. medic holds plasma bottle as South Vietnamese soldiers, showing strain of war, unload buddy **from** helicopter at Ban Me Thout in Vietnam's central highlands. Soldier was one of 50 injured when jet mistakenly bombed friendly troops.

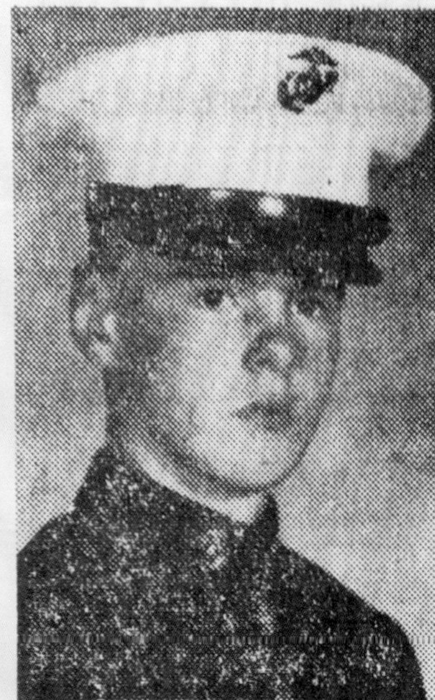

Pfc. Eric Lewis

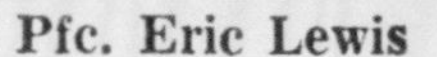

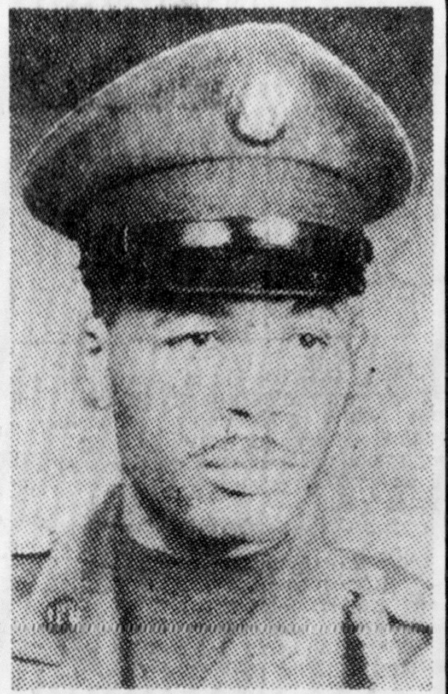

Pfc. Roosevelt G. Dockery

2 Buffalo Servicemen Are Killed in Vietnam

The Dept. of Defense announced Monday the combat deaths of two East Side servicemen.

Army Pfc. Roosevelt G. Dockery, 20, son of Mr. and Mrs. Roosevelt B. Dockery, 616 South Division St.

Marine Pfc. Eric Lewis, 18, son of Naron F. and Florence L. Lewis, 1019 Clinton St.

Dockery, a graduate of East High School, attended Erie Community College before entering the Army last May. He was killed last Wednesday while manning an artillery firing position. He served in Vietnam since October.

Besides his p a r e n t s, Pfc. Dockery is survived by three sisters, Mrs. Roosevelt Weather-

received
greed he
. Jackson
very five
ast letter
ly before
rance.
rrolls re-
ostscript:
you in 45

ly
the Car-
attending
and con-
d family,
arines as

has been
s part of
strength
did not
ns some-
Marines

ent with
Jackson
But he's
ting real
ng.
I'm even

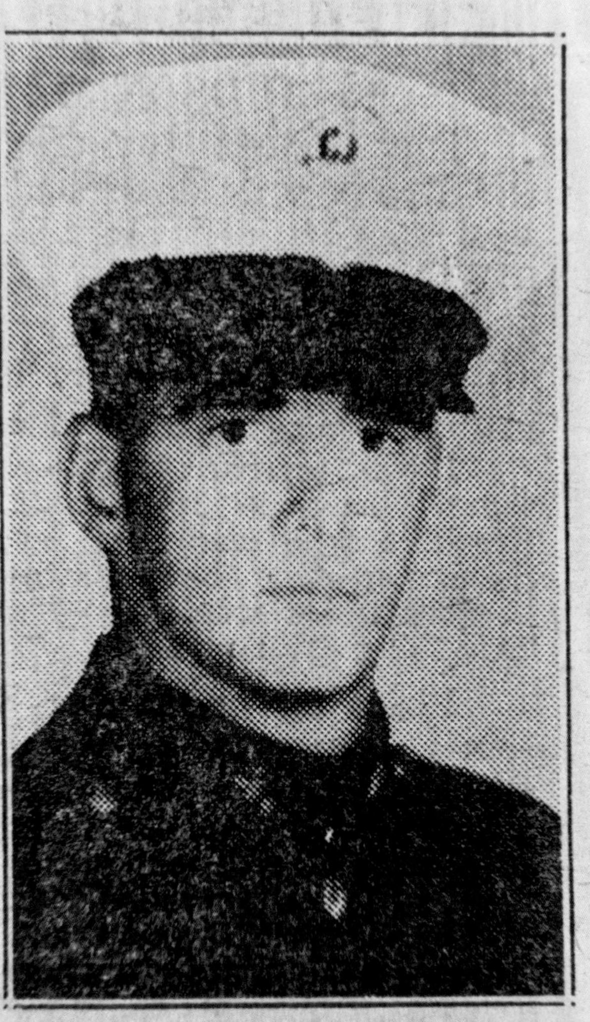

James Jackson Jr.
Missing since Sept. 21

beginning to give up hope. And
I've never done that in my life."

ttled North
terday for
e strategic

nks
ady
War

OREN
HE NEWS
— Defense
n drew a
picture to
saying
the Arab
ries were
ready to
a full-
war.
a special
g here, he
nted three
to justify
diagnosis:
crease in
military
th; inten-
ion of in-
rab orga-
ermed the
b public
for war.
e said, Is-
s fighting
that the
ntinue the
fare—par-
ighboring
rage ag-

ch raids,
to south-
left "a
d blood-
r Aqaba,

rist activ-
e occupied
increase
he called
would be
d. He did

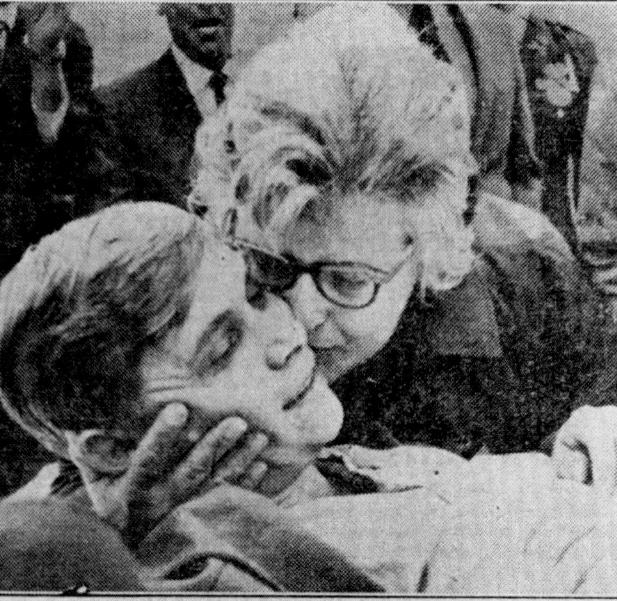

Pfc. James Strickland, who arrived at Fort Bragg, N.C., after 22
months of Viet Cong captivity, gets a kiss from his mother, Mrs.
John Strickland, Dunn, N.C.

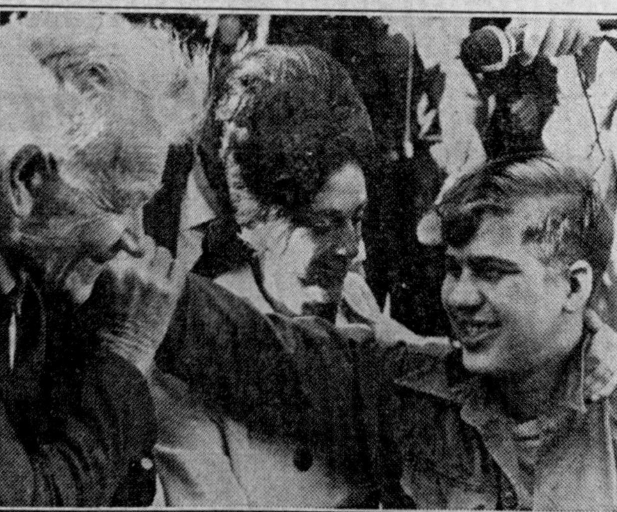

Pfc. Coy Tinsley is greeted by father Roscoe and wife Dorothy
on arrival at Fort Campbell, Ky. Tinsley, captured by Viet Cong
in March, was released Nov. 4.

looking
long dr
net ve
with go
of the
sleeves.
ting w
friends
Graham
the Ba
Rede w
just a
Paris. P
Brazilia
ried to
tional f
a brillia
crepe d
cabocho
and rin
rounded
can a gi
prepare
set is so

Mr.
tycoon),
ing rich.
cerise c
(discove
bassador
Sarnoff
made by
uine leop
Her bac
throws a

The
bassador
lettec. T
to the N
hold of s
What a

Mrs.
Joseph L
darling s
a jabot.
patchwo

and lime
tistics as
aire, fron
tion. Wha
there. It'
and spit

There
lery the
Enrico d'
had turne
New Yo

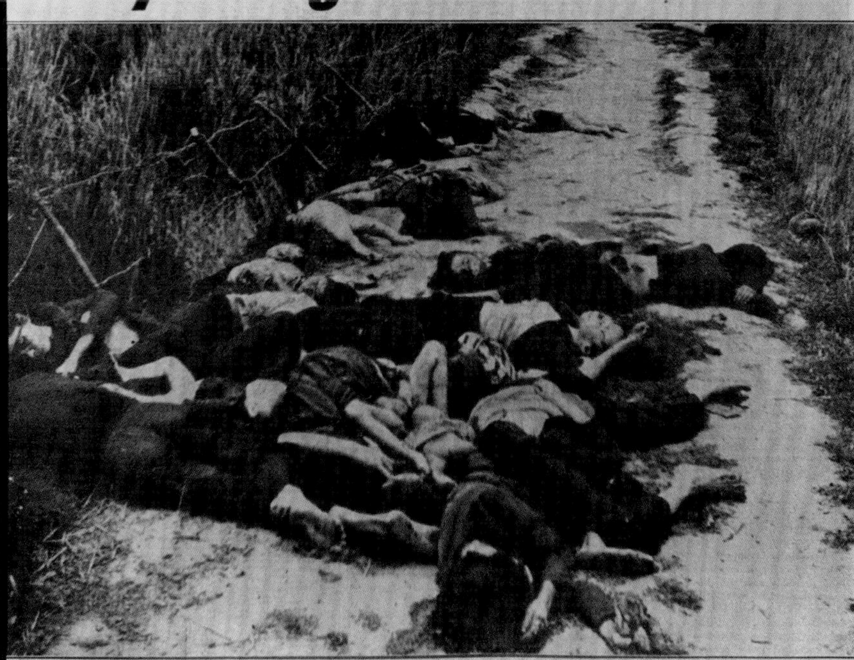

Scene of Horror. Bodies of women and children cover road outside village of My Lai, South Vietnam, site of alleged massacre in March 1968. Picture was taken by Ronald L. Haeberle, then serving as combat photographer, who accompanied U.S. troops on sweep into Viet Cong-controlled village complex of Song My, of which My Lai is part. —*Story p. 2*

Associated Press photo from Life magazine

w Study
Killings

...confidence in the ... incredibly hiding ...the alleged Songmy ... the time it oc-...onths ago."

...tor noted that the ...d committed atroc-...d: "Atrocities that ...ent occurance for ...he Vietcong do not ... none instance of ...rocity .

...t now have an in-...hat is scrupulously ... to the soldiers in-... fair to the truth, ...ow much it hurts."

...lied Criticism

...Resor and General ...d stressed that ...tment of General ...ot in itself mean ...ginal investigation ... were inadequate ...hat this was to be ...by the special in-

...iry that General ...arry out, they said, ...endent of the cur-...criminal investiga-...ing place. The gen-...e assisted by "a ... of legal and in-...xperts," including ... the assistant gen-...of the Army. ...ers is the chief of ...nponents of the ...he time of the ...

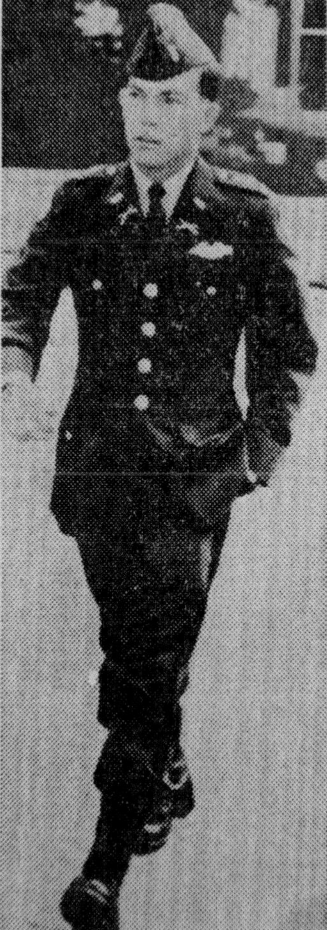

TO BE TRIED: First Lieut. William L. Calley Jr. at Fort Benning, Ga. He will be court-martialed by Army on charges of killing civilians in South Vietnam.

Associated Press

Army Sets

Continued From Page 1, C

...he visited his family in N

There was no mention ...today of a court-martia ...Staff Sgt. David Mitchell ...Francisville, La., a squad ...in Lieutenant Calley's pl ...Sergeant Mitchell has ...charged with assault wi ...tent to murder 30 Vietn ...civilians in the same in ...The sergeant is now sta ...at Fort Hood, Tex.

"That investigation is ...tinuing,' an officer said.

The six specific ...against Lieutenant ...charge that he violated A ...118 of the Uniform Co ...Military Justice. The artic ...fines the crimes under w ...person may be tried for ...lawfully" killing a huma ...ing "without justification ...cuse.'

The formal charges re ...the village as Mylai 4, th ...tary designation for the v ...of Songmy, which is one ...cluster of hamlets. Ame ...in the Quangngai area ...name dthe group of vi ..."Pinkville."

The first specific ...against Lieutenant Calley ...four murders, the secon ...for killing "not less than ...civilians, the third is for ...persons, the fifth charge ...one male and the sixth ...a 2-year-old child "whose ...and sex is unknown."

70 in Fourth Count

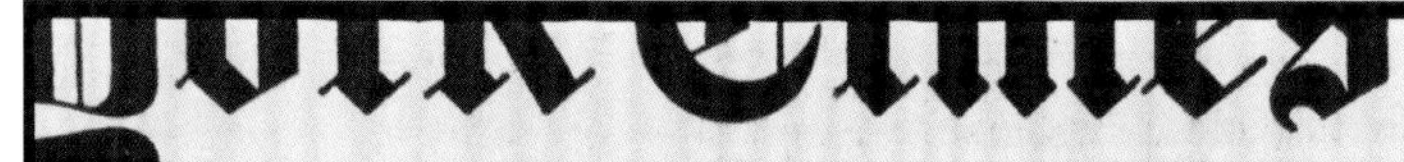

DAY, DECEMBER 12, 1969 —

d Johnson Confer on World Affairs

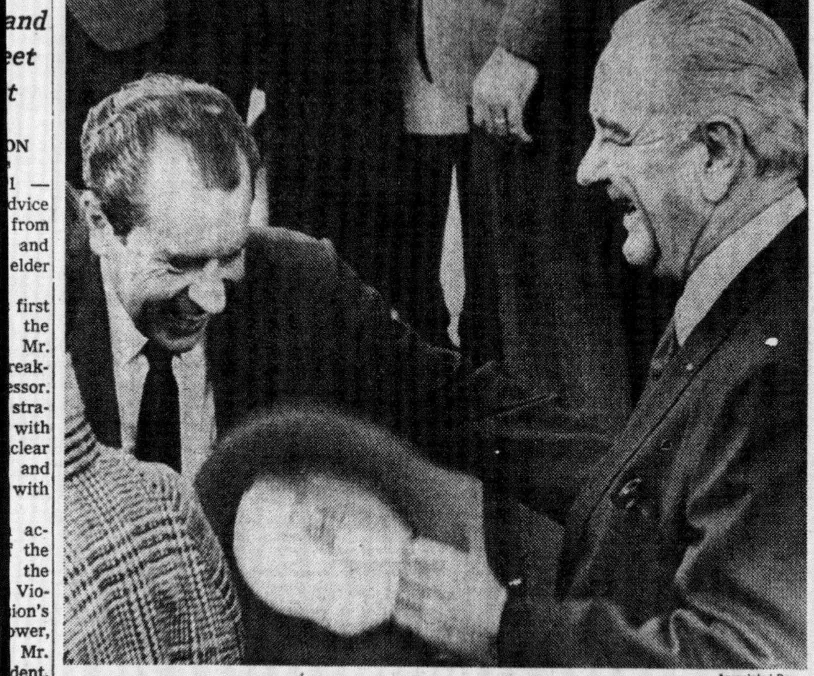

Associated Press

President Nixon sharing a joke with former President Lyndon B. Johnson after their two-hour breakfast meeting at the White House yesterday. They discussed major problems.

pearance of an effort by Mr. Nixon to seek broader support for his foreign and domestic policies.

Ronald L. Ziegler, the White House press secretary, continued to insist, however, that the talks did not signal any new developments. Mr. Ziegler said yssterday that the President "likes to talk with individuals who are well-versed in foreign policy matters from time to time, to get their thinking, to have a general exchange of views." The White House did

Continued on Page 20, Column 1

HARVARD OUSTS 75 IN BLACK PROTEST

Israeli Jets Down 3 MIG's In Battle Near Damascus

Wednesday, November 19, 1969

PEOPLE IN THE NEWS
the world...the nation...the area

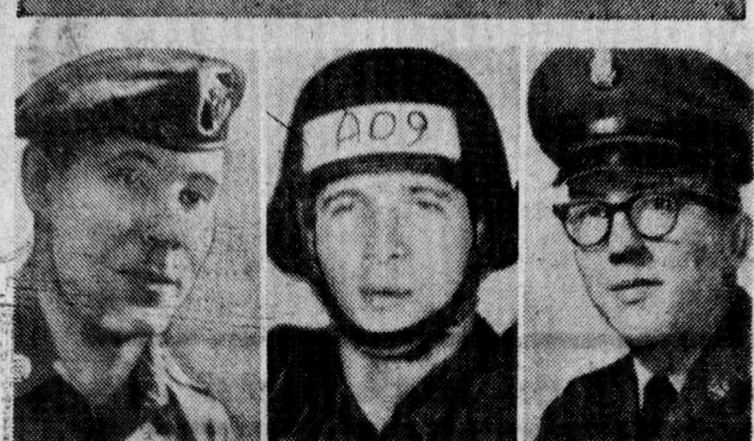

| Sgt. Yntema | Pfc. Lozada | Cpl. Wickam |

MEDAL WINNERS—Vice President Agnew presented Medals of Honor Tuesday to the widows of three soldiers killed in Vietnam while trying to save their comrades. The medals were awarded to Pfc. Carlos J. Lozada, 23, of the Bronx; Sgt. Gordon D. Yntema, 24, Bethesda, Md., and Cpl. Jerry W. Wickam, 27, Rockford, Ill.

(AP)

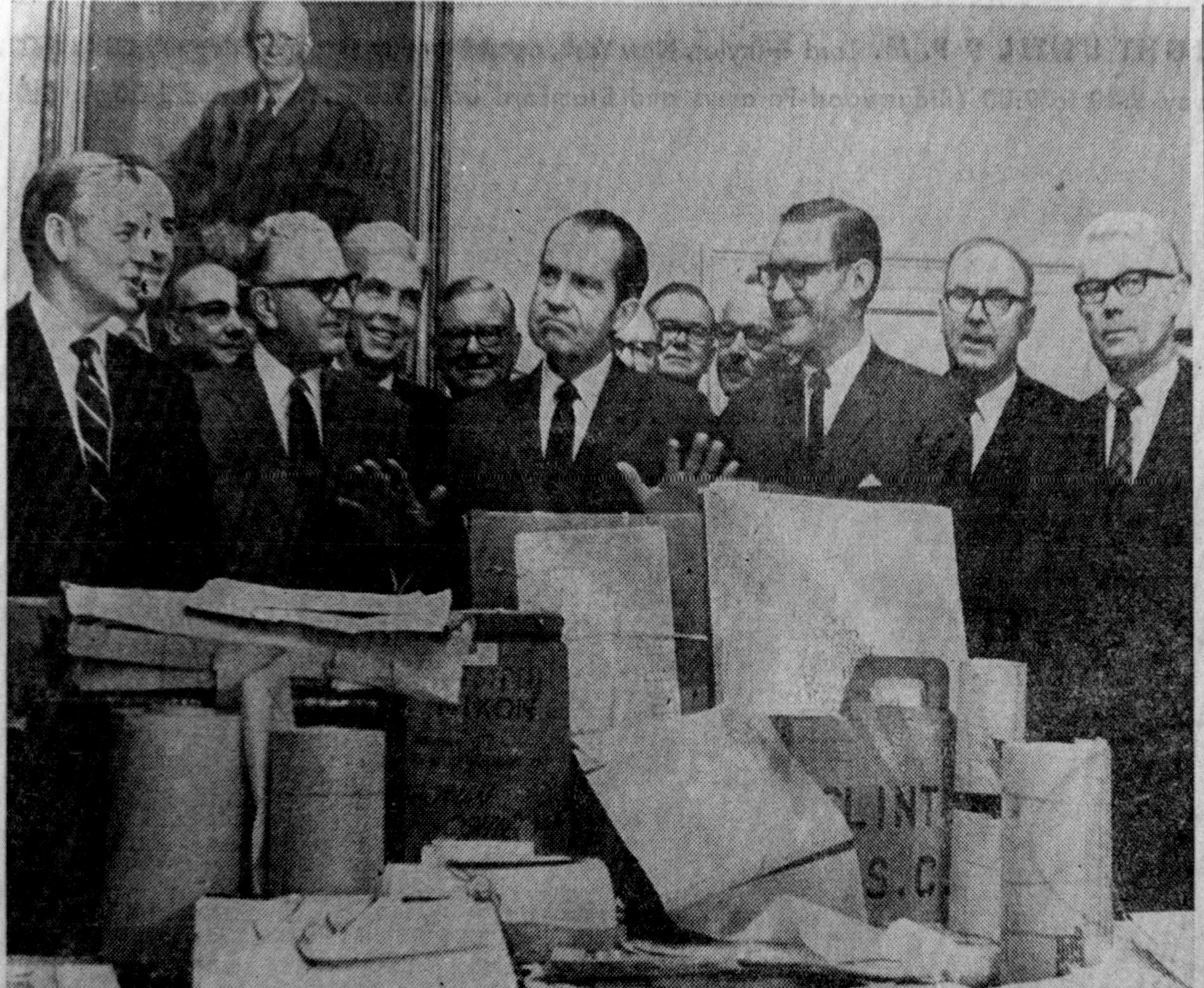

United Press International

GIVE VIETNAM PETITIONS TO THE PRESIDENT: Some of the 37 Representatives and Senators presenting lists of names to Mr. Nixon at the White House yesterday. The signers supported the Administration's Vietnam policies.

Nixon to Talk to Nation on Vietnam Soon

CLERGYMEN SEEK

PROTEST LEADERS UNSURE OF FUTURE

Abandon Plan for Escalating Antiwar Demonstrations

By DAVID E. ROSENBAUM
Special to The New York Times

WASHINGTON, Dec. 9—The coordinators of the Vietnam Moratorium Committee acknowledged today that they had reached a watershed point in their antiwar organizing.

The leaders of the group expressed uncertainty as to the future of the antiwar movement both in private conversations and at a news conference in which they announced plans for scattered and low-key protest activities this weekend.

They have definitelyy abandoned as impractical the original concept of an escalating number of days of protest each month — three in December, four in January and so on.

Marge Sklencar, one of the coordinators, said the group still hoped to have at least one protest each month. But she added, "What could we do for eight days in May?"

For a while, according to individuals close to the coordinators, there was serious thought about disbanding the committee.

An important factor was that the sources of money were running dry. Many of the wealthy liberals who contributed heavily in the early days of the comittee and many of the small contributors relieved to feel that they have given their share.

May Focus on Elections

Now, however, the thinking

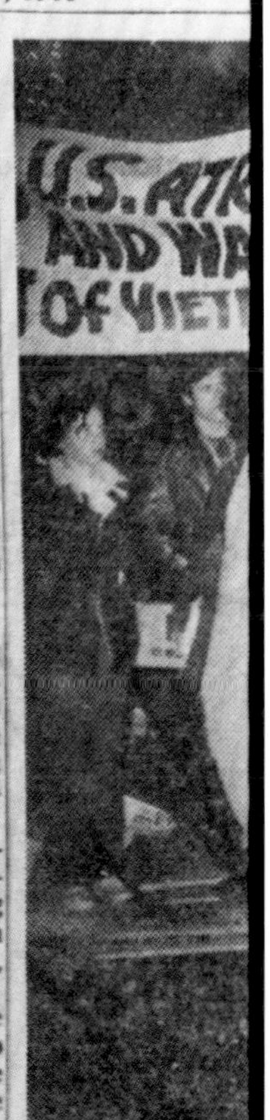

PROTESTING A
48th and 49th St
was in the city

Anti-N

By HOMER
Some 3,000 an
demonstrated tu
Park Avenue last
President Nixon,
tending the Nati

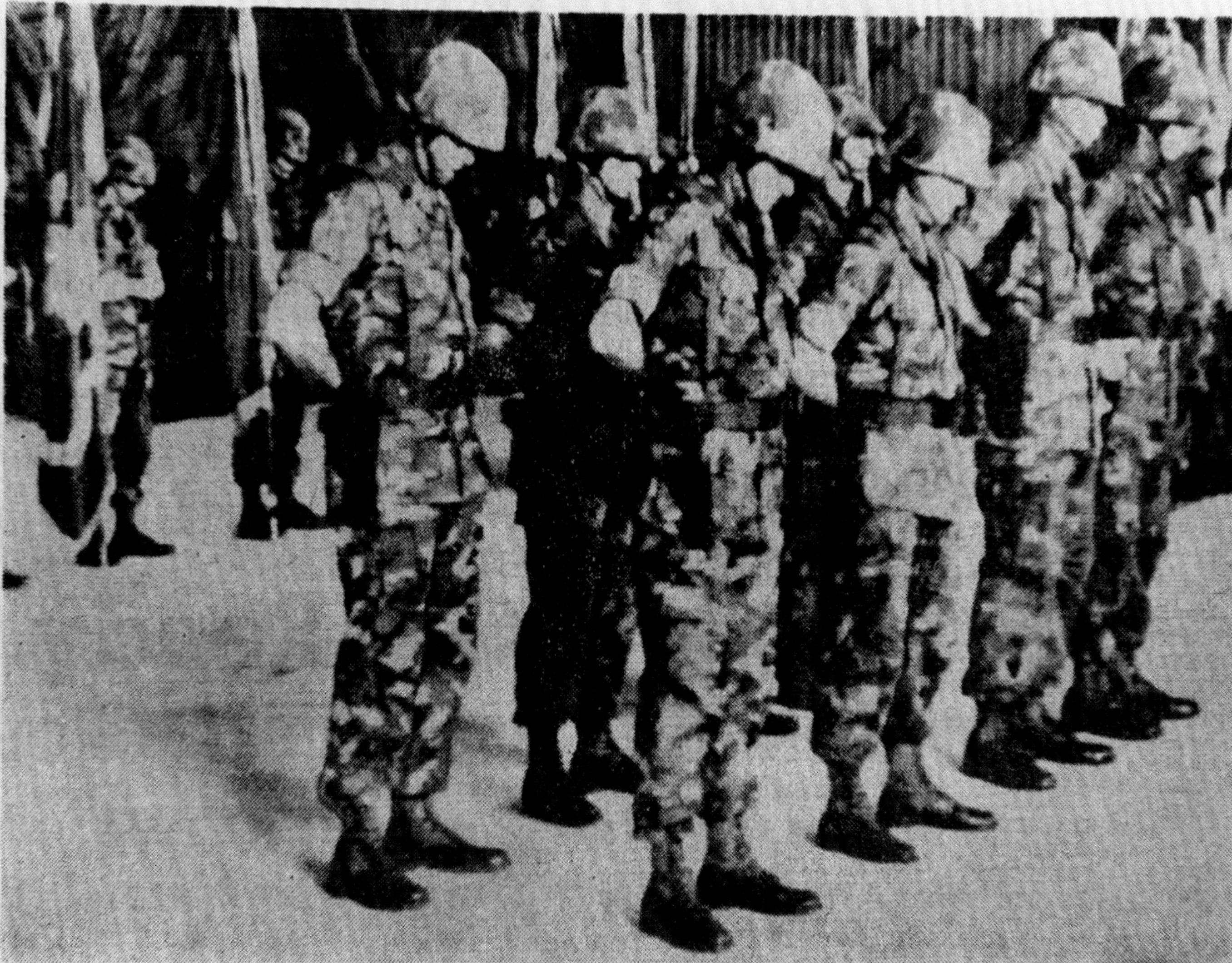

HONORING THE FALLEN — Members of the Third U. S. Marine Division's honor guard bow their heads during ceremony Friday honoring their dead as the unit leaves its Da Nang base for the States. The outfit lost about 5000 men during four years and eight months of Vietnam combat.　(AP)

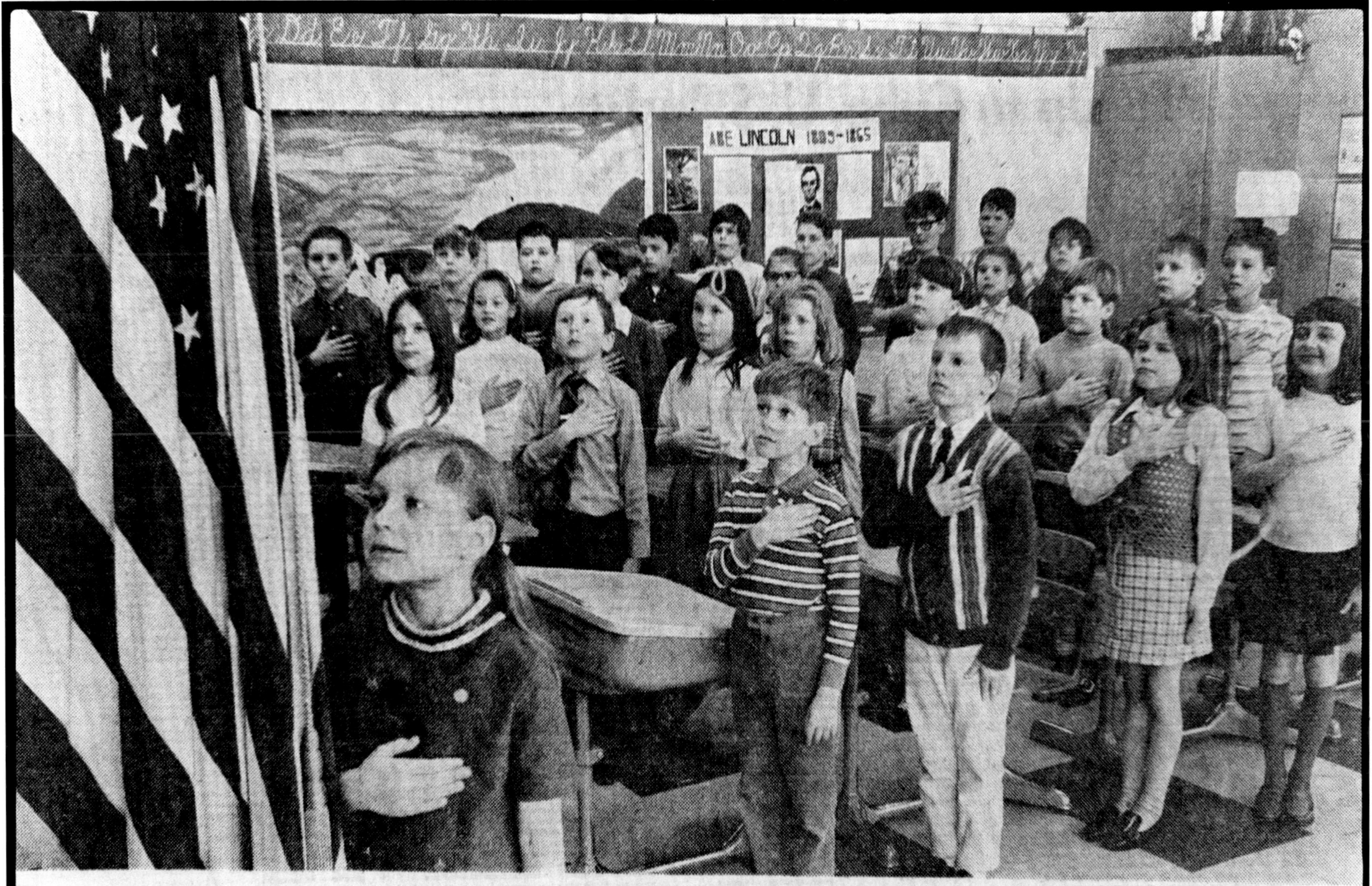

GOOD MORNING, FLAG—Susan Sommer, foreground, along with other members of the Third Grade at Cleveland Hill Primary School, gives the Pledge of Allegiance. They want to start a movement among other children to share their feeling for the flag.

That War Makes Boys Men

months in the Air Force. On Saturday his month's leave will terminate, and he will check in at Westover, Mass. Airbase.

STATIONED on the southern coast of Vietnam, Sgt. Barbarino had access to a beautiful beach and tennis courts. He was well satisfied with the meals served to the Air Force. Unlike Army veterans, who longed for fresh milk while serving in Vietnam, Sgt. Barbarino's outfit had fresh milk that was flown from Hawaii. Movies were shown nearly every night.

Despite this seemingly luxurious existence, the sergeant said, every American in Vietnam is in danger.

He carried a gun when repairing planes off the base.

IN SOUTH VIETNAM he knew a number of Koreans. They establish small businesses near American bases, he said.

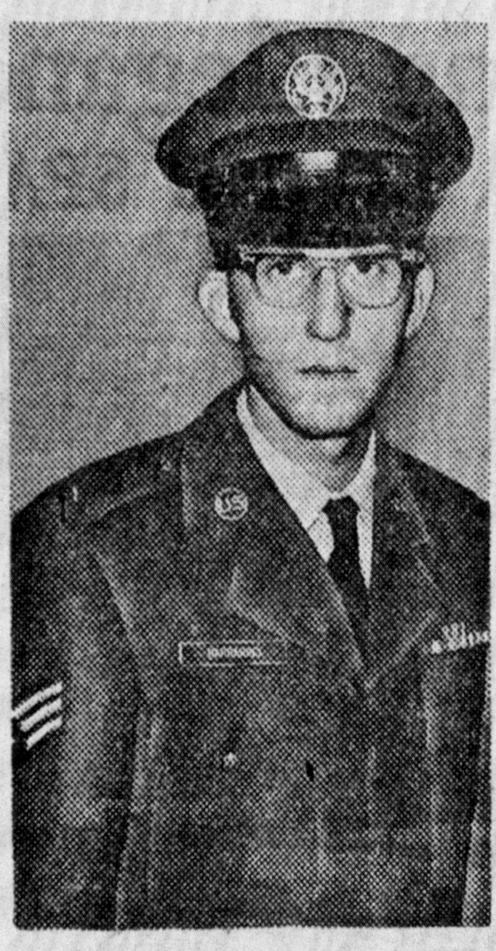

Sgt. Barbarino

Also, he learned karate from a Korean lieutenant. He achieved the brown belt, a high rank among karate students.

Sgt. Barbarino was among volunteers who built a school for South Vietnamese children. Last Christmas his outfit brought candy and cookies to an orphanage near their base.

"Every man serving in Vietnam genuinely appreciates any gift from the States," he said. "We hear of the antiwar protests which seem to indicate that our sacrifice is ignored. A gift from unknown Americans seems a tangible proof that we are not forgotten."

DURING a short stay in an Air Force hospital on the Nha Trang Base, Sgt. Barbarino was impressed with the excellent care he received.

Life in the military service in Vietnam is so different from civilian living in the United

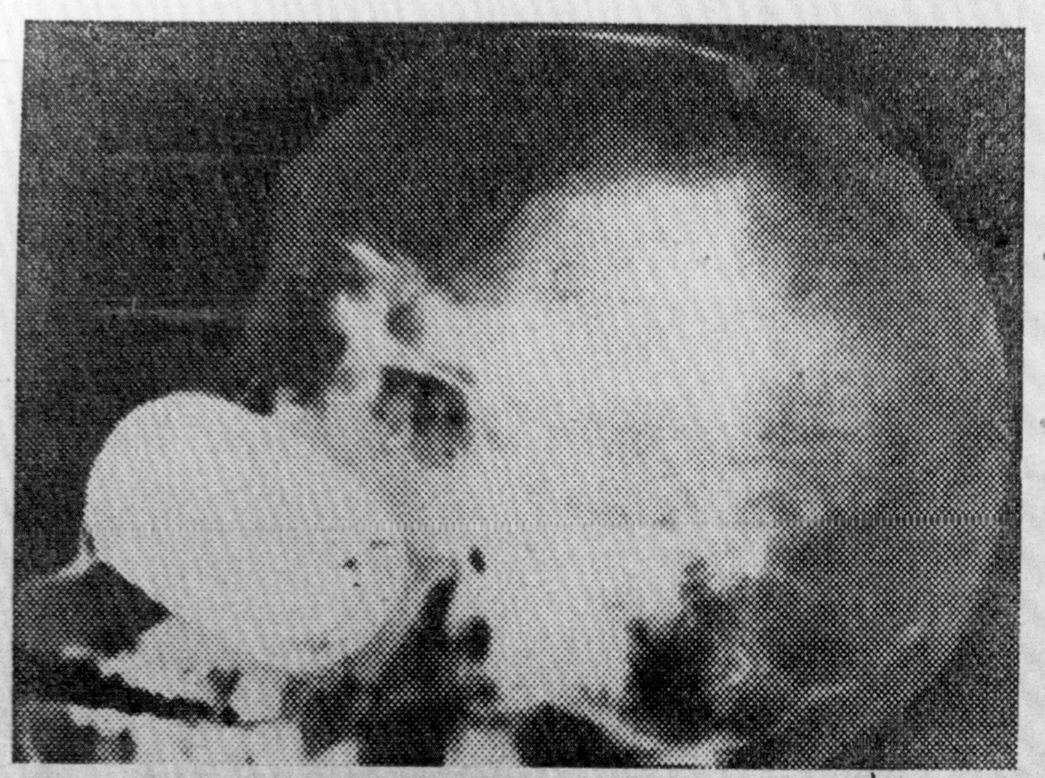
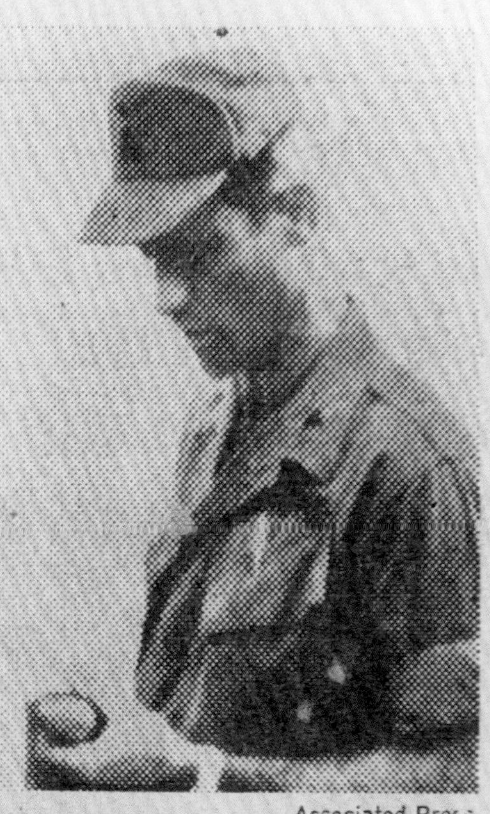

GRENADE AND SURGEON: Left: an X-ray of the live grenade lodged in the face of a prisoner captured by the army in South Vietnam. Right: U.S. Air Force Lieut. Col. Thomas H. Witschi of Wading River, L. I., holding the M-79 after he used a pocket knife and forceps to extract the grenade outside army hospital in Quinhon several weeks ago.

Grenade Is Cut From Prisoner's Face

More Charges Filed Over My Lai; Delay in Investigation Expected

By the Associated Press

WASHINGTON, Jan. 9— With four soldiers now charged, Army sources say it may take another three months to complete investigations of 22 other men suspected of involvement in the alleged massacre of Vietnamese civilians at My Lai.

Formal charges of premeditated murder were filed Thursday against Sgt. Charles E. Hutto, 21, of Tallulah, La., and Pvt. Gerald A. Smith, 22, of Chicago. Sgt. Hutto also was accused of assault with intent to commit murder.

A sex-crime angle entered the case for the first time as Sgt. Hutto also was charged wtih rape and Pvt. Smith with "indecent assault on a Vietnamese female."

Due Out Tuesday

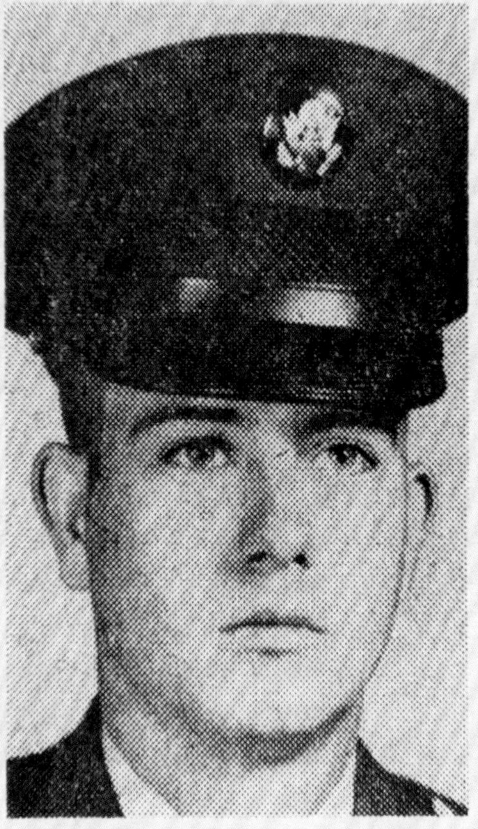

SGT. CHARLES E. HUTTO

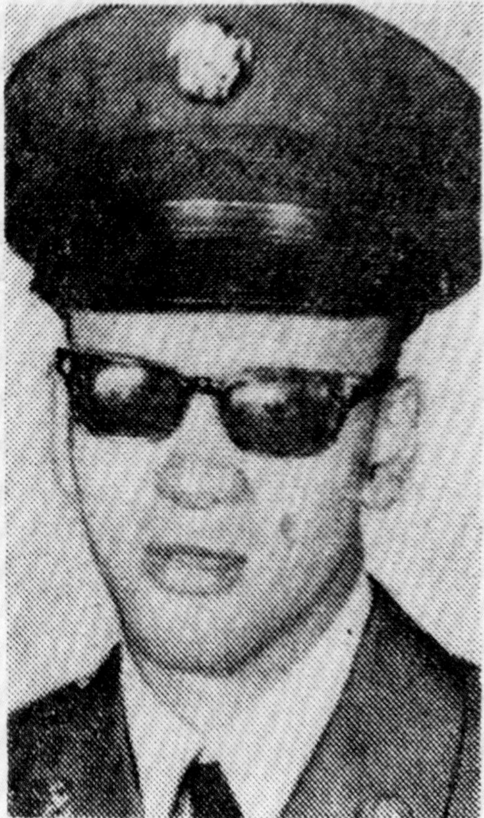

PVT. GERALD A. SMITH

A Sex-Crime Angle Enters the Case

ATROCITY CHARGE STIRRING BRITISH

Debate Sought in Commons or at Labor M.P. Meeting

By ANTHONY LEWIS
Special to The New York Times

LONDON, Nov. 21 — The allegations of atrocities by American soldiers in South Vietnam will almost certainly be debated in the British House of Commons or before a meeting of the Parliamentary Labor party.

Pressure for a formal debate on the reports of mass murder — and the whole question of British policy toward the American involvement in Vietnam — grew markedly today. Public interest in the charges of a massacre in a Vietnamese village in March, 1968, is running extremely high in Britain.

The object of the pressure, which comes from back-bench members of the Labor party, is to have a debate before Parliament takes its Christmas recess. That way, members could make their feelings known before Prime Minister Wilson goes to Washington to meet President Nixon in January.

Reports Dominate Press

The reports about the alleged massacre in the village of Songmy, near Danang, dominated much of the press today. A number of commentators remarked that the concern about the charges seemed more intense here than in the United States, and were puzzled at the relative coolness with which the charges were being reported and discussed in America.

ion should be shocked at such detailed allegations. Even if they are substantiated to the extent of only 1 per cent, they would leave forever a blot on American military honor. It must be assumed that the inves-

torial headed "A Brutal Affair" that "military and civil authorities will have to set up a full and open investigation if American and world opinion is to be satisfied that such incidents are not only exceptional and punishable but that adequate steps

Thus a junior minister regarded as on the party's right was highly critical in private today of a further comment by Mr. Brown that there had been atrocities by the Communist side.

600 Clocks Lost in Fire

BEL AIR, Md., Nov. 20 (AP) —From 600 to 800 grandfather clocks being finished for the Christmas trade were destroyed Thursday by a fire that caused total damage estimated at near-

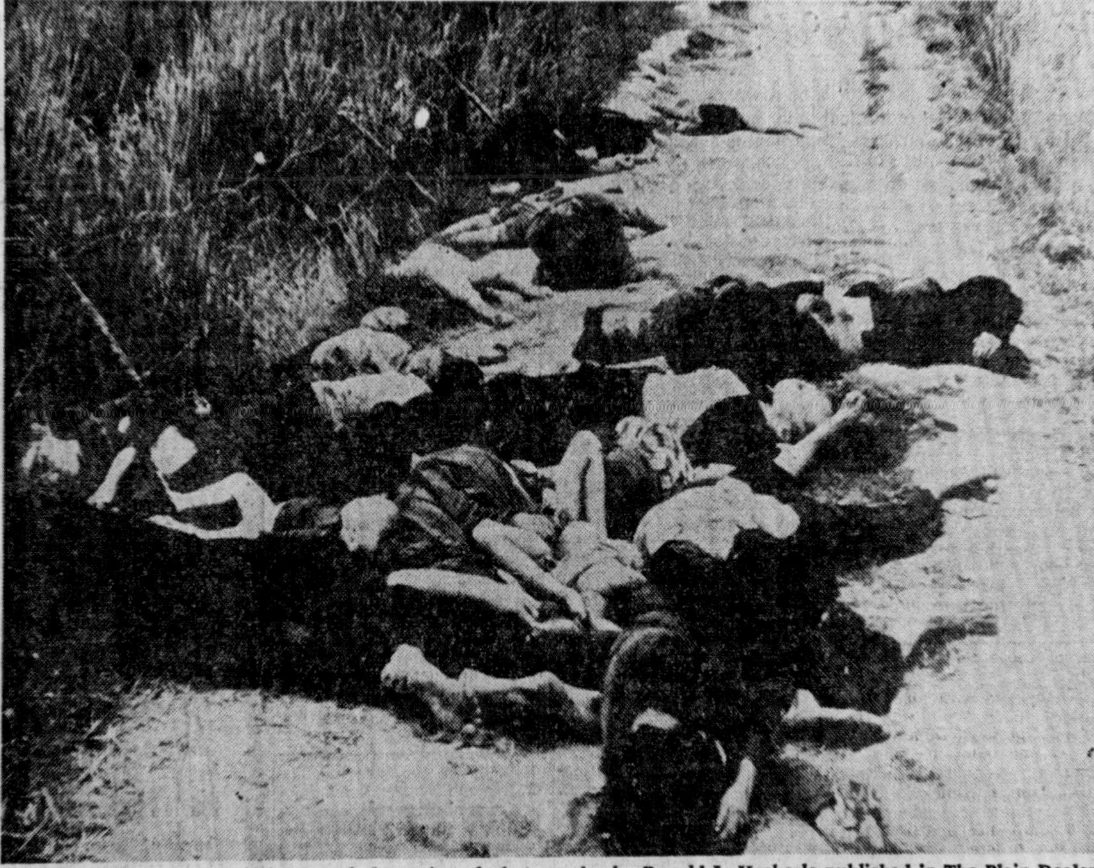

DEATH IN VIETNAM: This is one of the series of photographs by Ronald L. Haeberle published in The Plain Dealer

FORMER G.I. TOOK PICTURES OF DEAD

Says He Saw 100 Slayings and Gave Photos to Army

The accompanying photograph, published on Thursday in The Cleveland Plain Dealer, was taken by Ronald L. Haeberle of Cleveland while he was serving in Vietnam as an Army sergeant assigned to public information duties.

When published, the photograph was labeled "©1969, Ronald L. Haeberle." The photograph accompanied an interview with Mr. Haeberle by Joseph Eszterhas of The Plain Dealer staff.

In the interview, it was reported that Mr. Haeberle took this picture and several others while accompanying C Company, First Battalion, 20th Infantry Regiment, 11th Light Infantry Brigade, when its troops entered a South Vietnamese village where civilian residents were allegedly massacred by American troops in March, 1968.

Mr. Haeberle has said that he supplied the Army with copies of these photographs. The Army declined to comment on either the photographs or the alleged shootings in the village, saying that an investigation was under way and that it did not want to prejudice the case.

In the interview published in The Plain Dealer, Mr. Haeberle reported that he saw "as many as 30 American soldiers murder as many of 100 South Vietnamese civilians, many of them women and babies, many left in lifeless clumps."

He said the killings had been carried out with M-16 rifles

m News Wire Services
INGTON, Nov. 21—The
iving rose four-tenths of
t in October, continuing
n's sharpest inflation in
the Labor Department
y.

r, consumers got a
en food prices declined
s of 1 per cent, notably
and vegetables.

partment attributed the
price rise mainly to
costs for both new and
s, clothing and most
of so-called consumer

tober rise was smaller
five-tenths of 1 per
ease in September and
one in July, but was
to the four-tenths of 1
jump in August.

abor Department said
er figures represented
off of the rate of con-
ice increases since mid-

ower Down

Popkin, assistant com-
of the Bureau of Labor
said relative stability
te of price increases

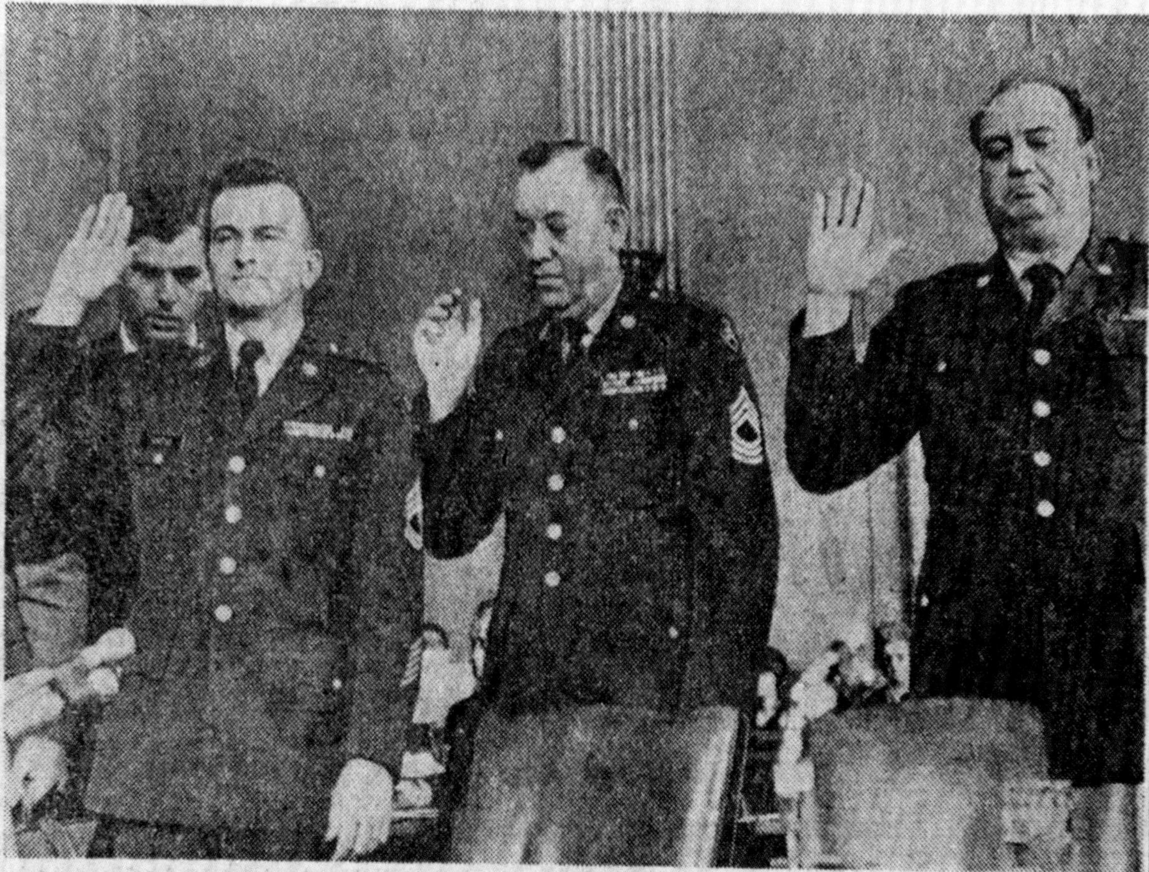

BEFORE TAKING THE FIFTH—Three Army sergeants accused of bleeding GIs in Vietnam with kickback and war profiteering schemes used the Fifth Amendment today before the Senate Permanent Investigating Subcommittee. They are, from left, James D. Givens, Ted Dickerson and Billy J. Dugger, all former custodians of Army clubs in Vietnam.—Story on Page 20. (UPI)

Agnew Press Critique | Five Desperadoes

B
Bu
WASHINGTON,
to confirm the nom
worth Jr. to the
President his choice
in 39 years. The vot

Twenty-six Republic
19 Democrats—mainly
ers — voted for conf
Against were 38 Demo
17 Republicans.

The margin of 10 aga
firmation was larger
been anticipated and
a last-minute decision
the U. S. Court of
judge by a majority
senators who had been
fence-sitters.

President Nixon said
deeply regretted the S
jection of Judge Hayns
the Supreme Court. H
Mr. Haynsworth an ou
jurist and said he woul
another Supreme Court
tion in January.

The President calle
Haynsworth at Greenvi

Q I've heard that there was never any formal request by the South Vietnamese government asking the U.S. for military aid. Is this true? — J.L., Chicago.

A Yes, according to South Vietnamese Vice President Marshal Ky. "America's policy was wrong when 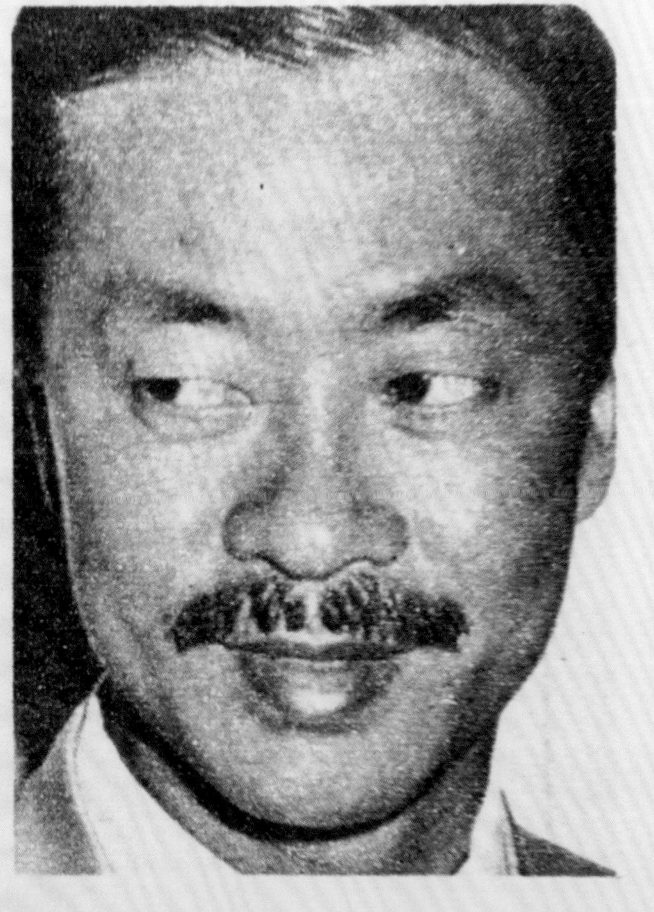 it poured in troops to win the guerrilla war," he says. "I told them they should modernize and train our army instead."

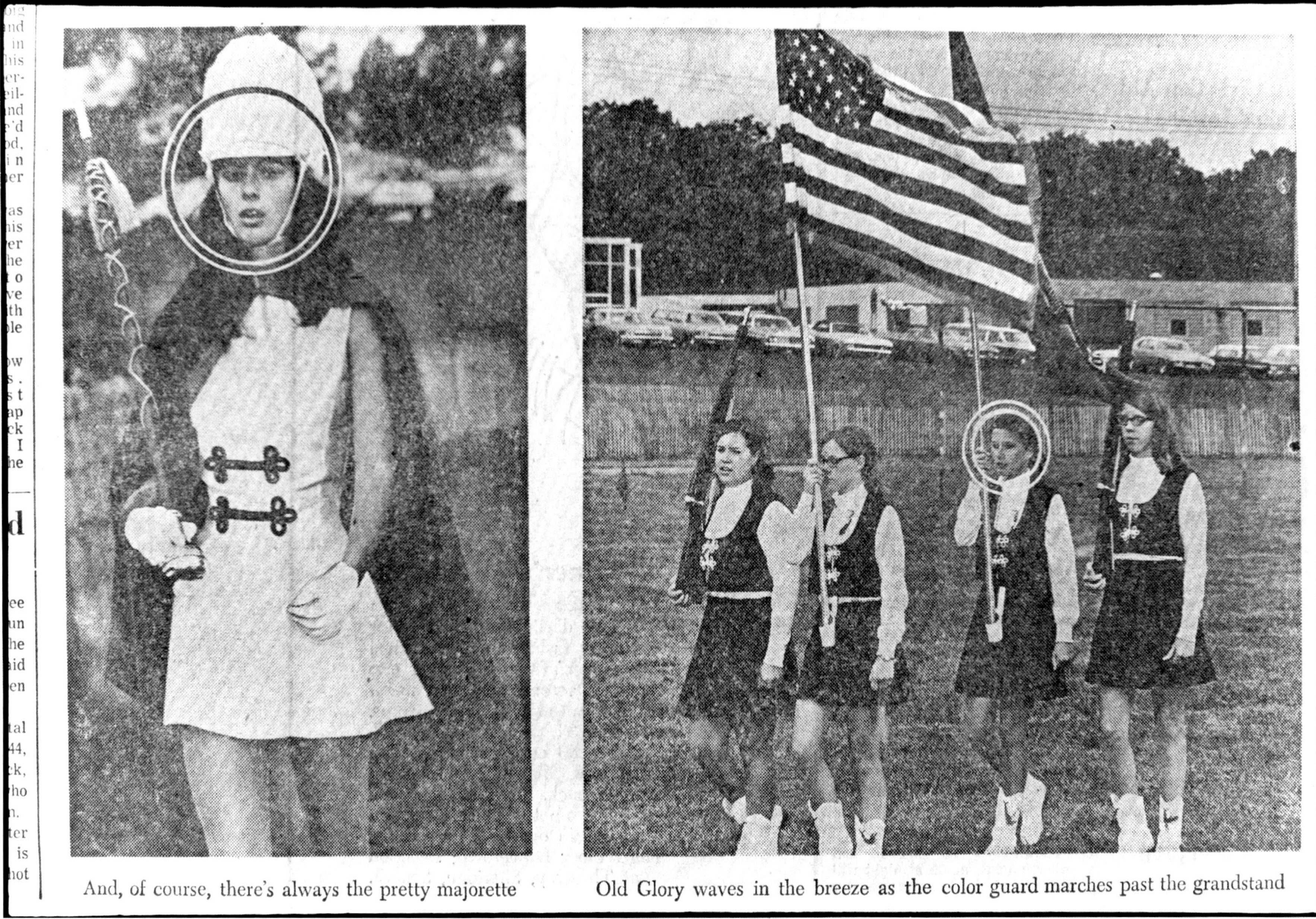

And, of course, there's always the pretty majorette

Old Glory waves in the breeze as the color guard marches past the grandstand

ill Bring War's End

Vows New Pullout At Yuletide

Plan Not Tied To Parleys

WASHINGTON (AP) — President Nixon promised the nation Monday night a Christmastime announcement of new U.S. troop withdrawals from South Vietnam, and said his current policy will bring the conflict to a conclusion no matter what happens at the nego-

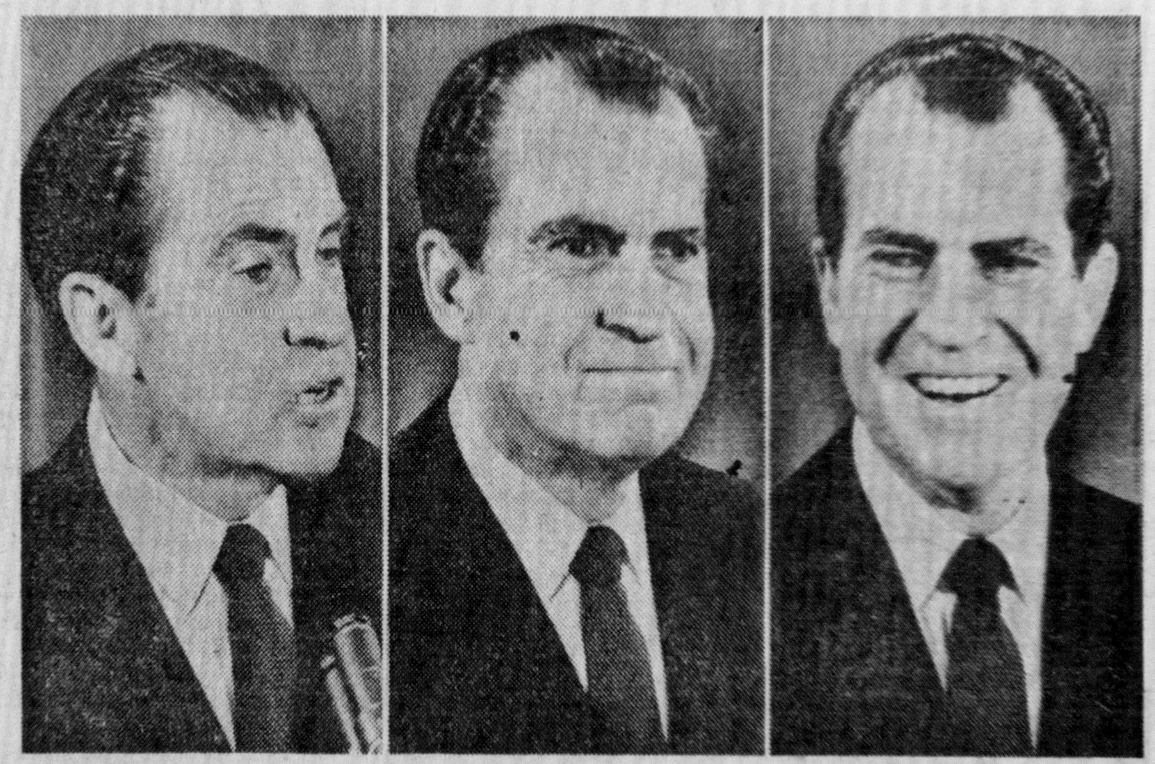

President Nixon's expressions reflect variety of questions and answers

... during news conference

Group Says Mass Unrest

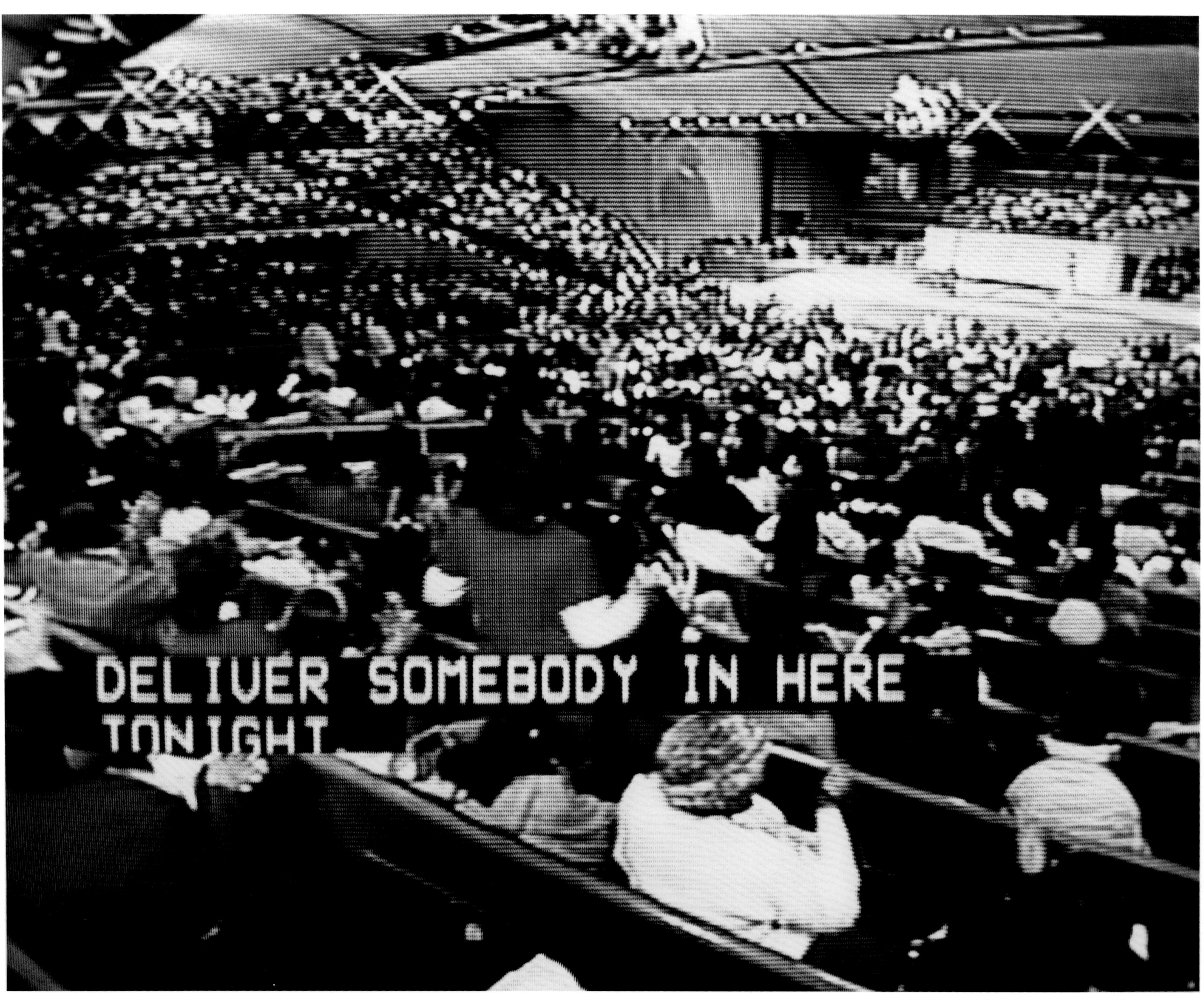
DELIVER SOMEBODY IN HERE
TONIGHT

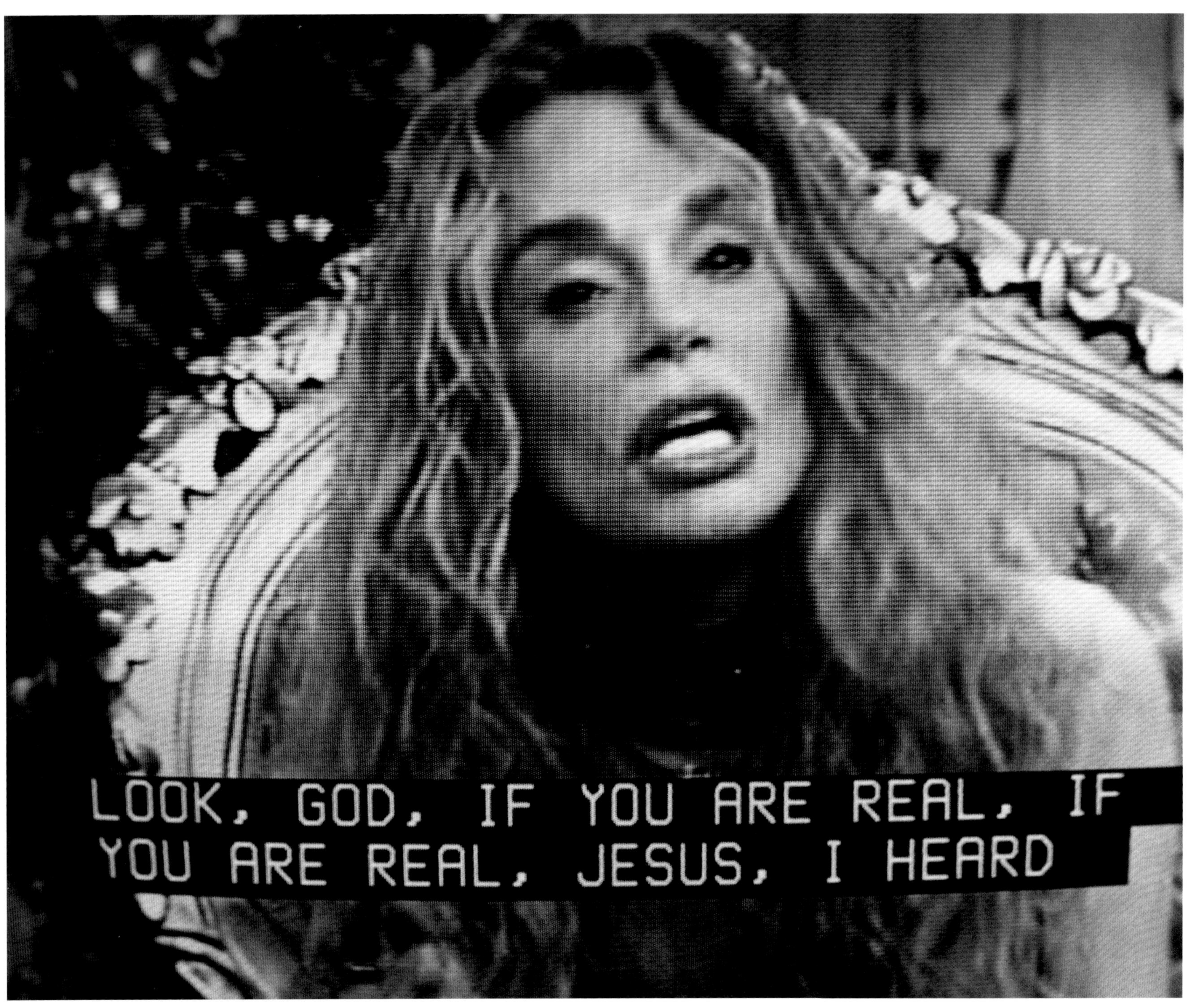

LOOK, GOD, IF YOU ARE REAL, IF
YOU ARE REAL, JESUS, I HEARD

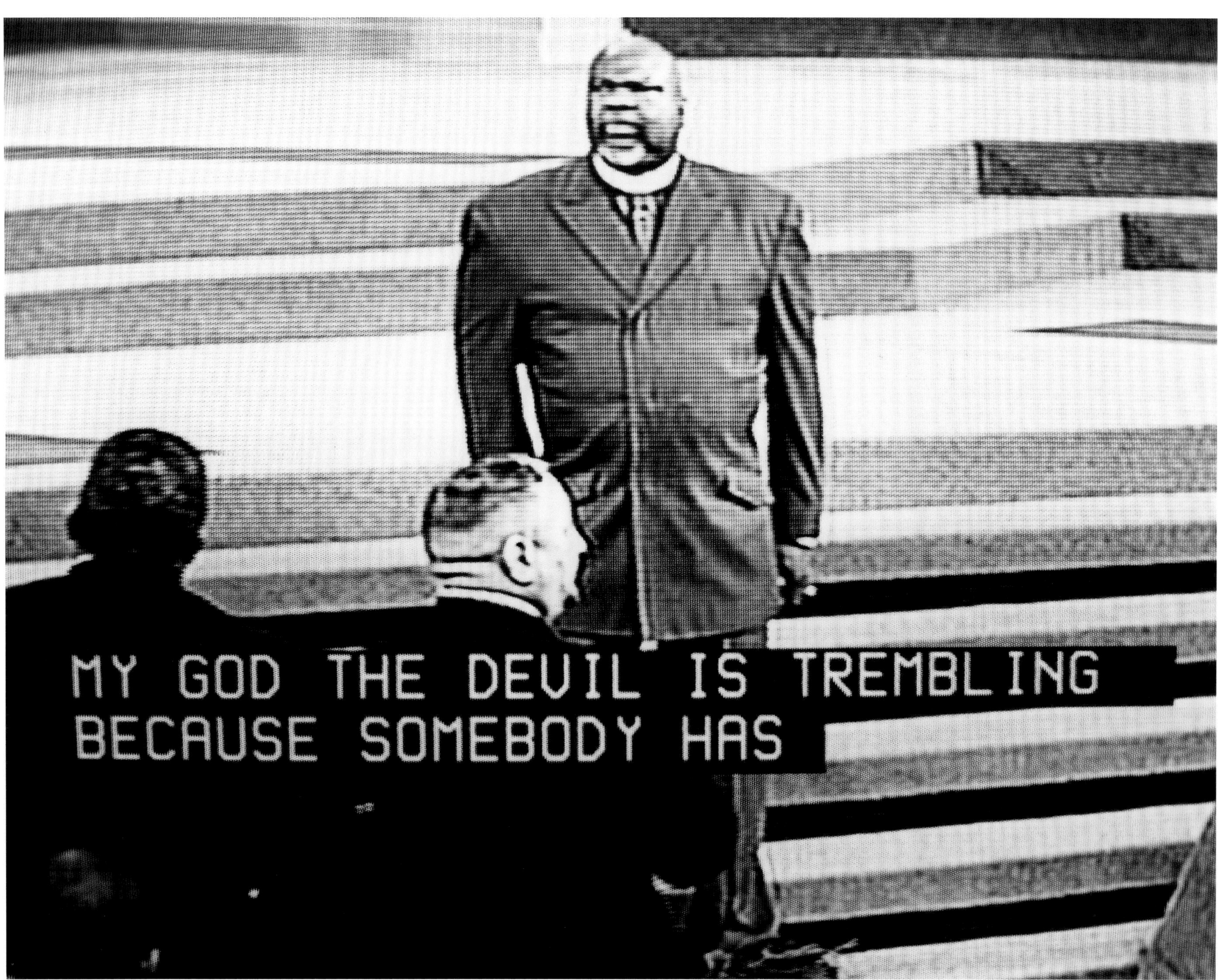
MY GOD THE DEVIL IS TREMBLING
BECAUSE SOMEBODY HAS

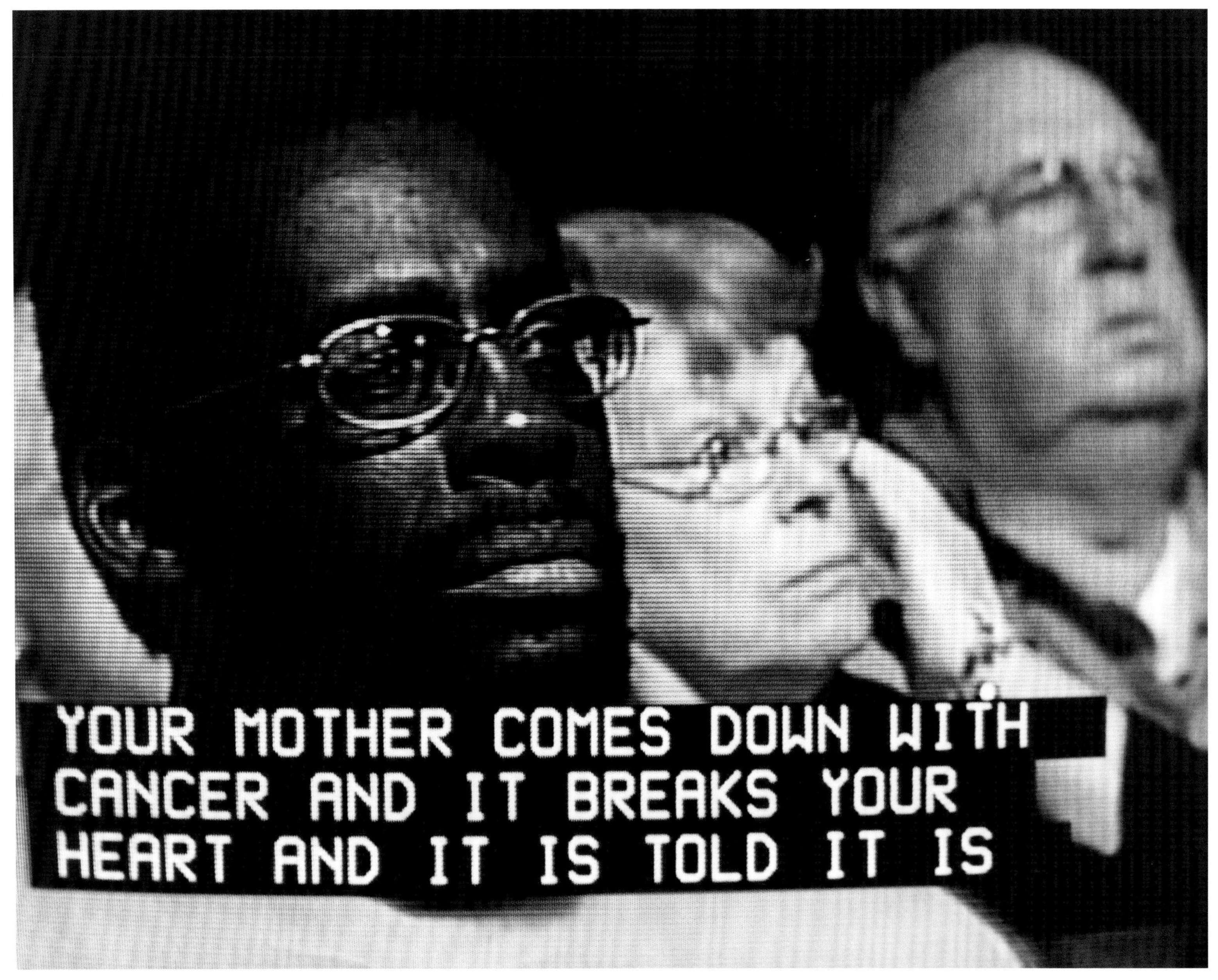

YOUR MOTHER COMES DOWN WITH
CANCER AND IT BREAKS YOUR
HEART AND IT IS TOLD IT IS

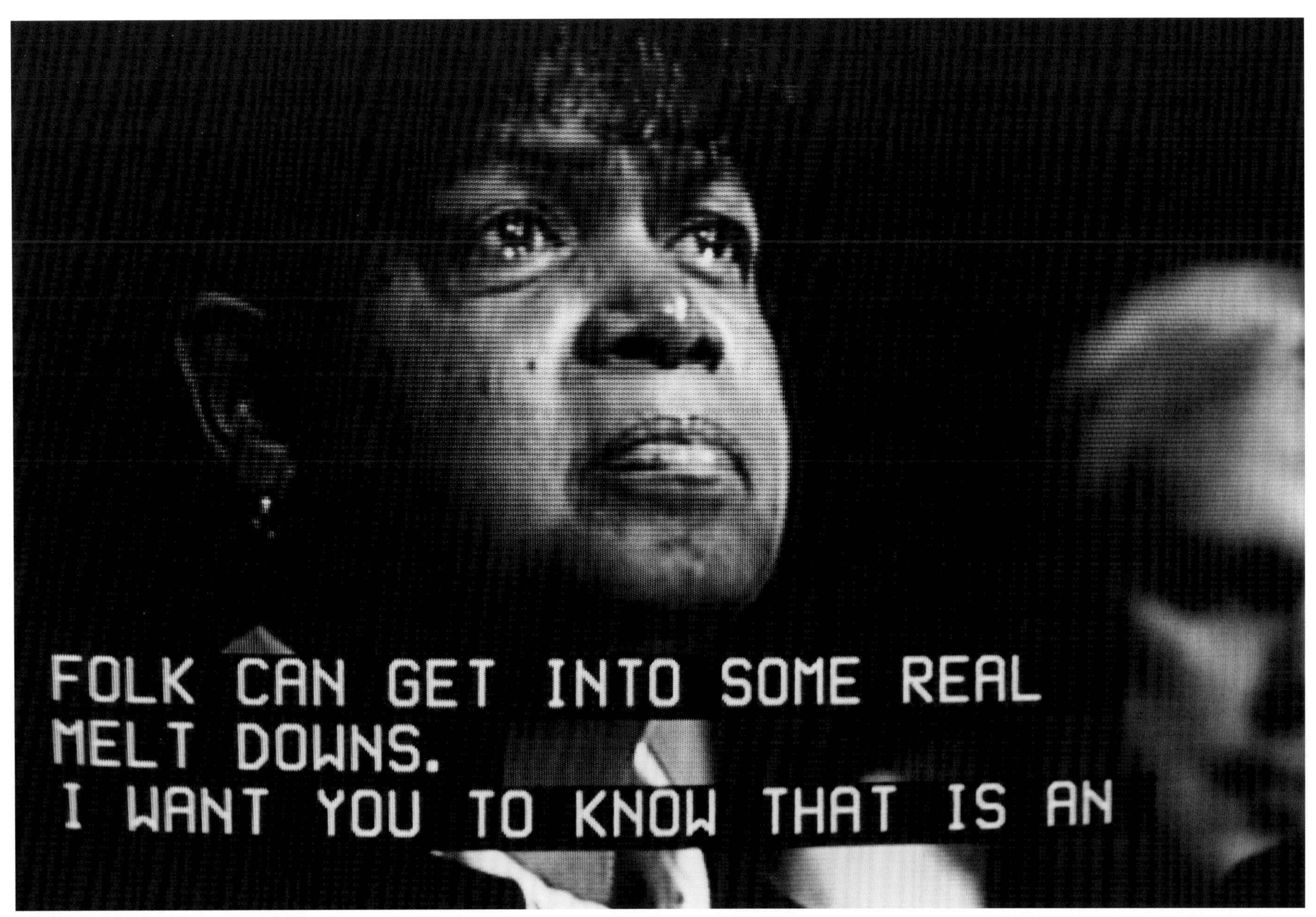
FOLK CAN GET INTO SOME REAL
MELT DOWNS.
I WANT YOU TO KNOW THAT IS AN

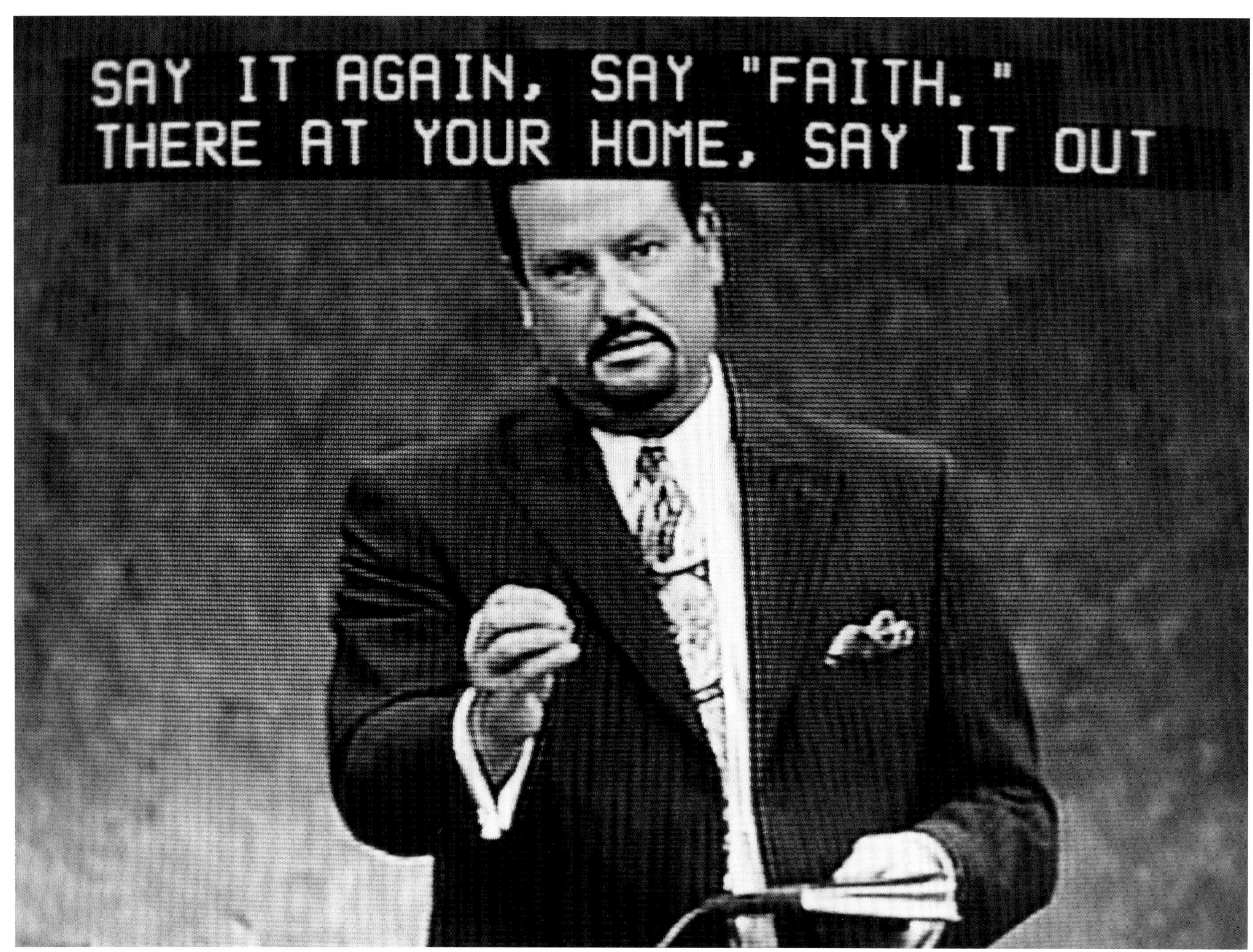

SAY IT AGAIN, SAY "FAITH."
THERE AT YOUR HOME, SAY IT OUT

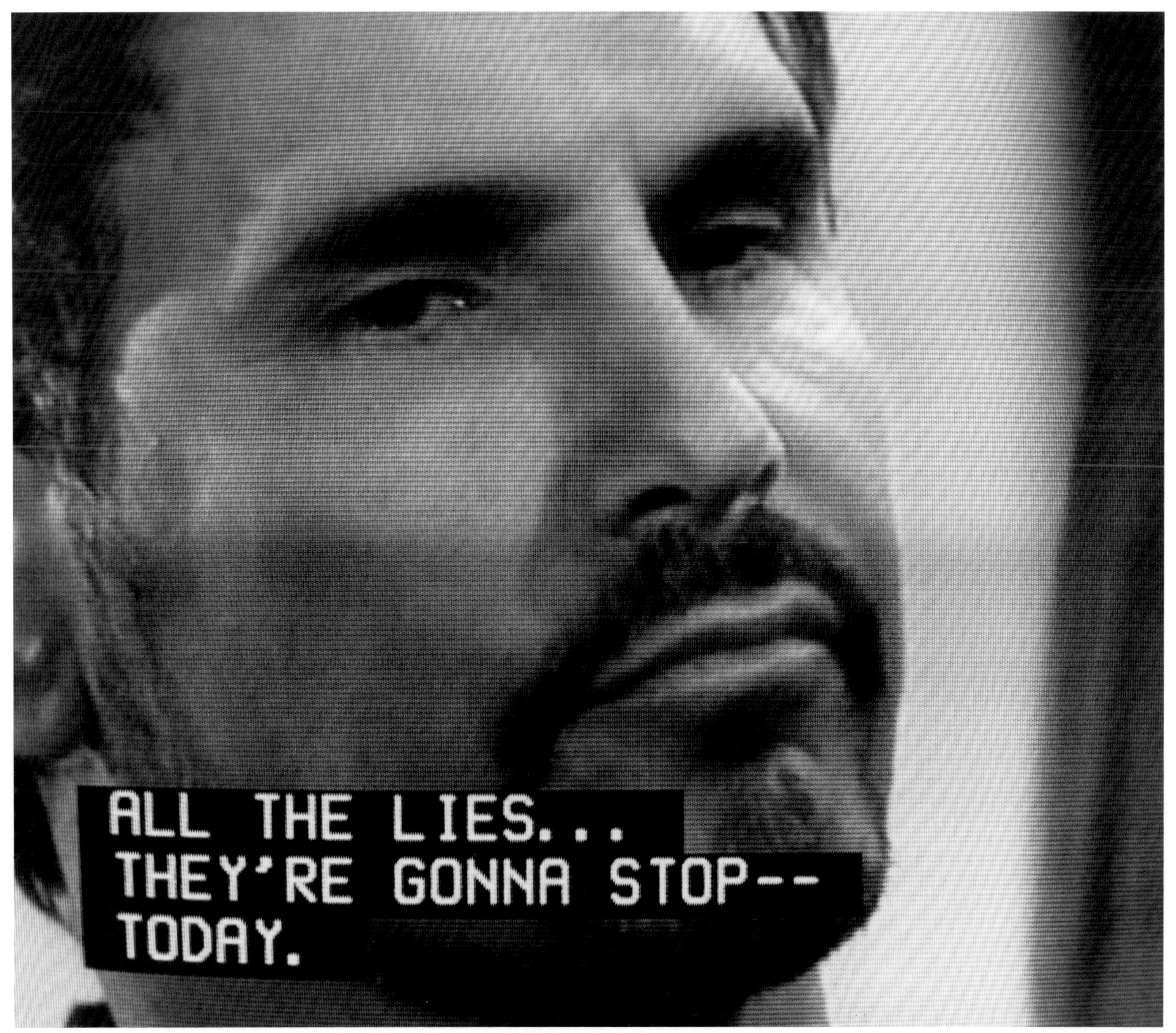

ALL THE LIES...
THEY'RE GONNA STOP--
TODAY.

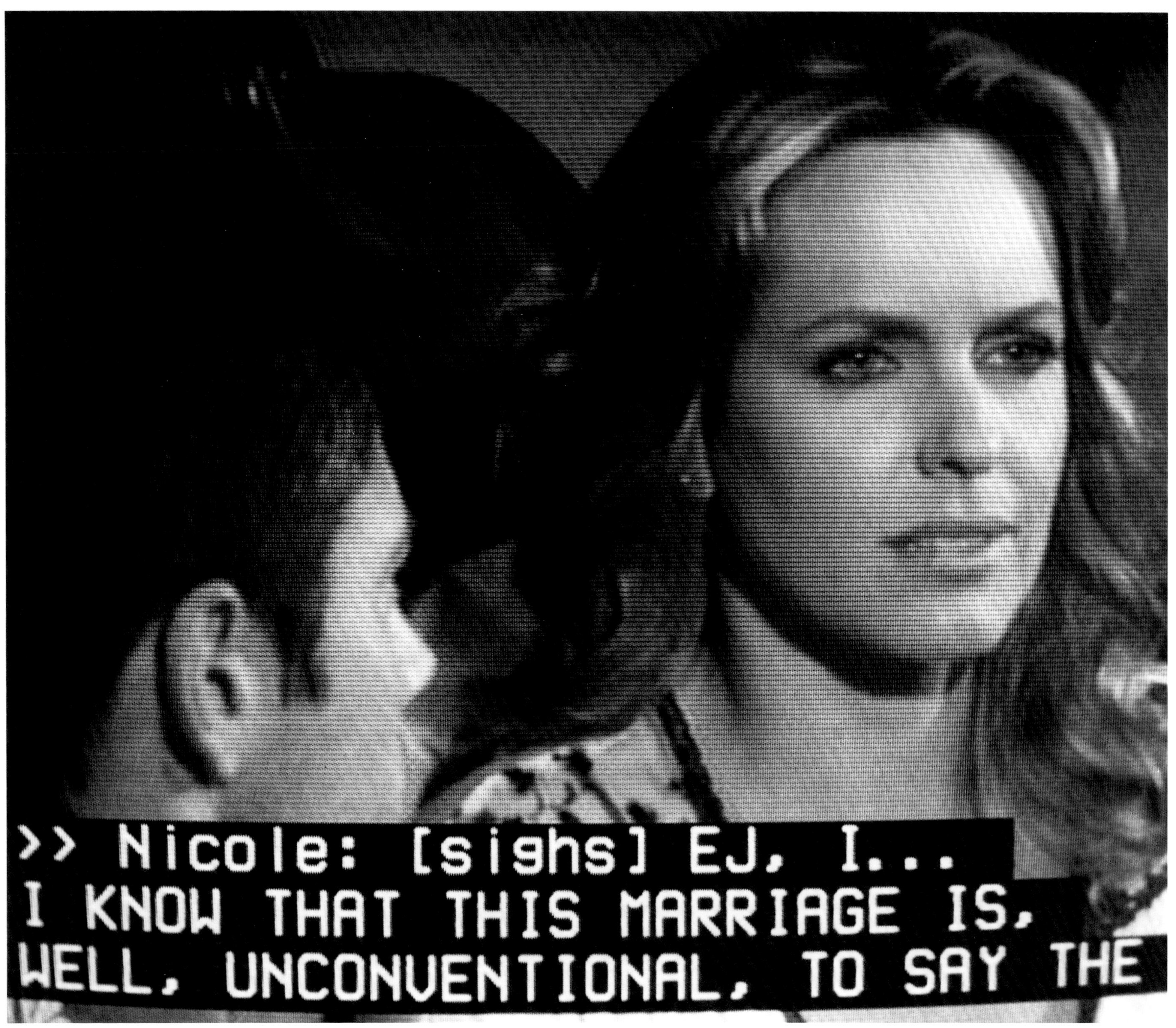

>> Nicole: [sighs] EJ, I...
I KNOW THAT THIS MARRIAGE IS,
WELL, UNCONVENTIONAL, TO SAY THE

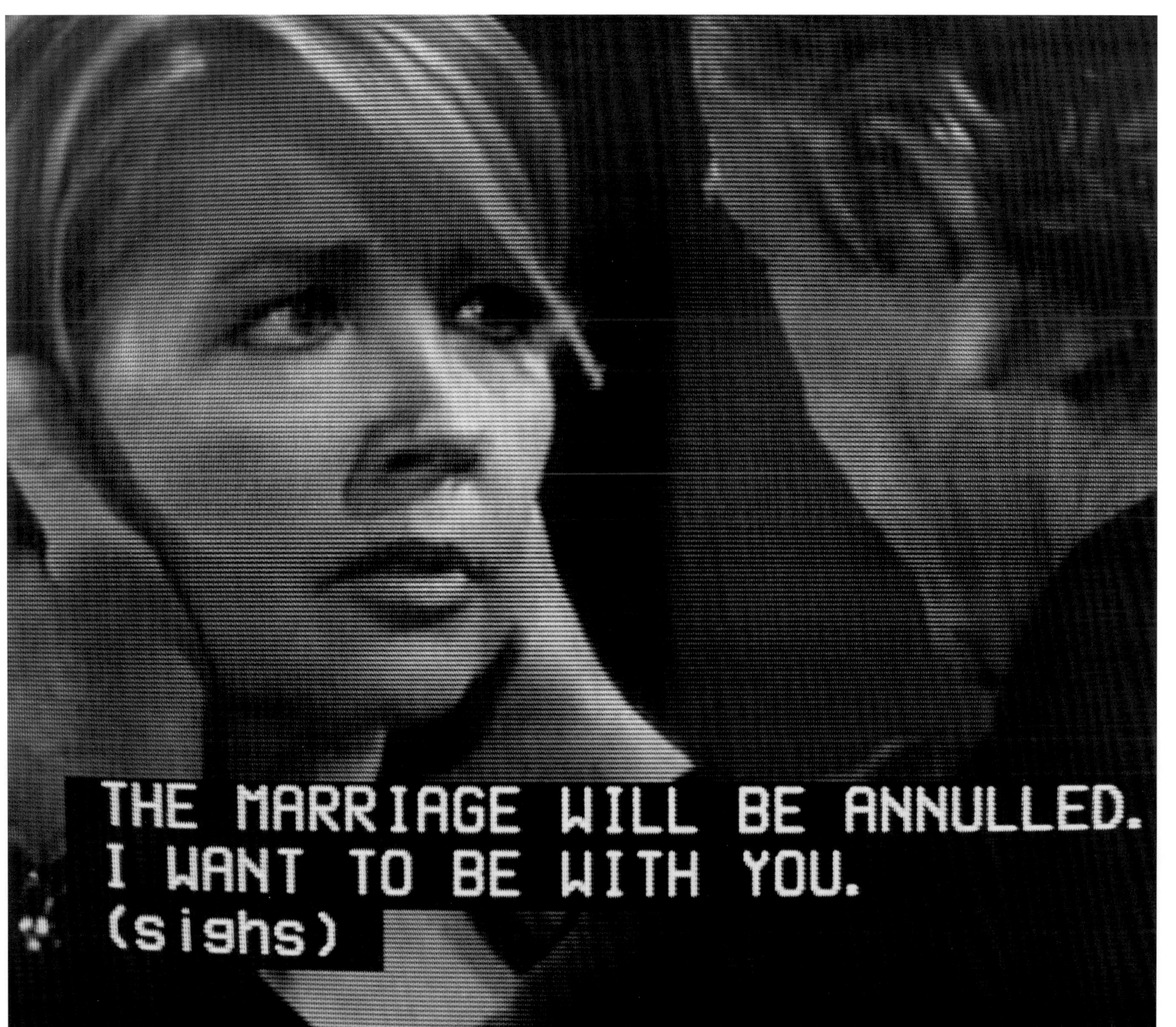

THE MARRIAGE WILL BE ANNULLED.
I WANT TO BE WITH YOU.
(sighs)

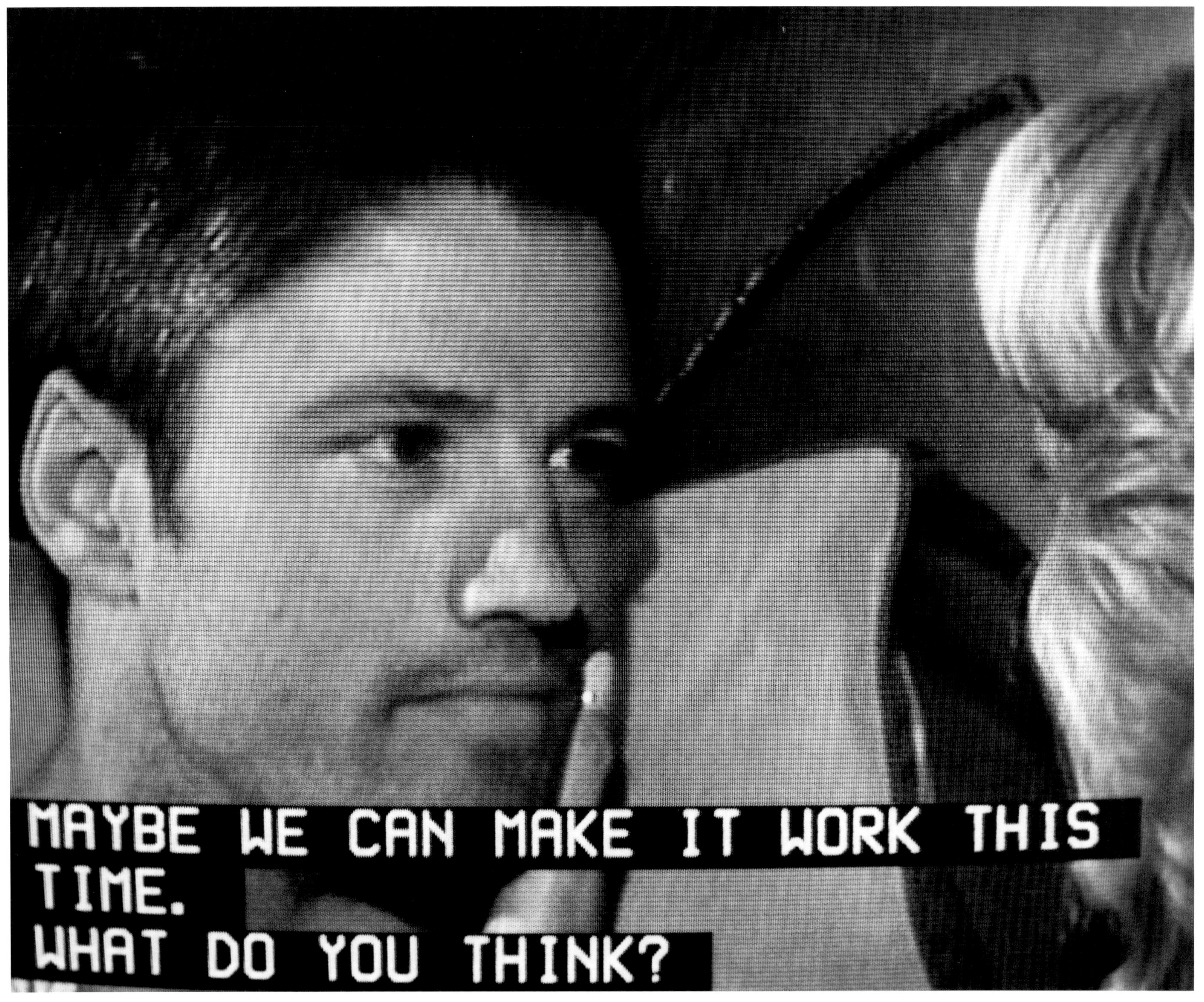
MAYBE WE CAN MAKE IT WORK THIS
TIME.
WHAT DO YOU THINK?

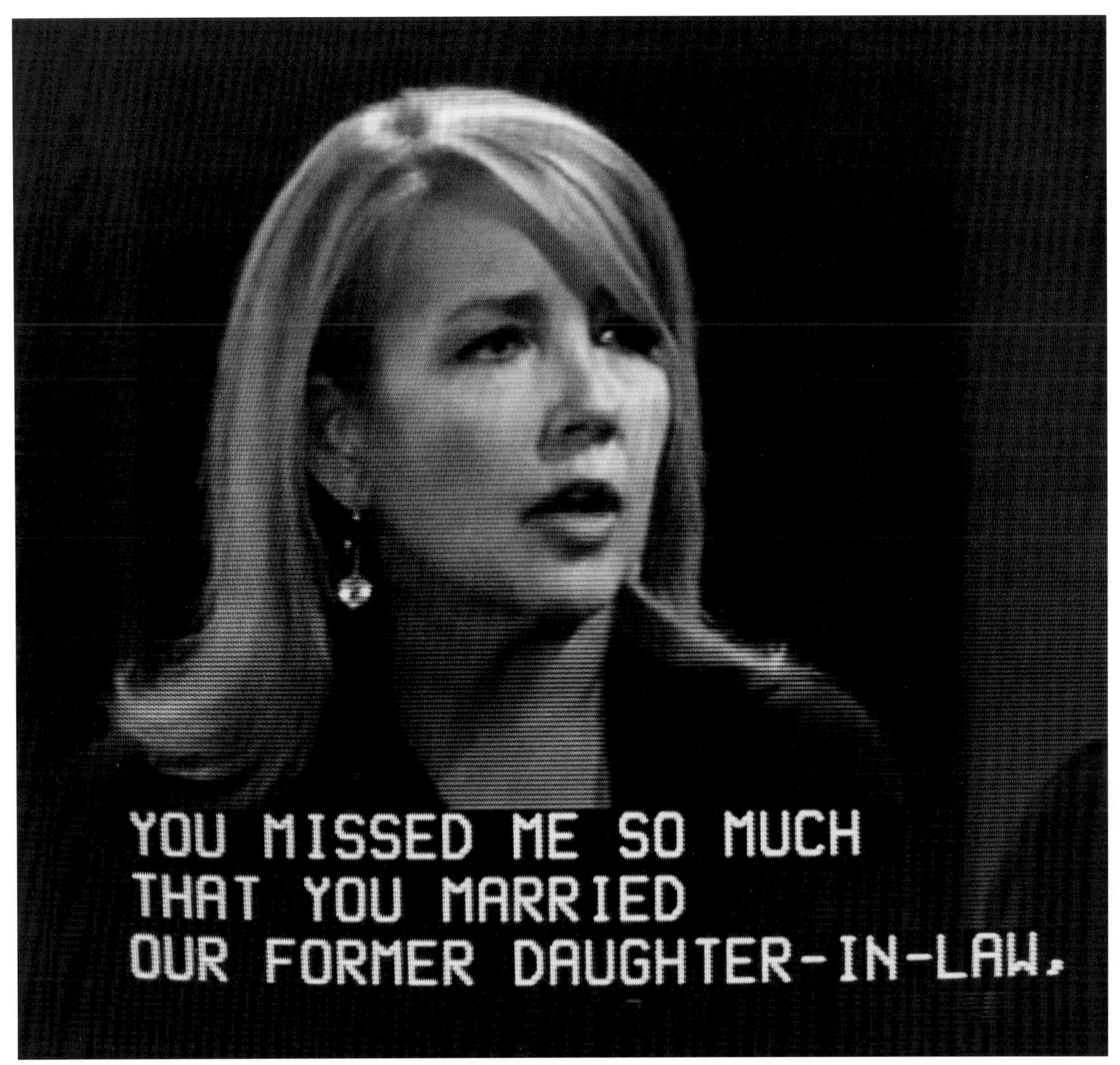

YOU MISSED ME SO MUCH
THAT YOU MARRIED
OUR FORMER DAUGHTER-IN-LAW.

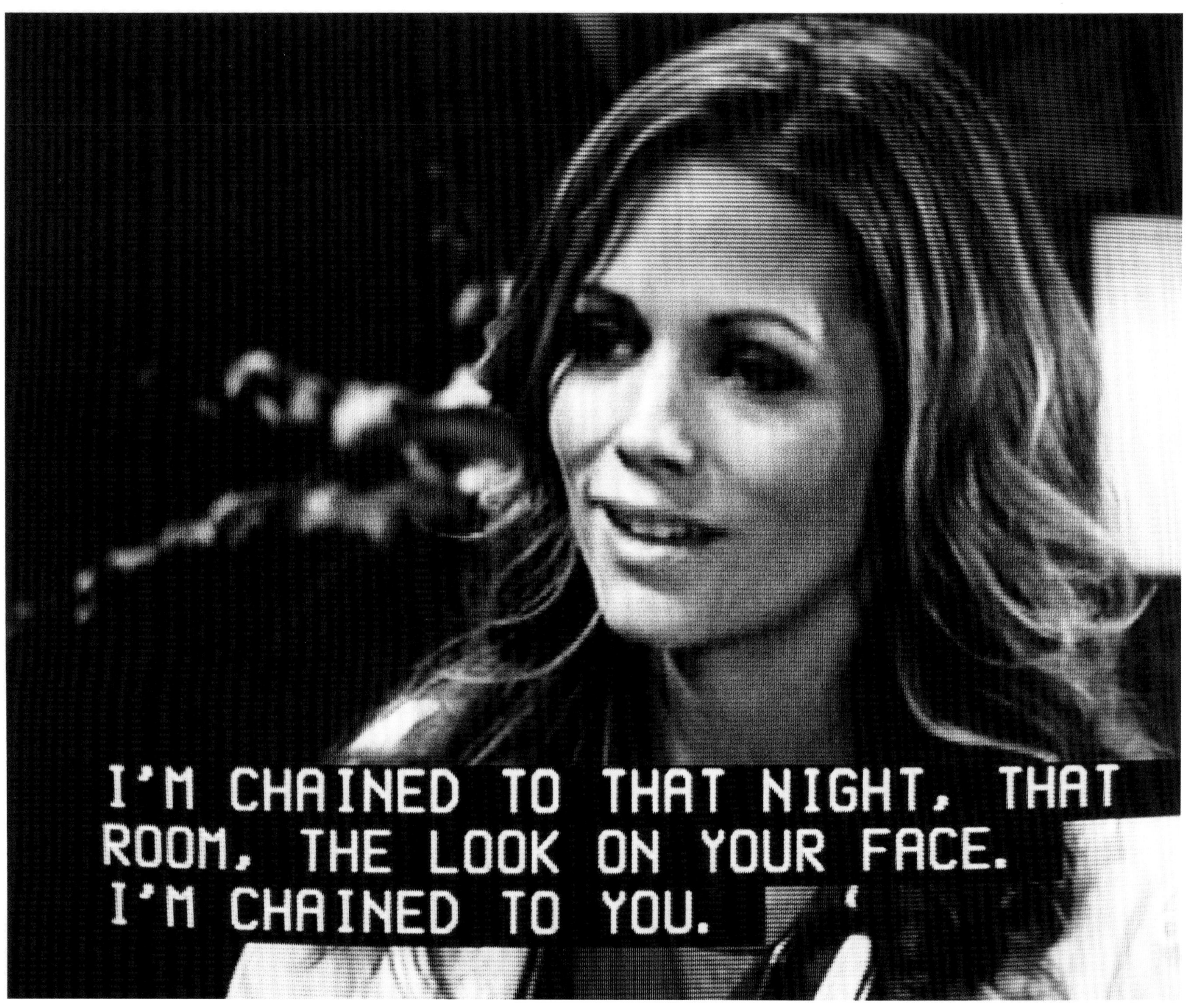
I'M CHAINED TO THAT NIGHT, THAT
ROOM, THE LOOK ON YOUR FACE.
I'M CHAINED TO YOU.

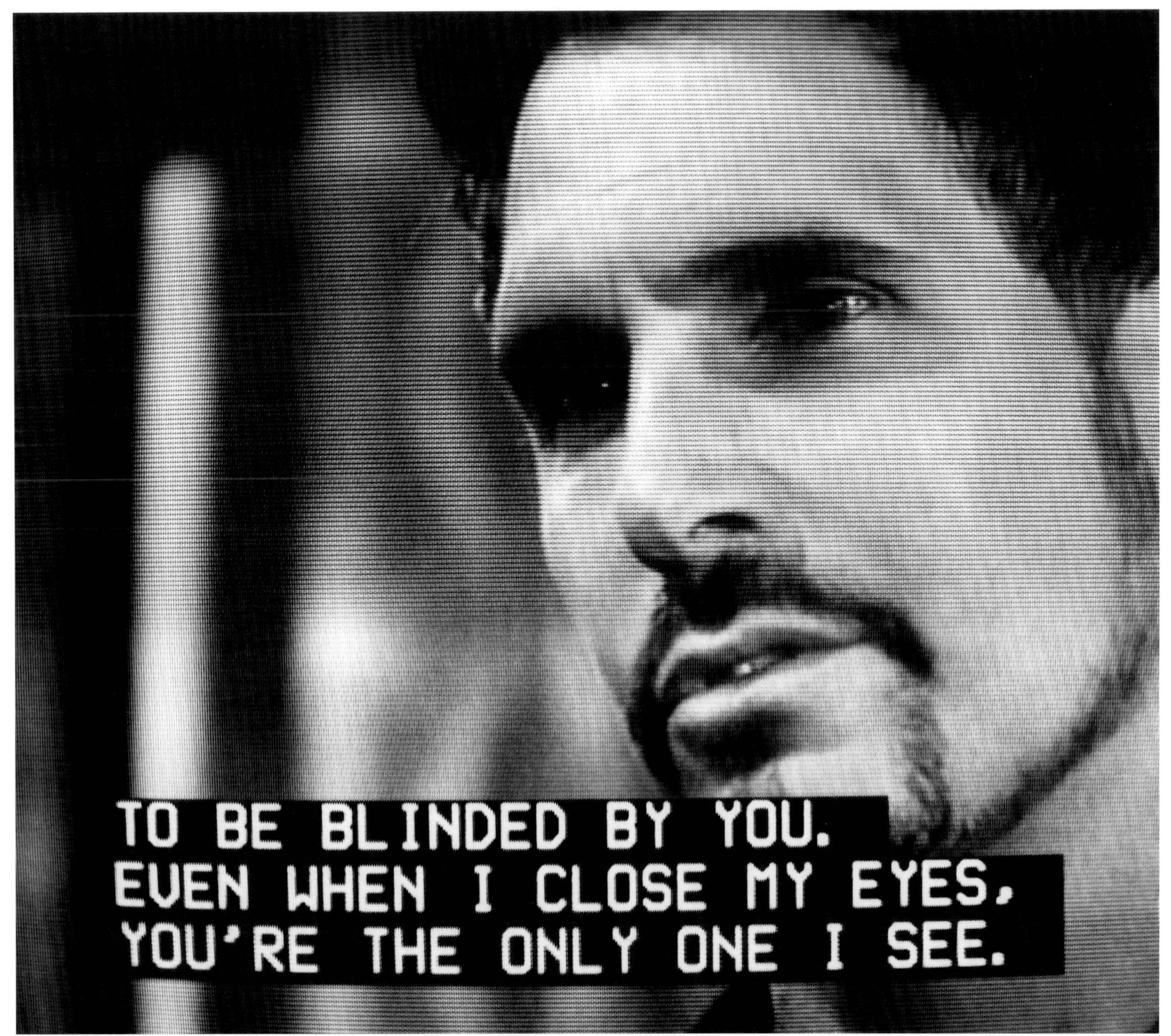

TO BE BLINDED BY YOU.
EVEN WHEN I CLOSE MY EYES,
YOU'RE THE ONLY ONE I SEE.

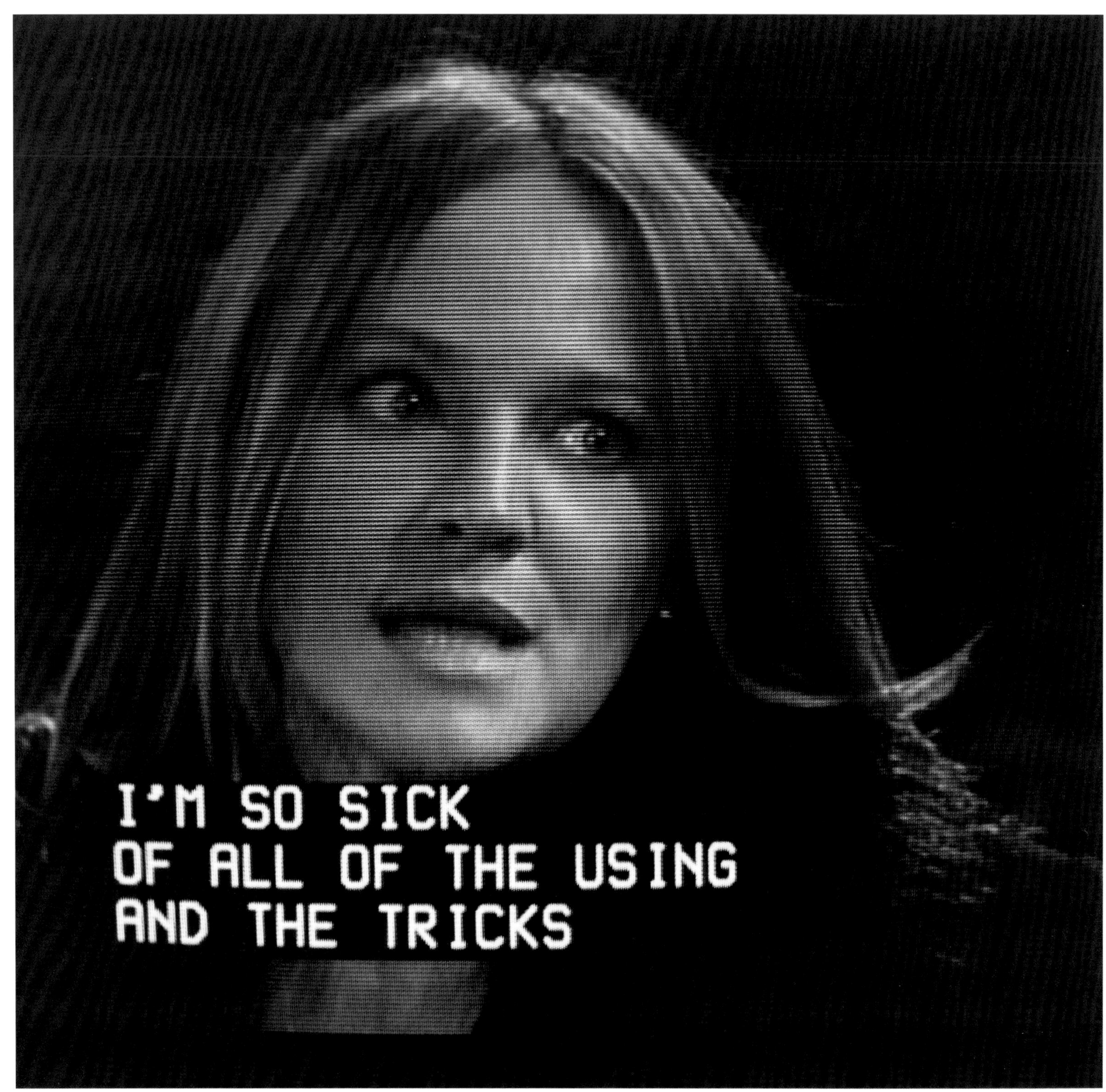

I'M SO SICK
OF ALL OF THE USING
AND THE TRICKS

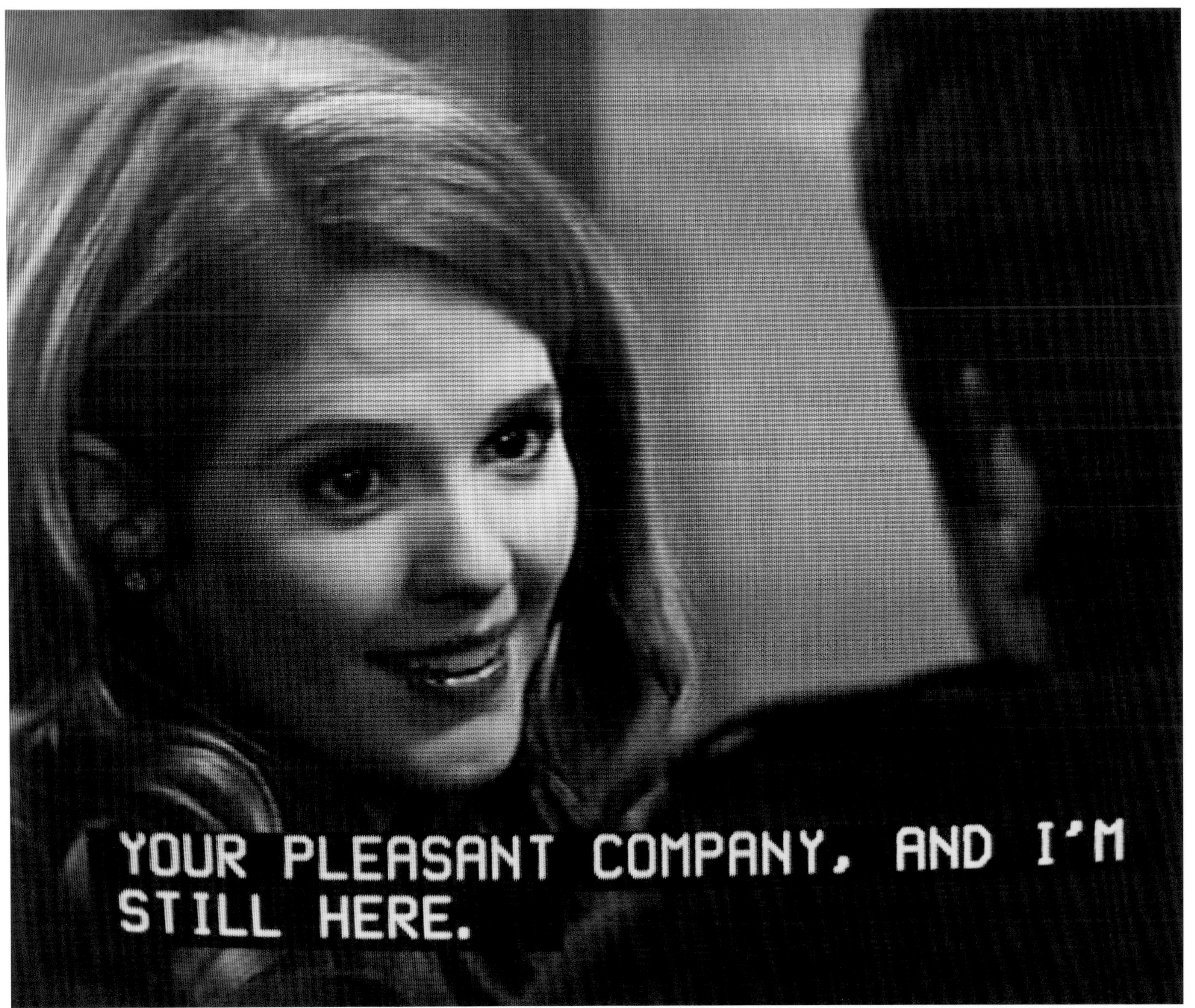

YOUR PLEASANT COMPANY, AND I'M
STILL HERE.

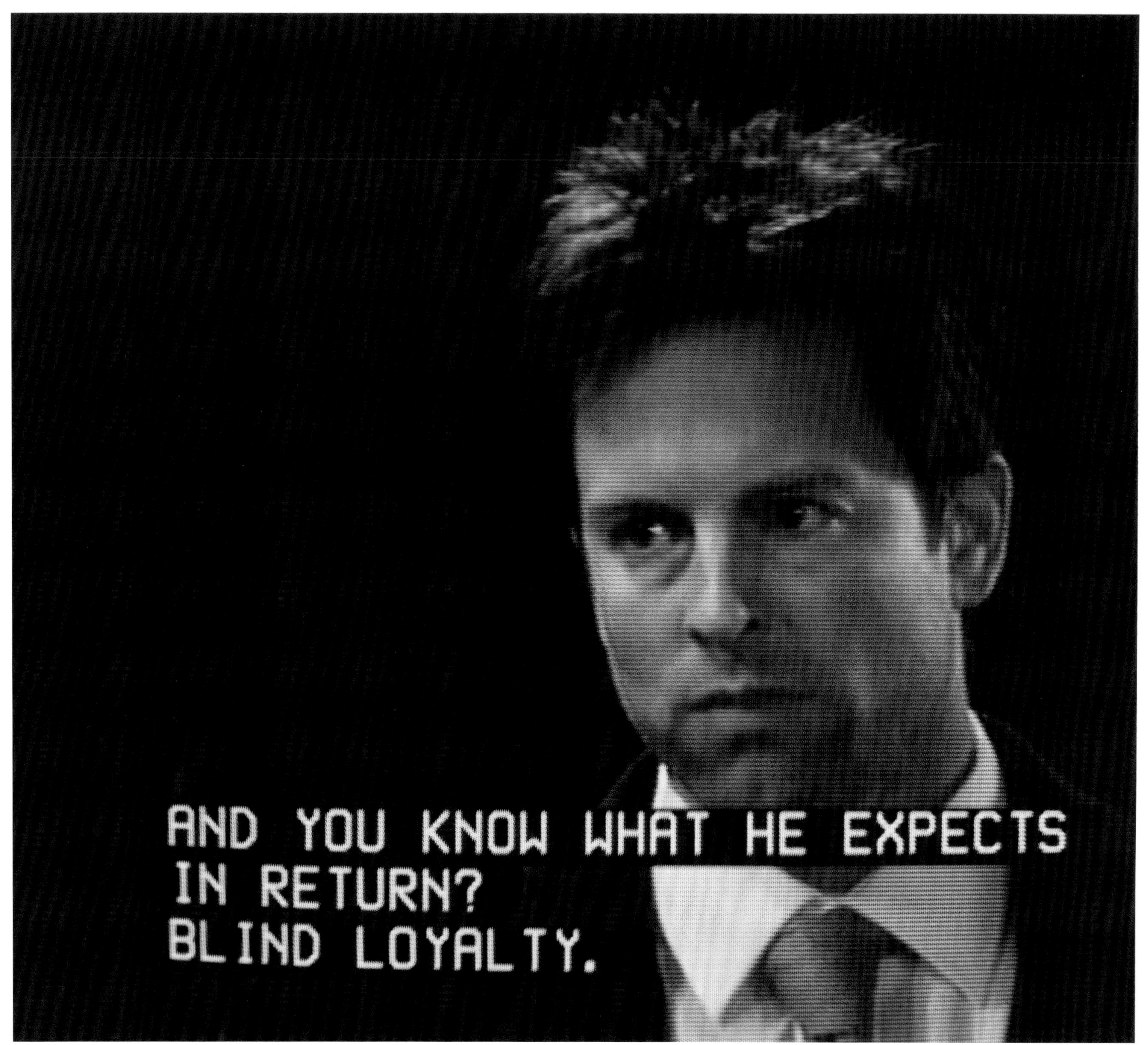
AND YOU KNOW WHAT HE EXPECTS
IN RETURN?
BLIND LOYALTY.

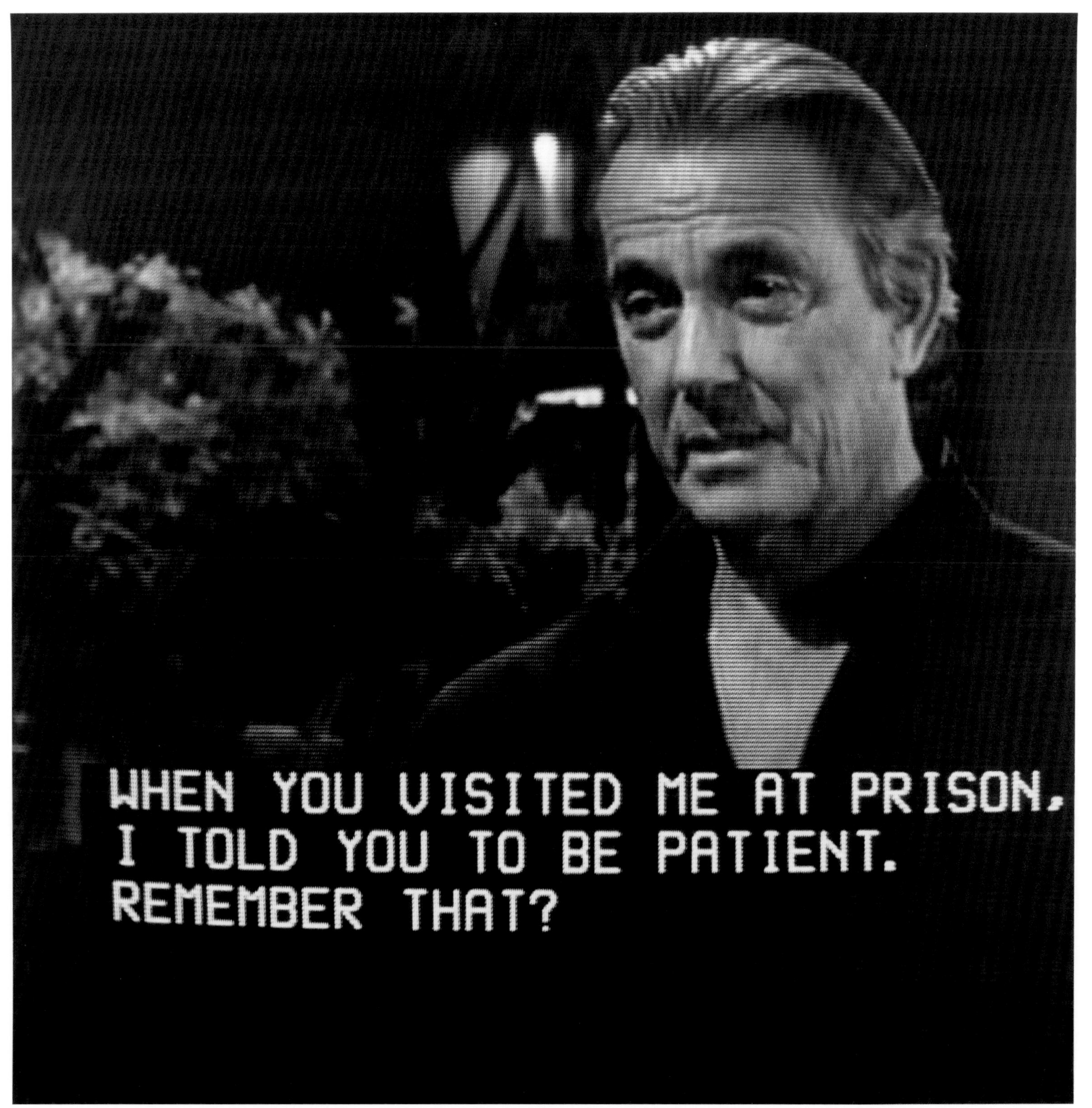
WHEN YOU VISITED ME AT PRISON,
I TOLD YOU TO BE PATIENT.
REMEMBER THAT?

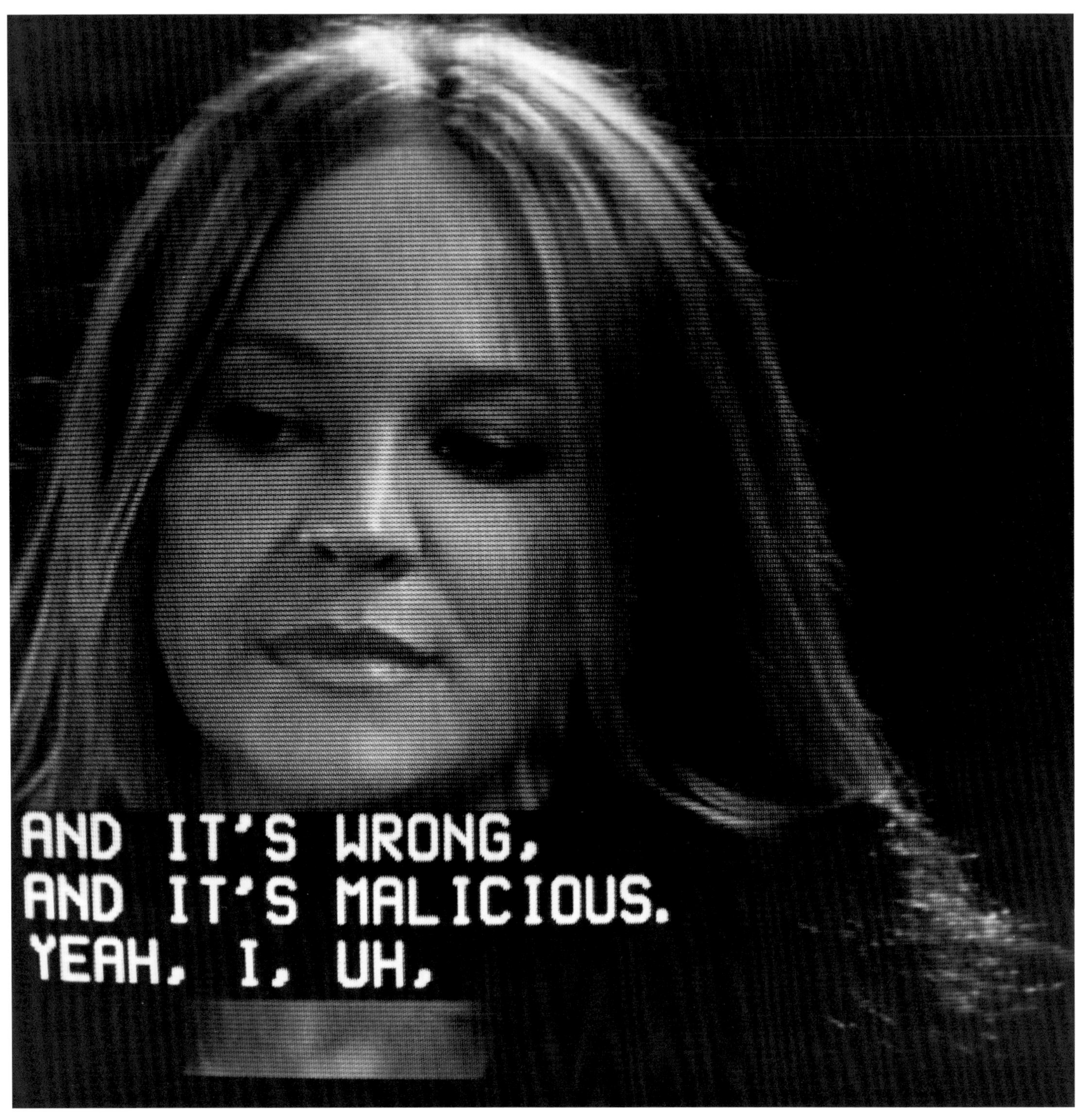

AND IT'S WRONG,
AND IT'S MALICIOUS.
YEAH, I, UH,

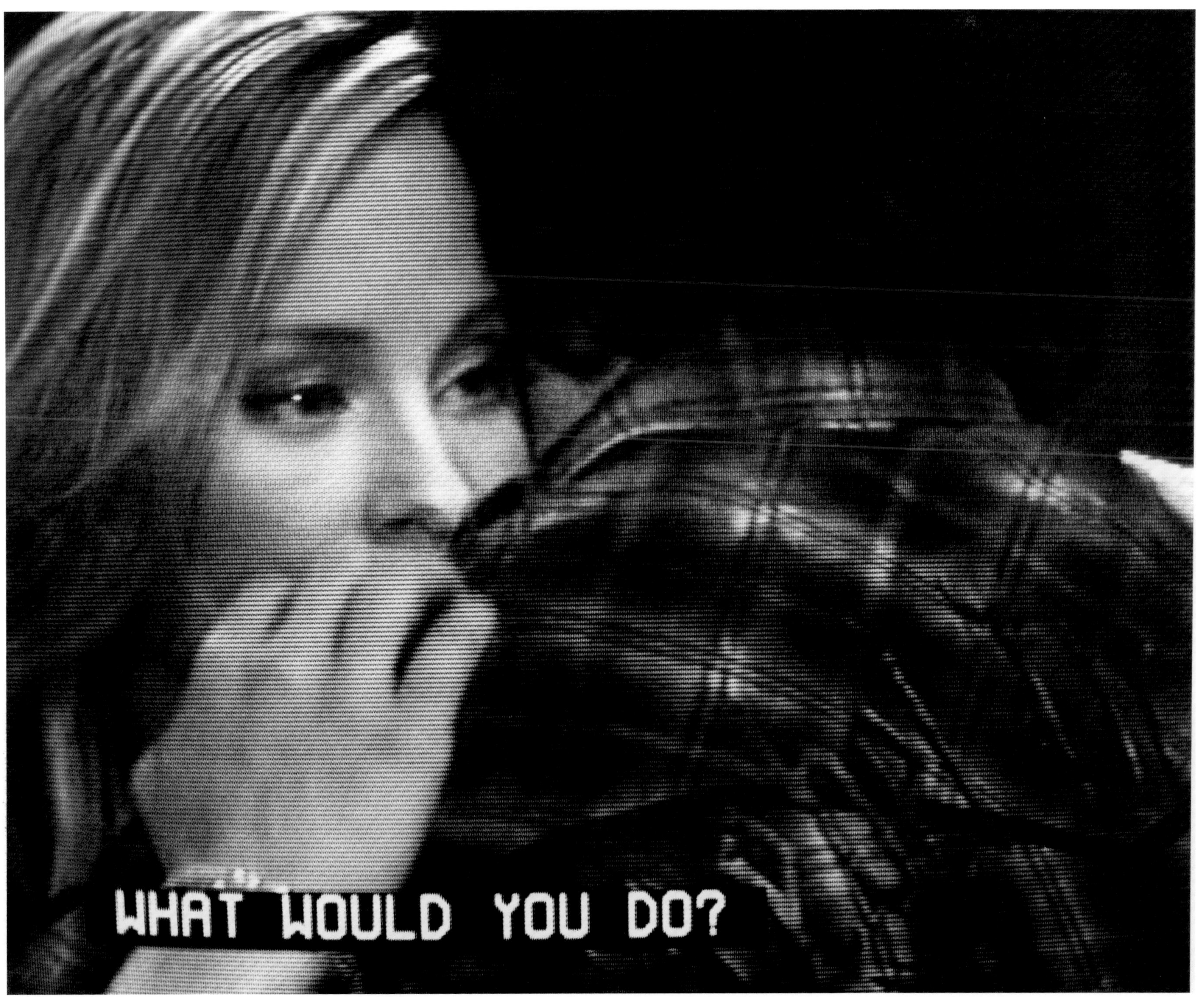

WHAT WOULD YOU DO?

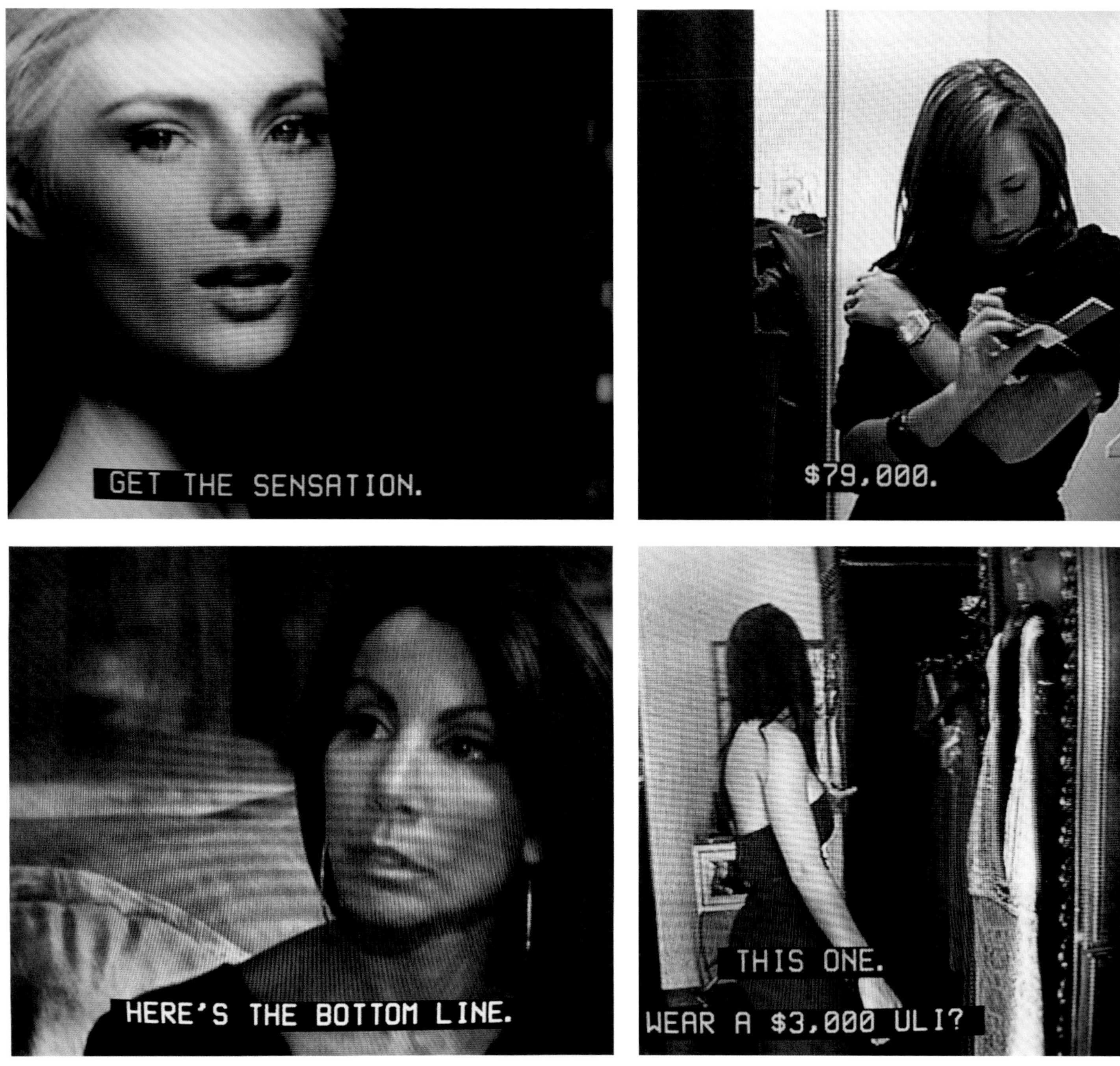
GET THE SENSATION.
$79,000.
HERE'S THE BOTTOM LINE.
THIS ONE.
WEAR A $3,000 ULI?

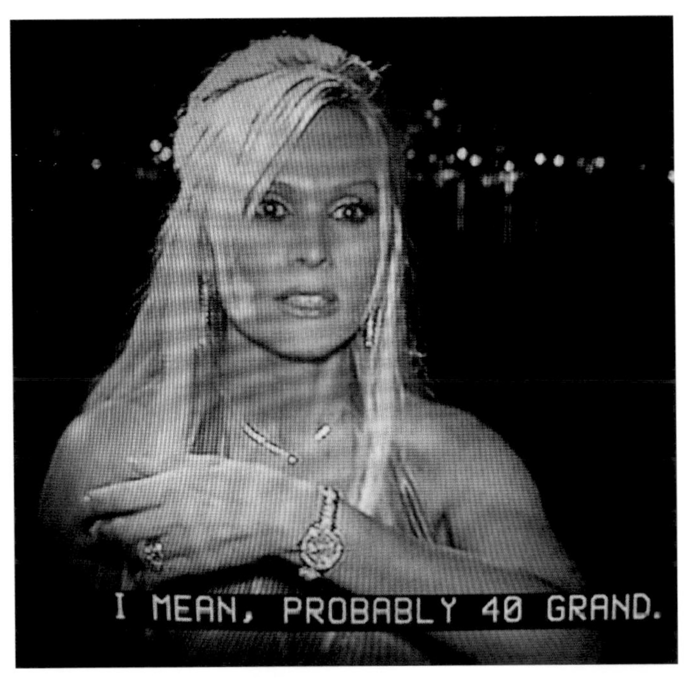
I MEAN, PROBABLY 40 GRAND.

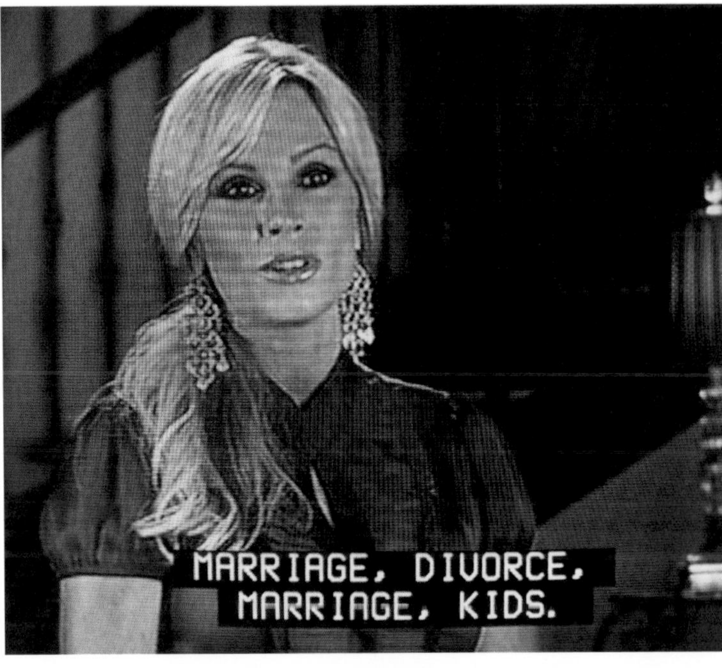
MARRIAGE, DIVORCE,
MARRIAGE, KIDS.

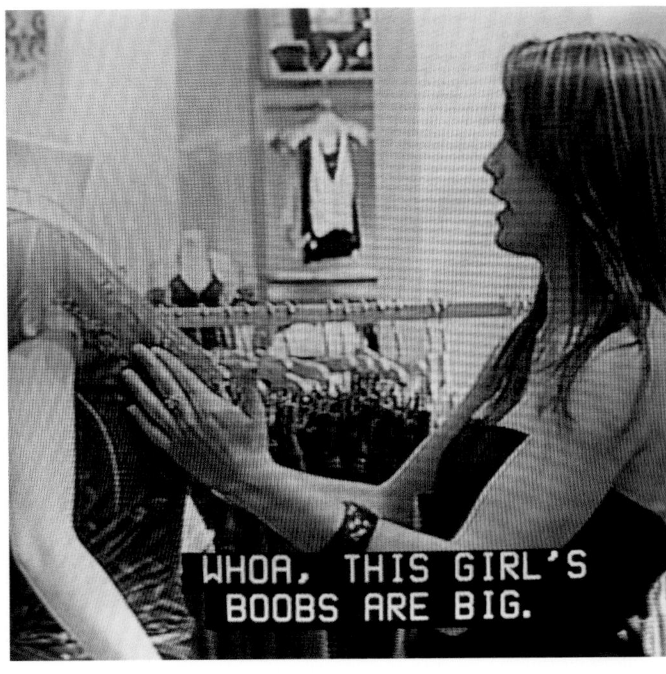
WHOA, THIS GIRL'S
BOOBS ARE BIG.

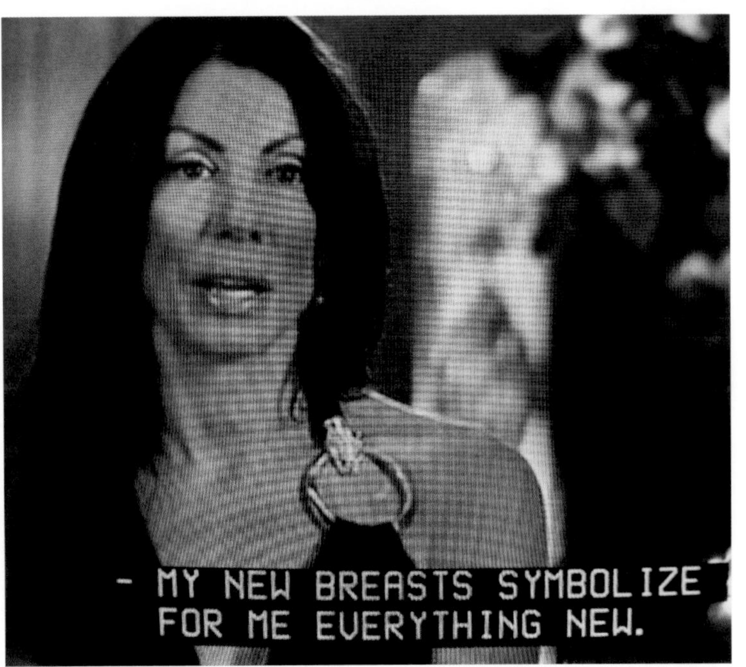
- MY NEW BREASTS SYMBOLIZE
FOR ME EVERYTHING NEW.

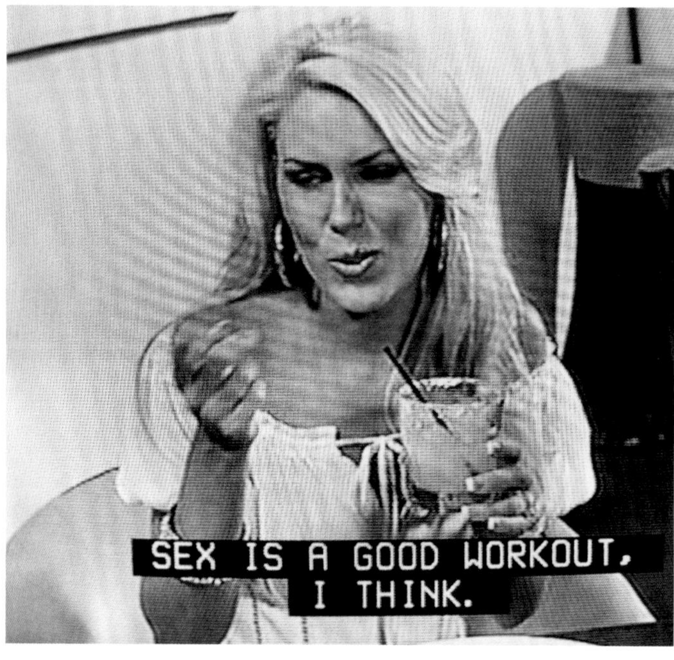
SEX IS A GOOD WORKOUT,
I THINK.

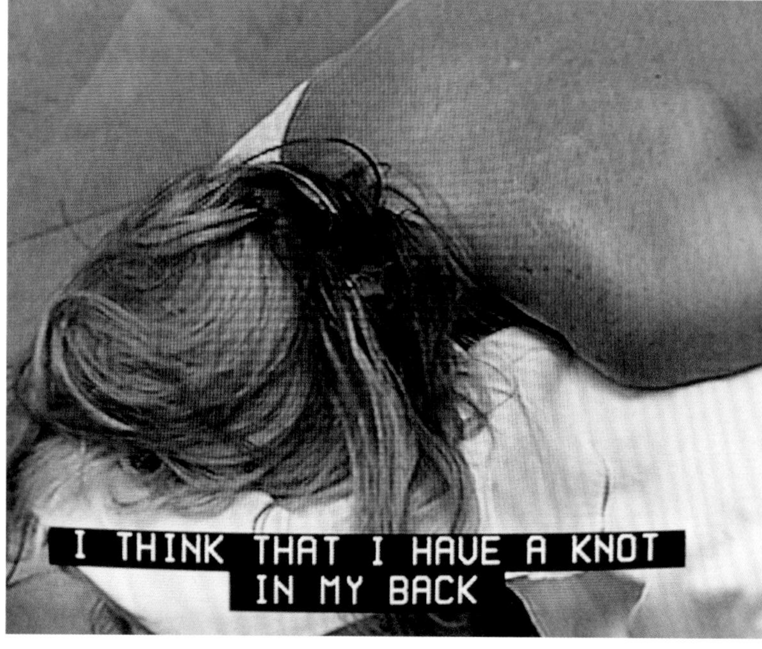
I THINK THAT I HAVE A KNOT
IN MY BACK

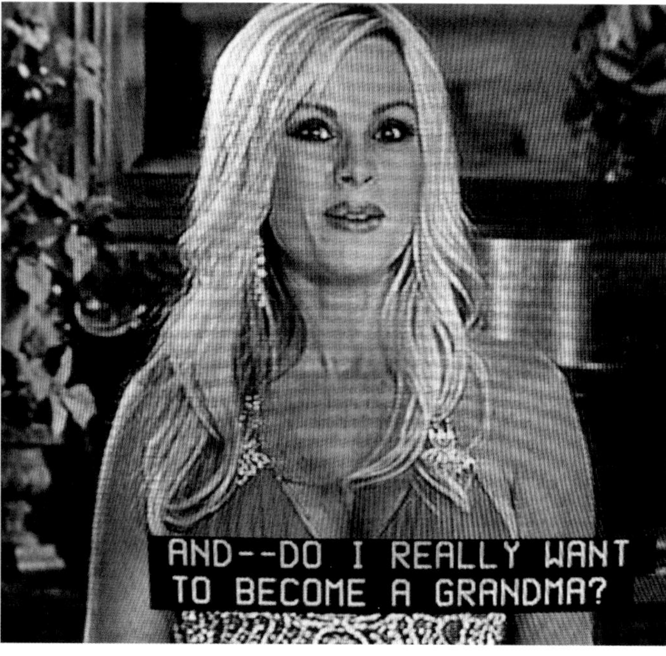
AND--DO I REALLY WANT
TO BECOME A GRANDMA?

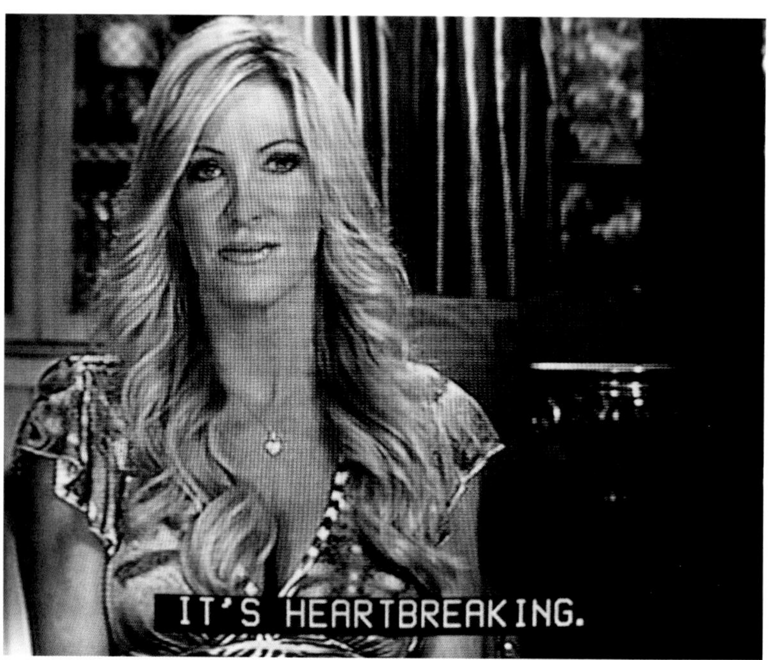
IT'S HEARTBREAKING.

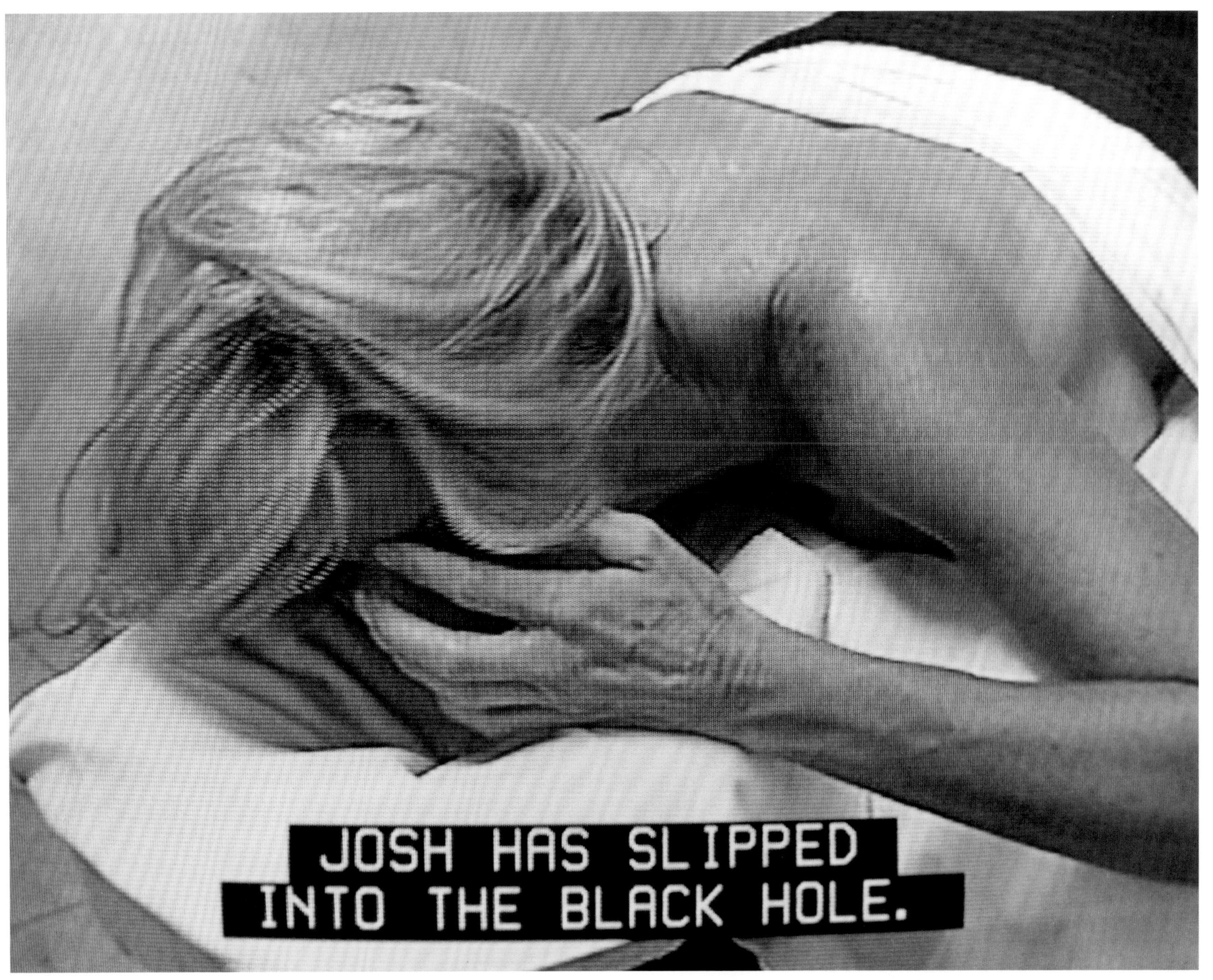
JOSH HAS SLIPPED
INTO THE BLACK HOLE.

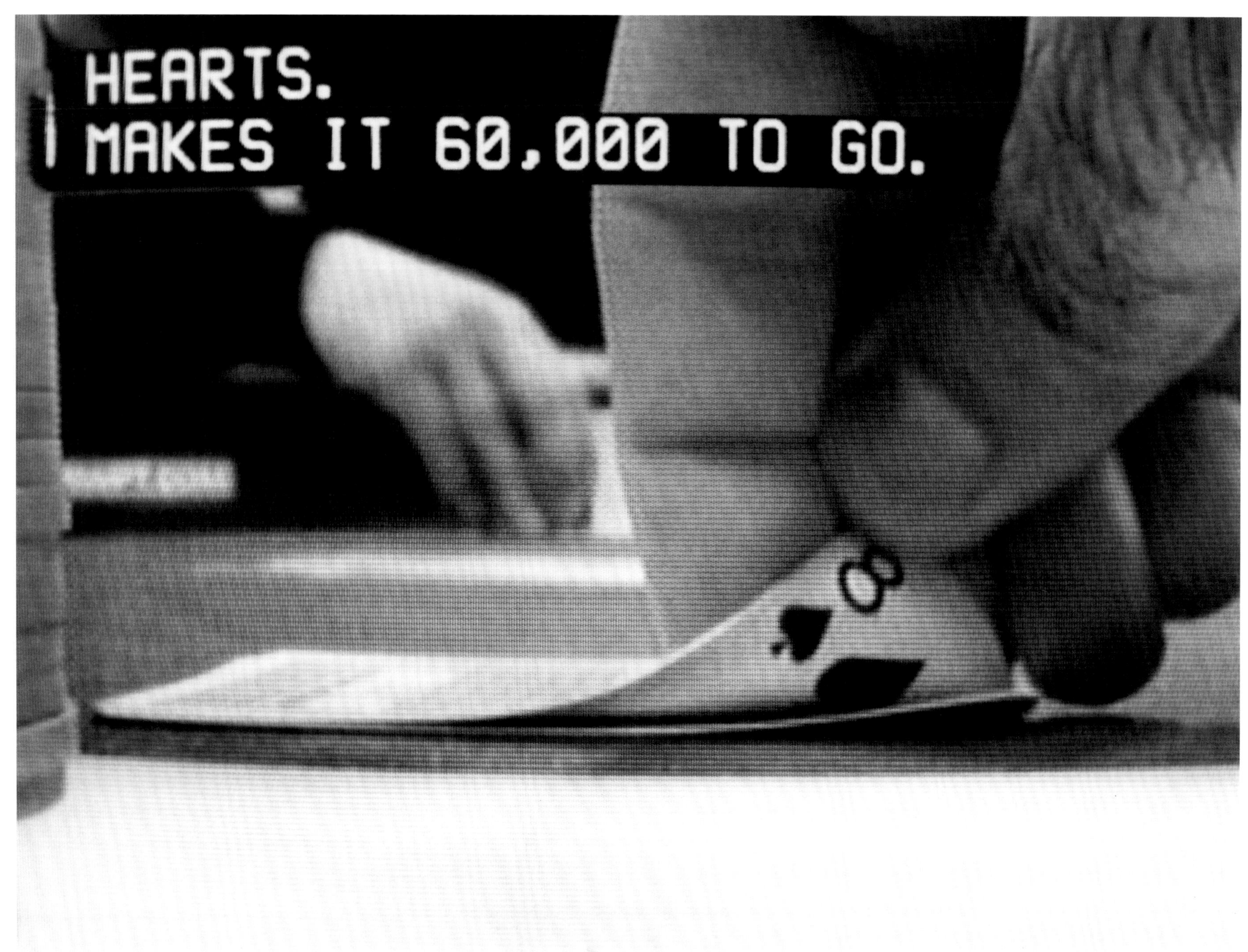
HEARTS.
MAKES IT 60,000 TO GO.

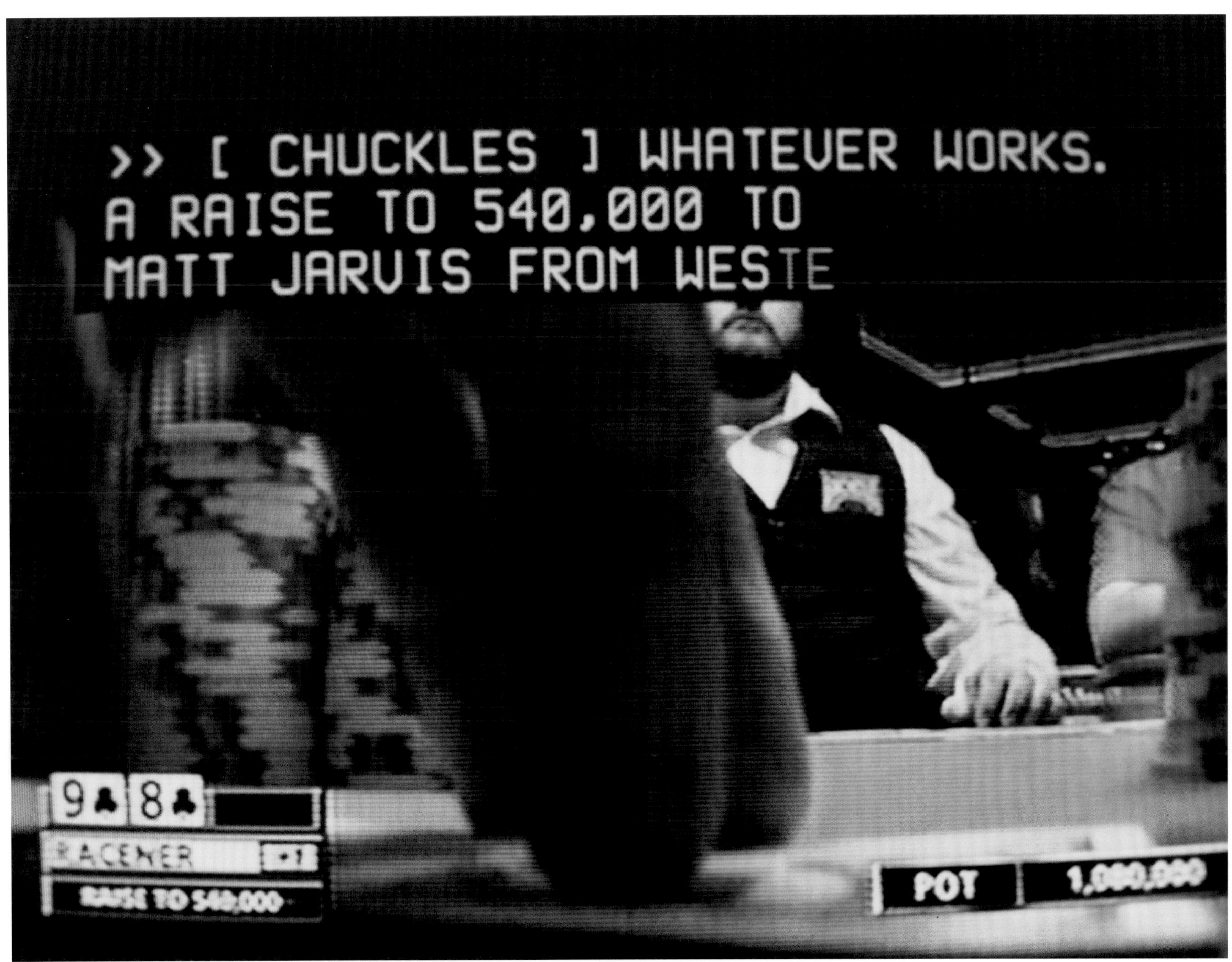
>> [CHUCKLES] WHATEVER WORKS.
A RAISE TO 540,000 TO
MATT JARVIS FROM WESTE
9♣ 8♣
RACENER   #1
RAISE TO 540,000
POT   1,000,000

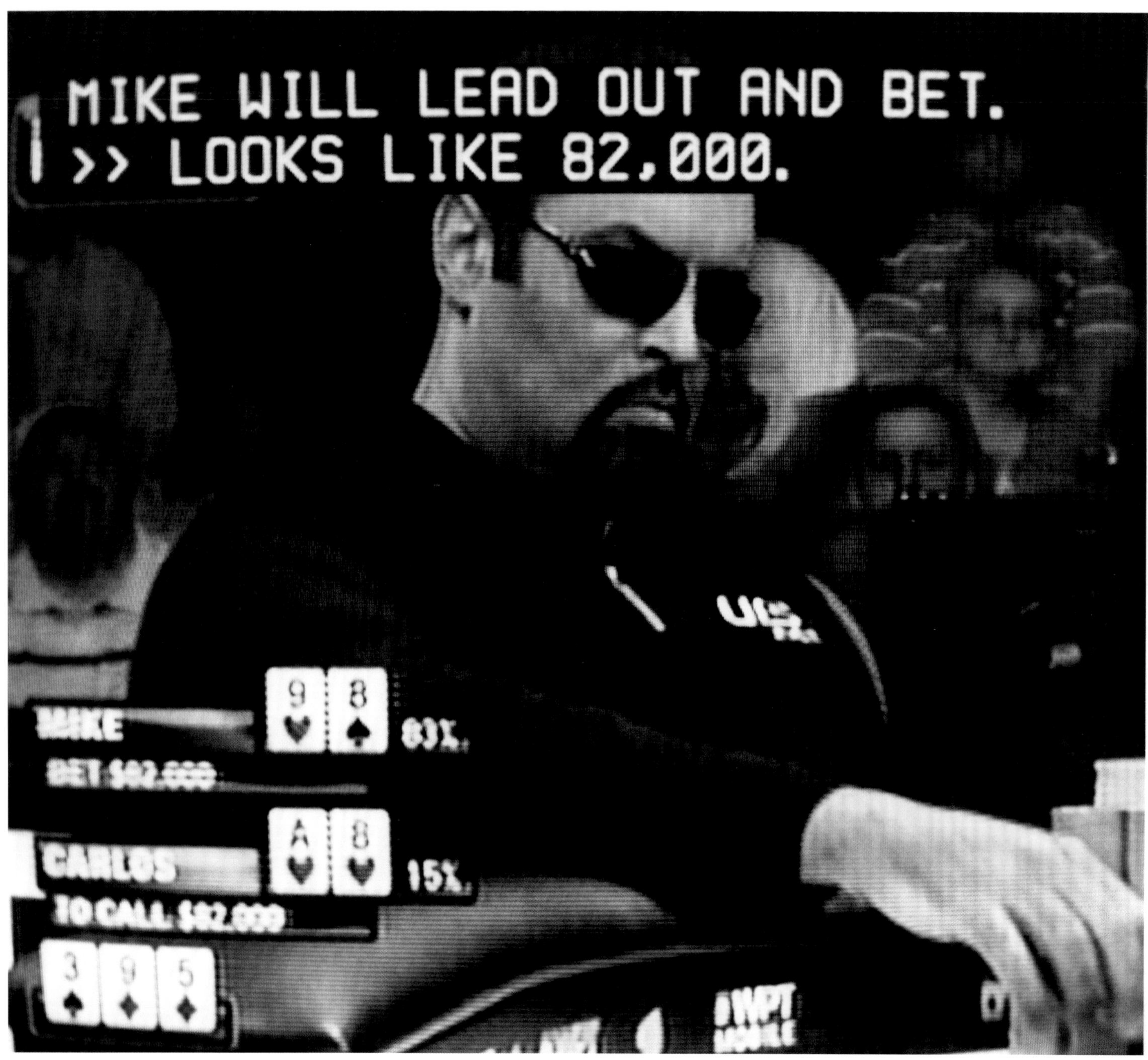

MIKE WILL LEAD OUT AND BET.
>> LOOKS LIKE 82,000.
MIKE
BET $82,000
CARLOS
TO CALL $82,000

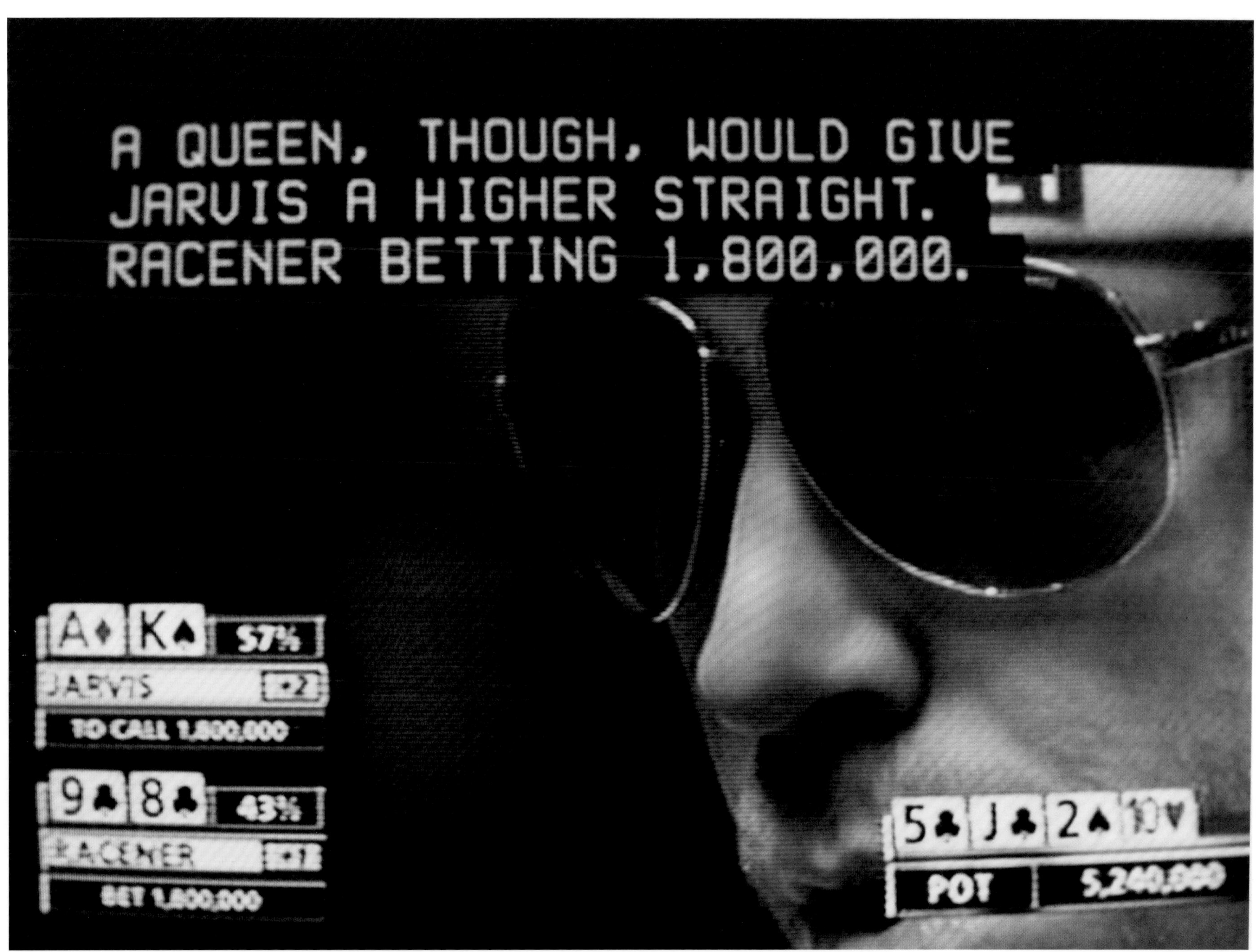

A QUEEN, THOUGH, WOULD GIVE JARVIS A HIGHER STRAIGHT. RACENER BETTING 1,800,000.
A♦ K♠ 57%
JARVIS
TO CALL 1,800,000
9♣ 8♣ 43%
RACENER
BET 1,800,000
5♣ J♣ 2♠ 10♥
POT 5,240,000

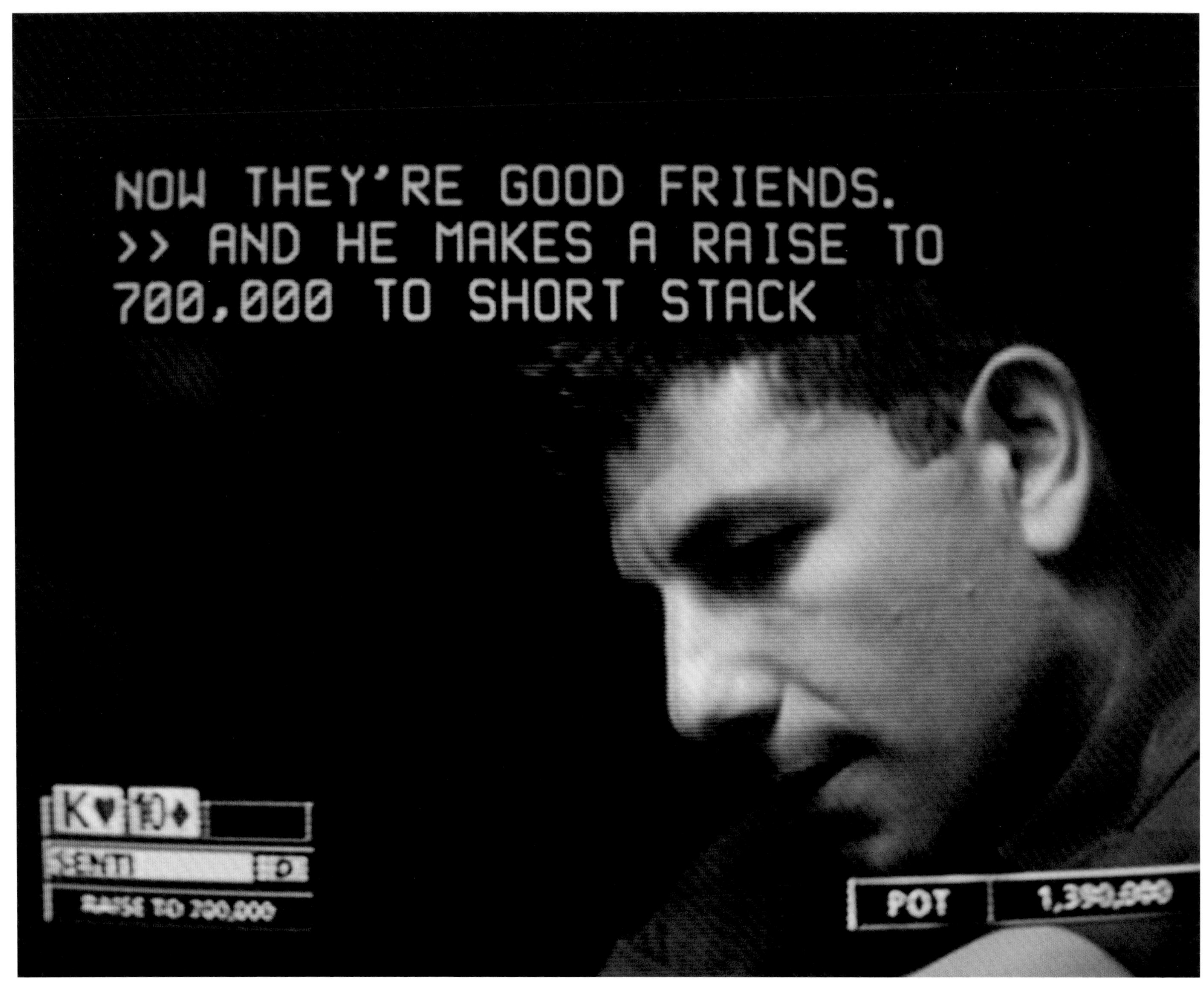

NOW THEY'RE GOOD FRIENDS.
>> AND HE MAKES A RAISE TO
700,000 TO SHORT STACK
RAISE TO 700,000
POT 1,390,000

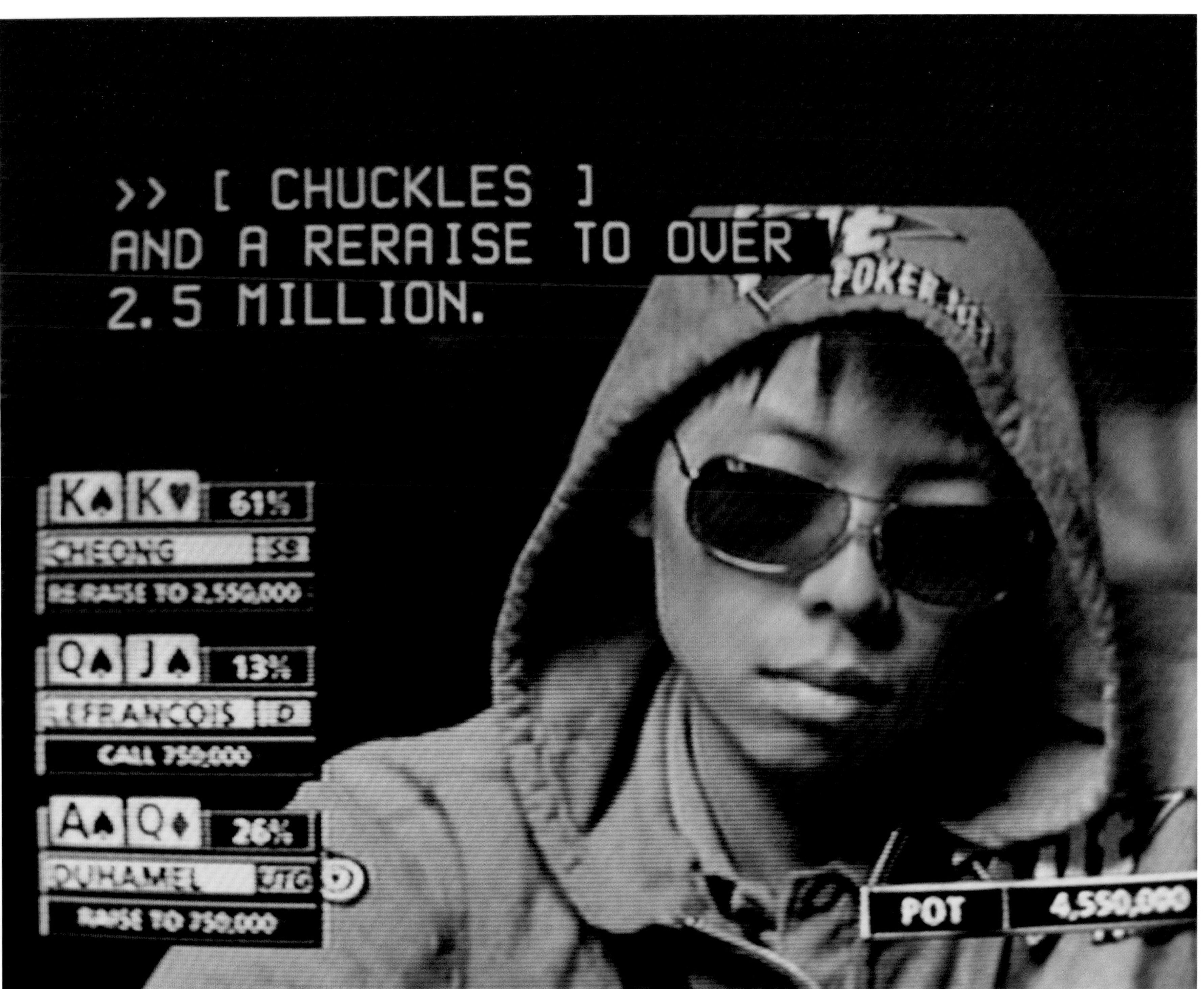
>> [CHUCKLES]
AND A RERAISE TO OVER
2.5 MILLION.
K♠ K♥ 61%
CHEONG 59
RE-RAISE TO 2,550,000
Q♠ J♠ 13%
FRANCOIS D
CALL 750,000
A♠ Q♦ 26%
DUHAMEL STG
RAISE TO 750,000
POT 4,550,000

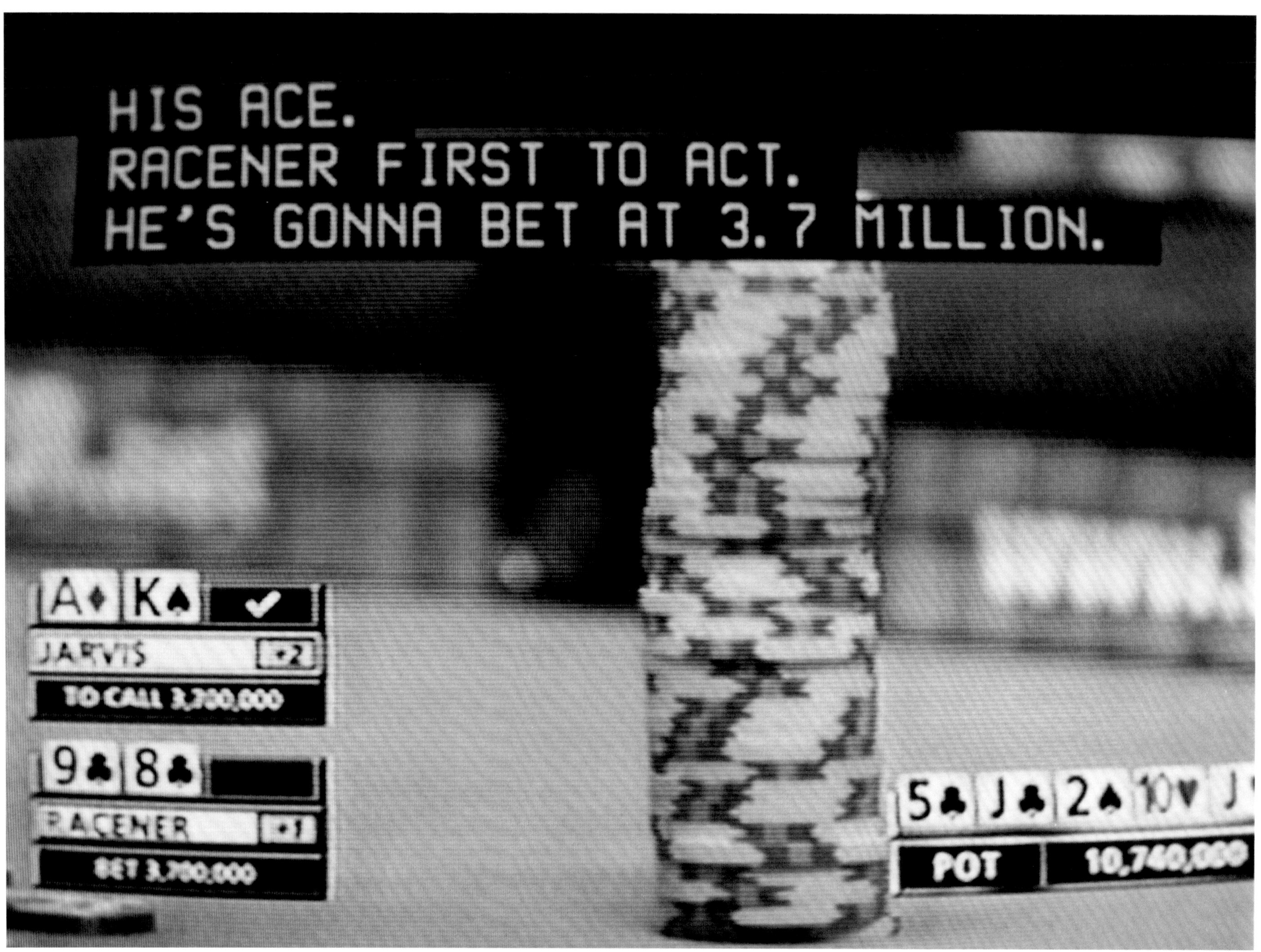
HIS ACE.
RACENER FIRST TO ACT.
HE'S GONNA BET AT 3.7 MILLION.
A♦ K♠ ✔
JARVIS +2
TO CALL 3,700,000
9♣ 8♣
RACENER +1
BET 3,700,000
5♣ J♣ 2♠ 10♥ J
POT 10,740,000

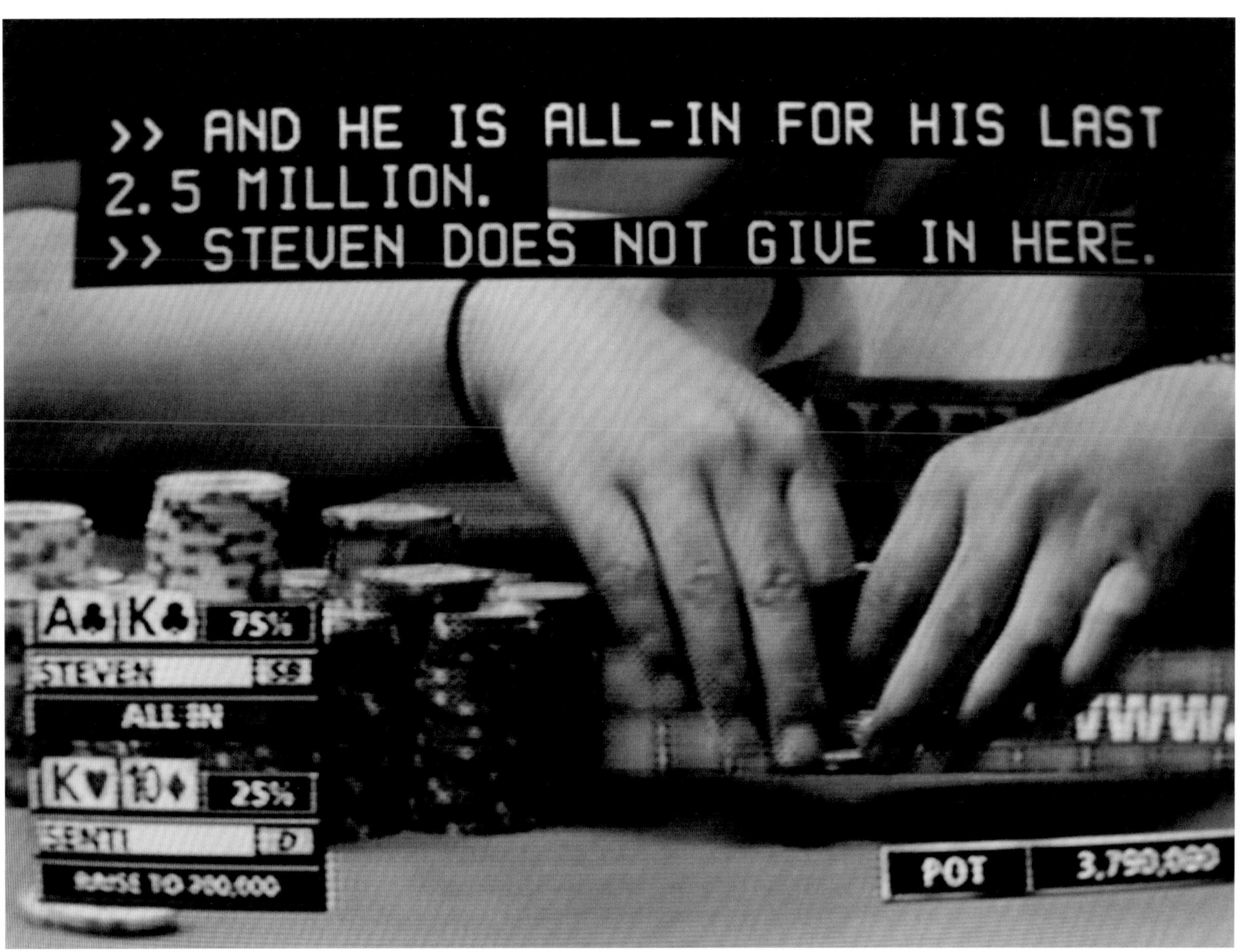

>> AND HE IS ALL-IN FOR HIS LAST
2.5 MILLION.
>> STEVEN DOES NOT GIVE IN HERE.
A♣ K♣ 75%
STEVEN 59
ALL IN
K♥ 10♦ 25%
SENTI ED
RAISE TO 700,000
POT 3,790,000

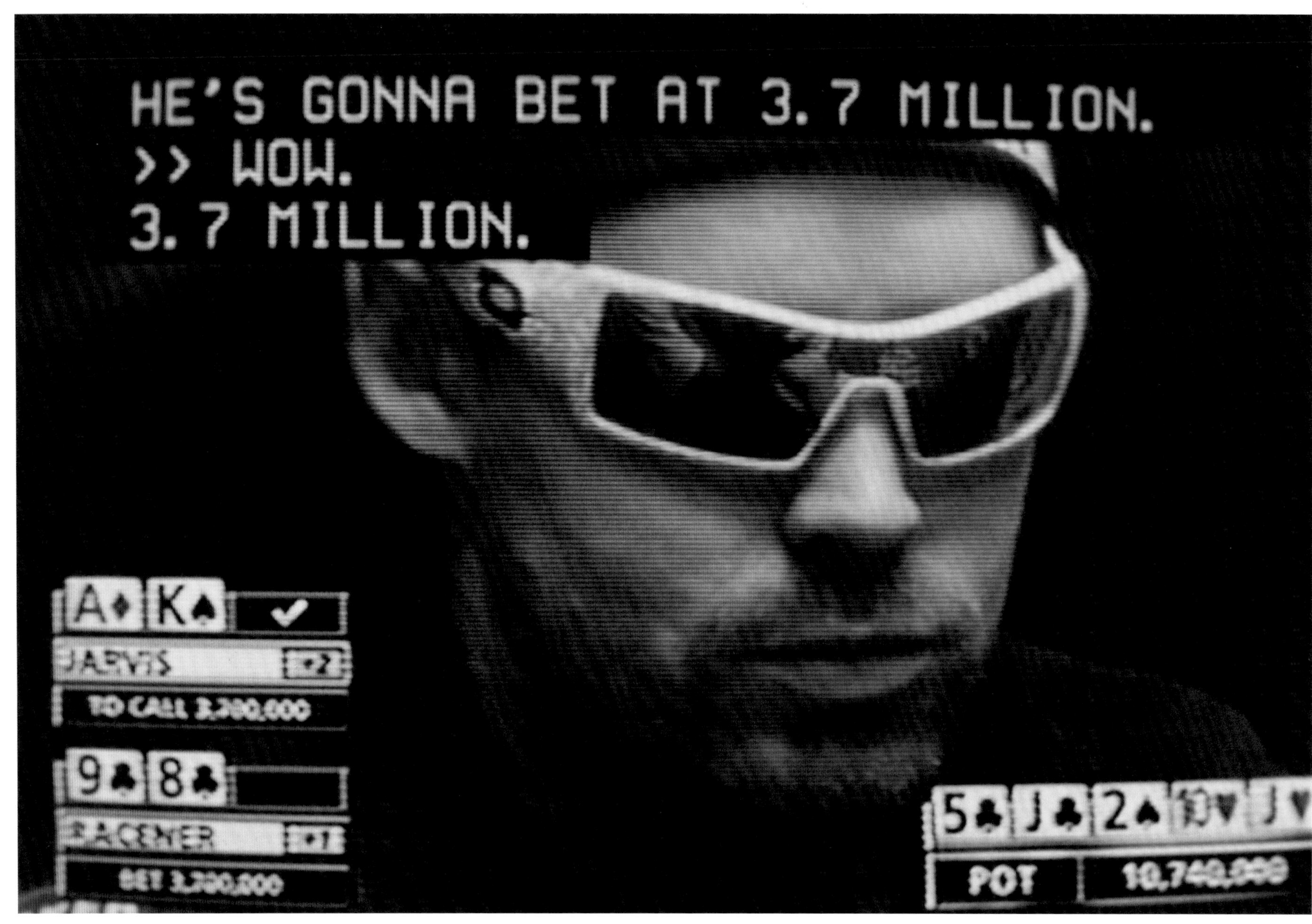
HE'S GONNA BET AT 3.7 MILLION.
>> WOW.
3.7 MILLION.

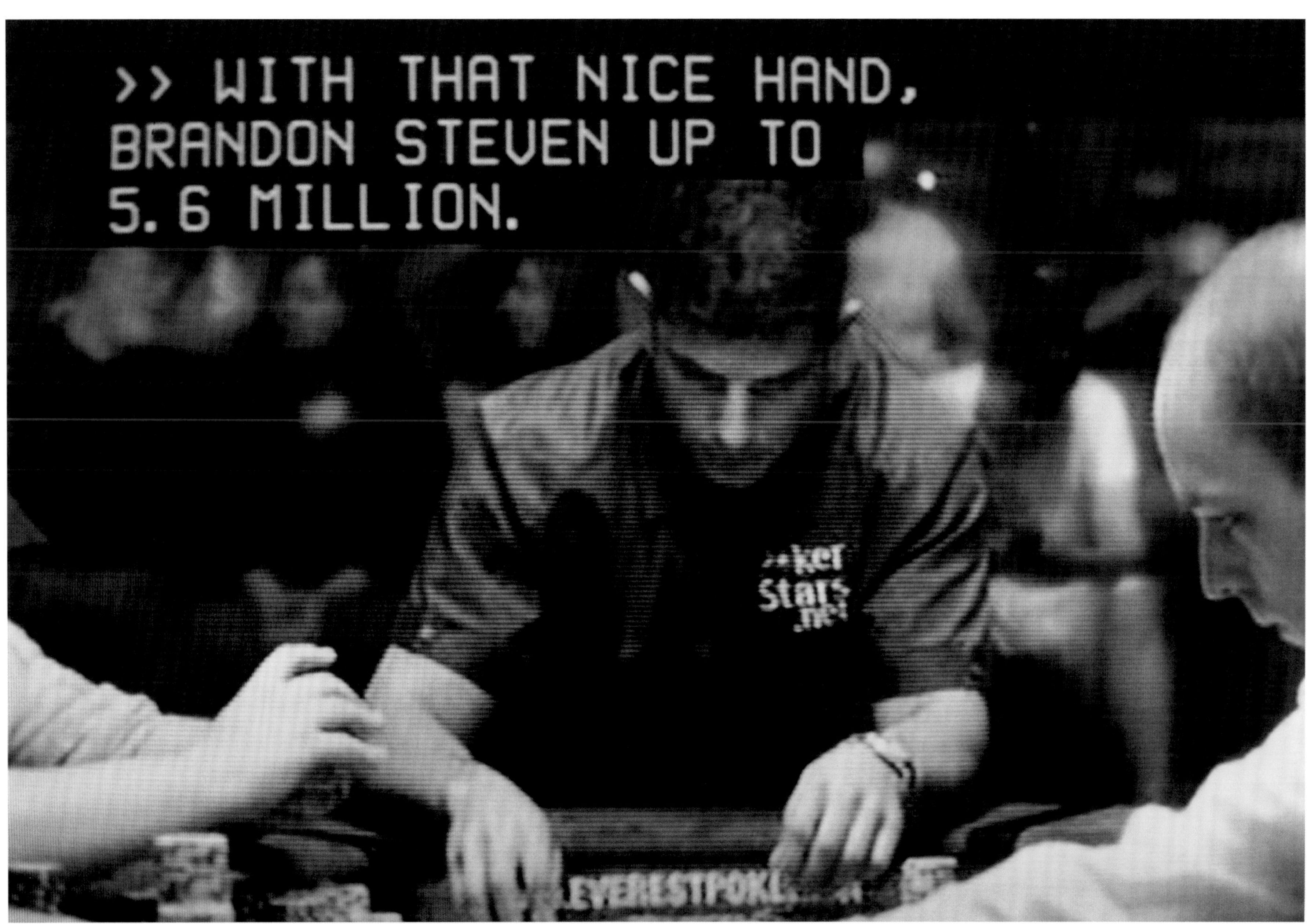

>> WITH THAT NICE HAND,
BRANDON STEVEN UP TO
5.6 MILLION.

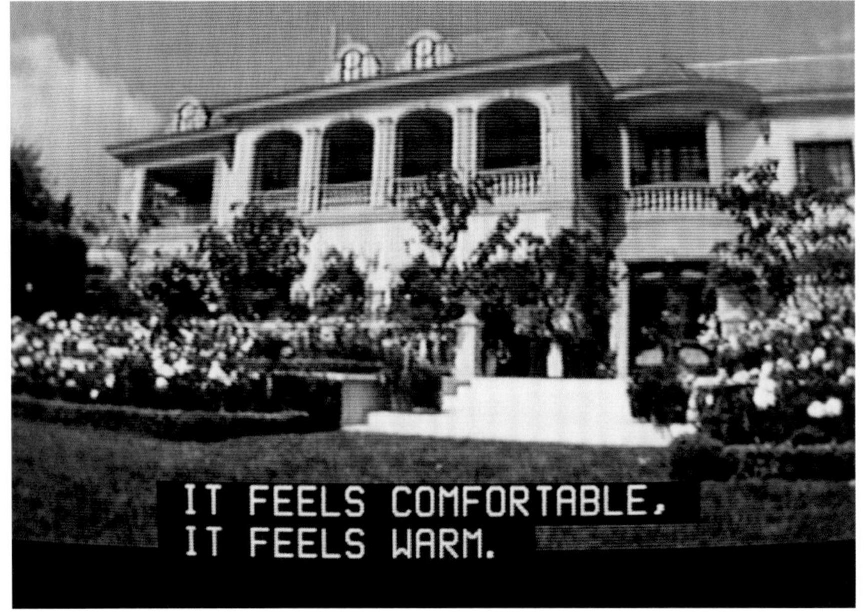
IT FEELS COMFORTABLE,
IT FEELS WARM.

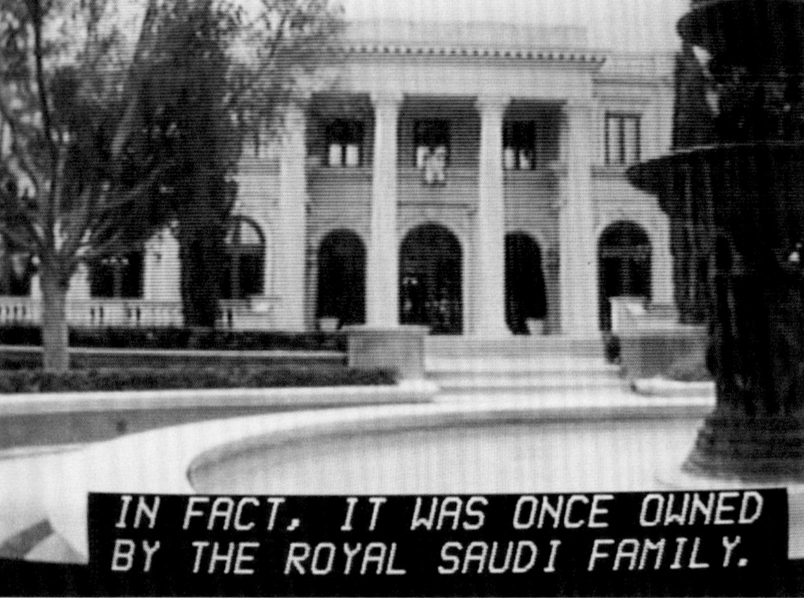
IN FACT, IT WAS ONCE OWNED
BY THE ROYAL SAUDI FAMILY.

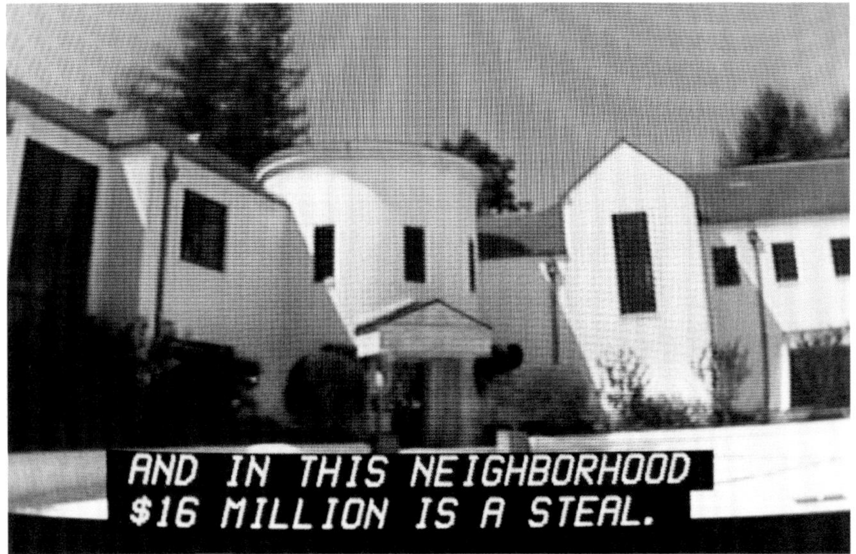
AND IN THIS NEIGHBORHOOD
$16 MILLION IS A STEAL.

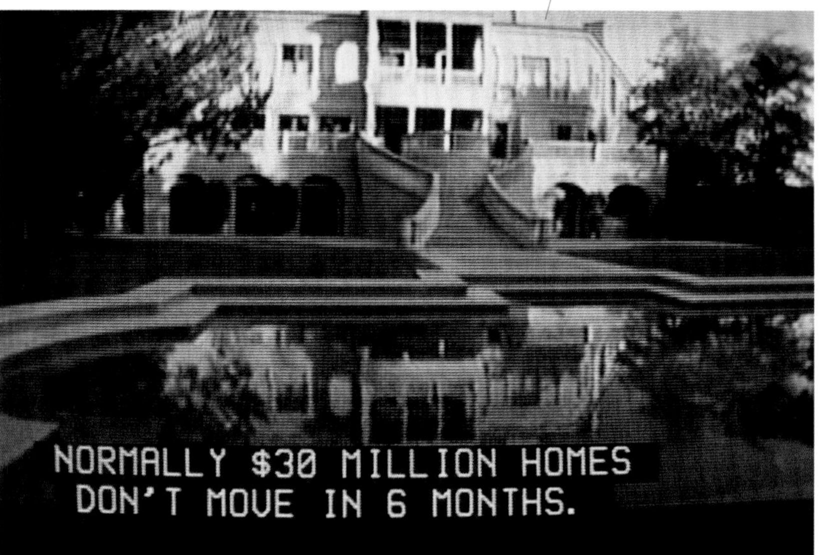
NORMALLY $30 MILLION HOMES
DON'T MOVE IN 6 MONTHS.

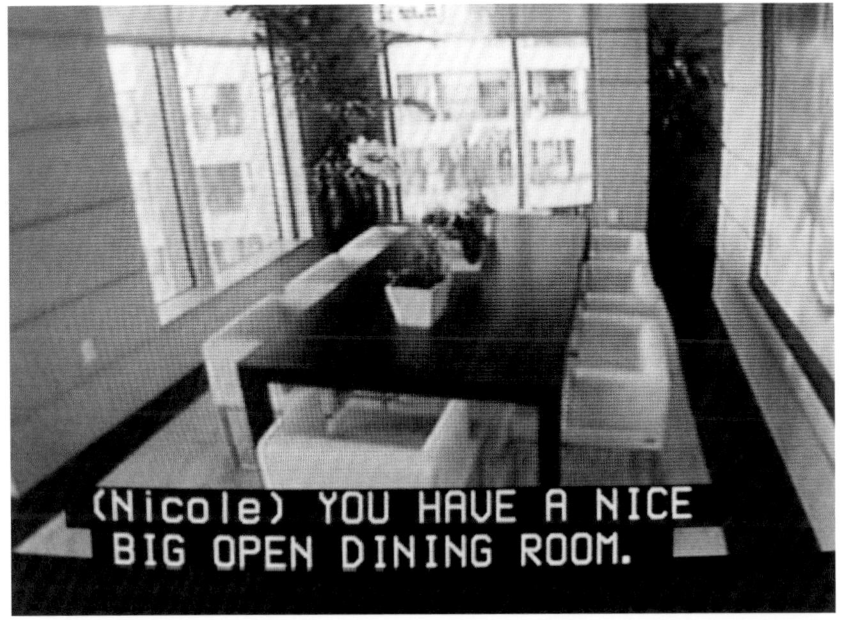
(Nicole) YOU HAVE A NICE
BIG OPEN DINING ROOM.

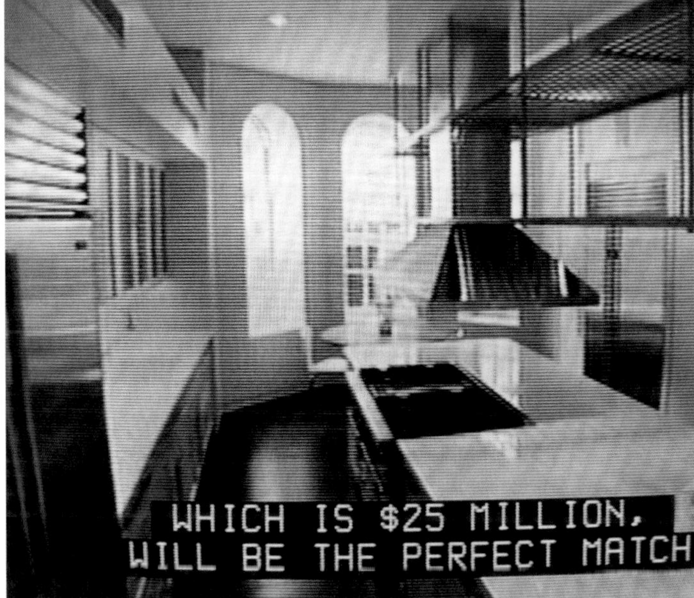
WHICH IS $25 MILLION,
WILL BE THE PERFECT MATCH

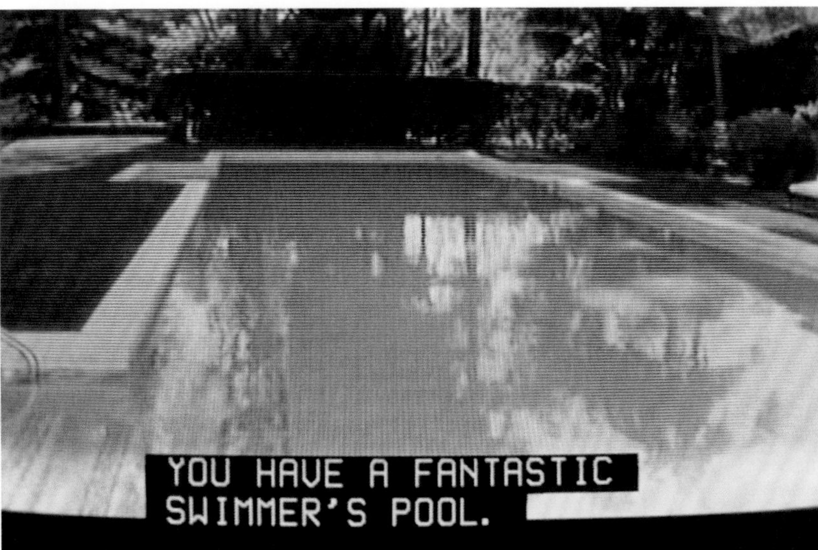
YOU HAVE A FANTASTIC
SWIMMER'S POOL.

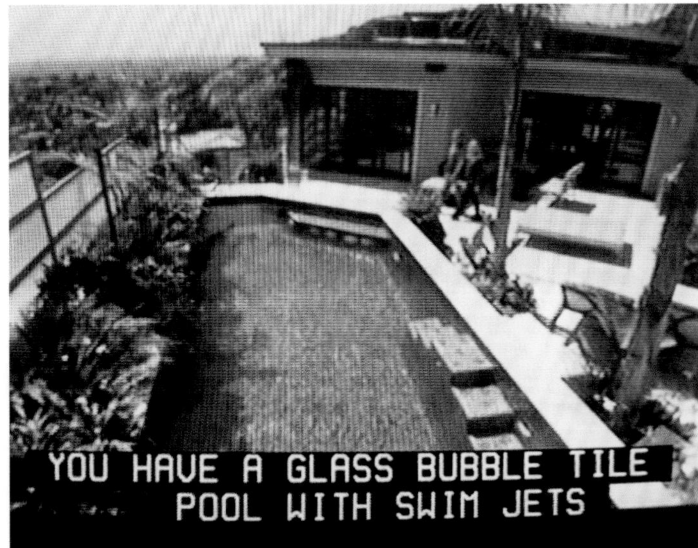
YOU HAVE A GLASS BUBBLE TILE
POOL WITH SWIM JETS

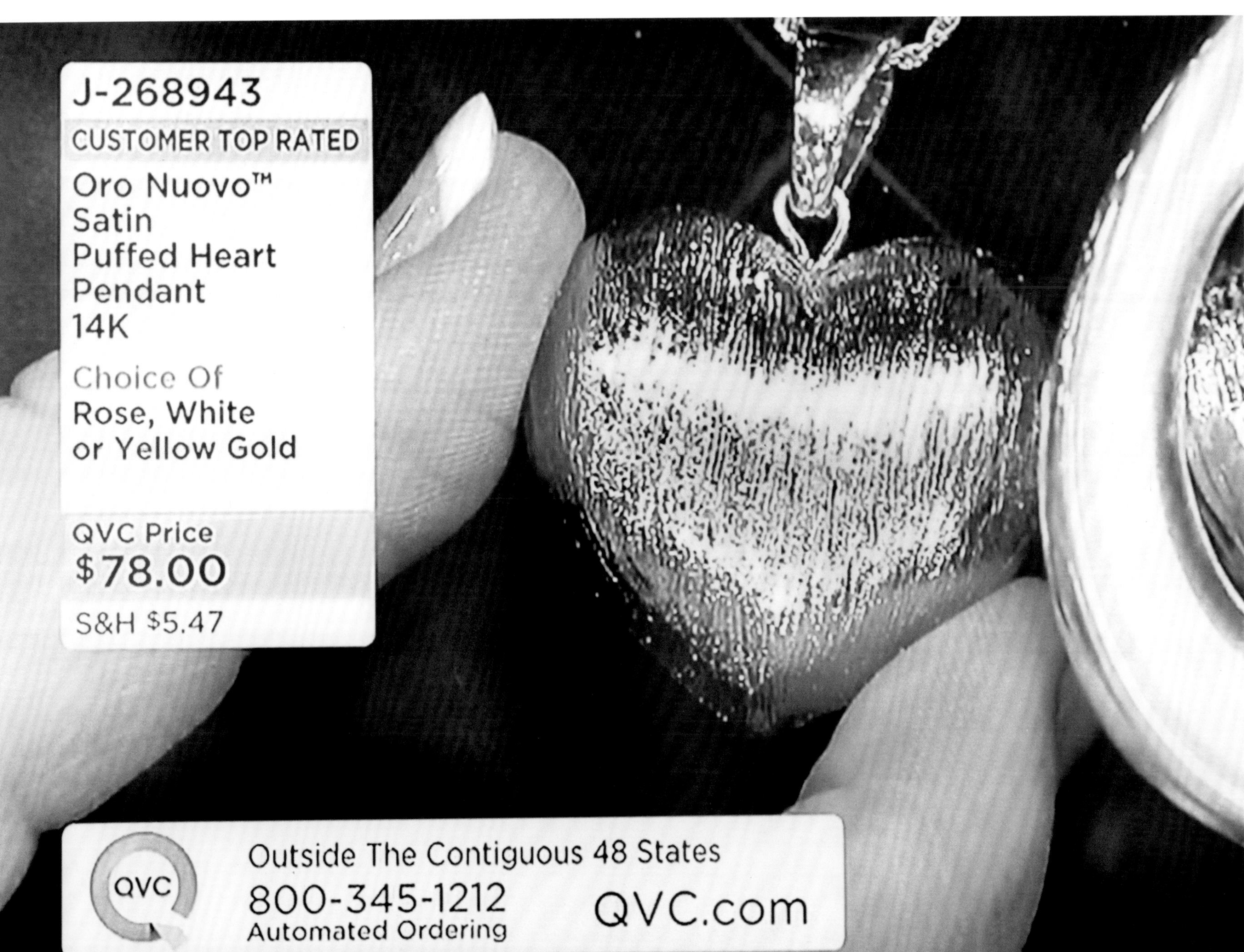

J-268943
CUSTOMER TOP RATED
Oro Nuovo™
Satin
Puffed Heart
Pendant
14K
Choice Of
Rose, White
or Yellow Gold
QVC Price
$78.00
S&H $5.47
Outside The Contiguous 48 States
800-345-1212
Automated Ordering
QVC.com

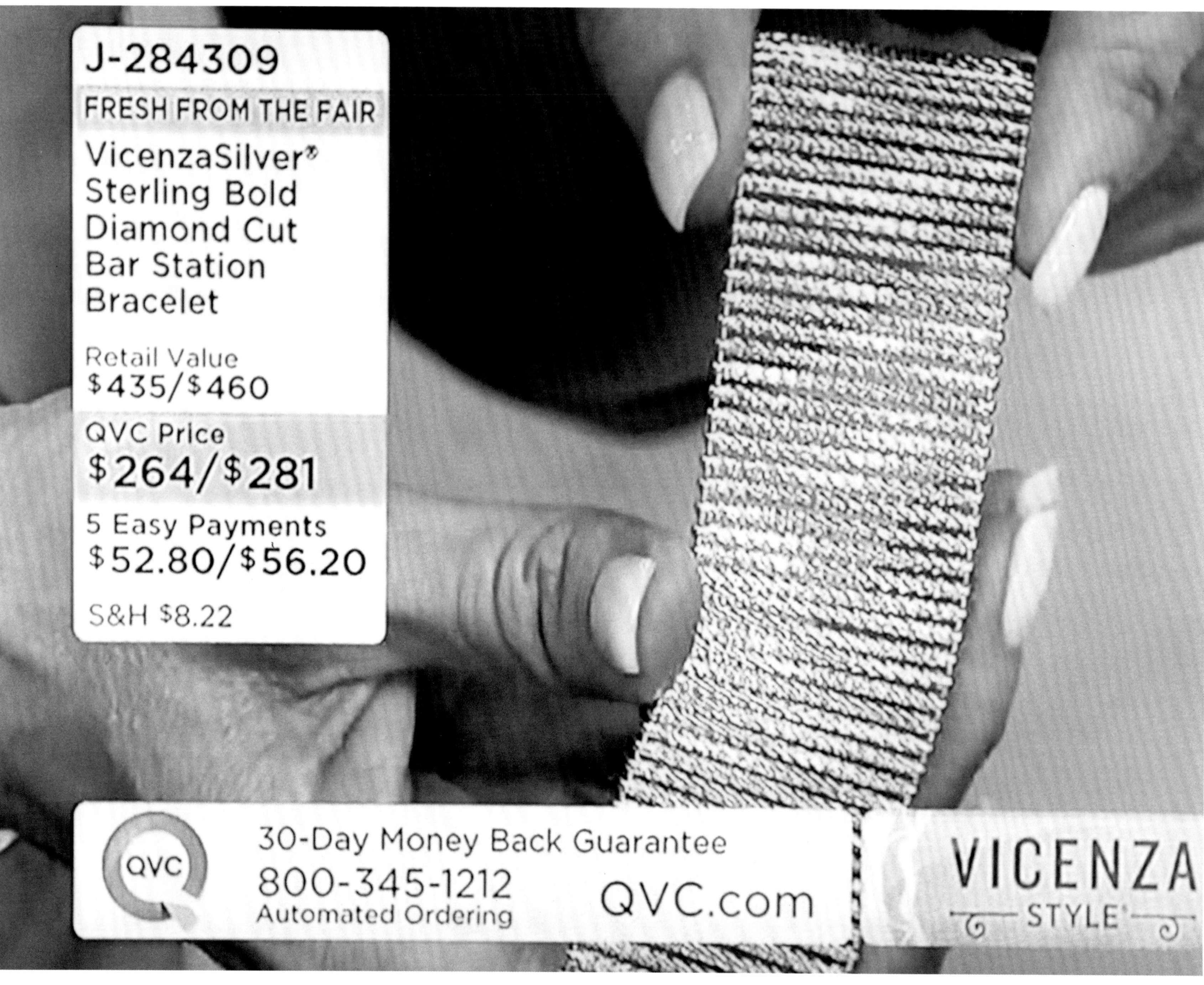

J-284309

FRESH FROM THE FAIR

VicenzaSilver®
Sterling Bold
Diamond Cut
Bar Station
Bracelet

Retail Value
$435/$460

QVC Price
$264/$281

5 Easy Payments
$52.80/$56.20

S&H $8.22

QVC
30-Day Money Back Guarantee
800-345-1212
Automated Ordering
QVC.com

VICENZA
STYLE

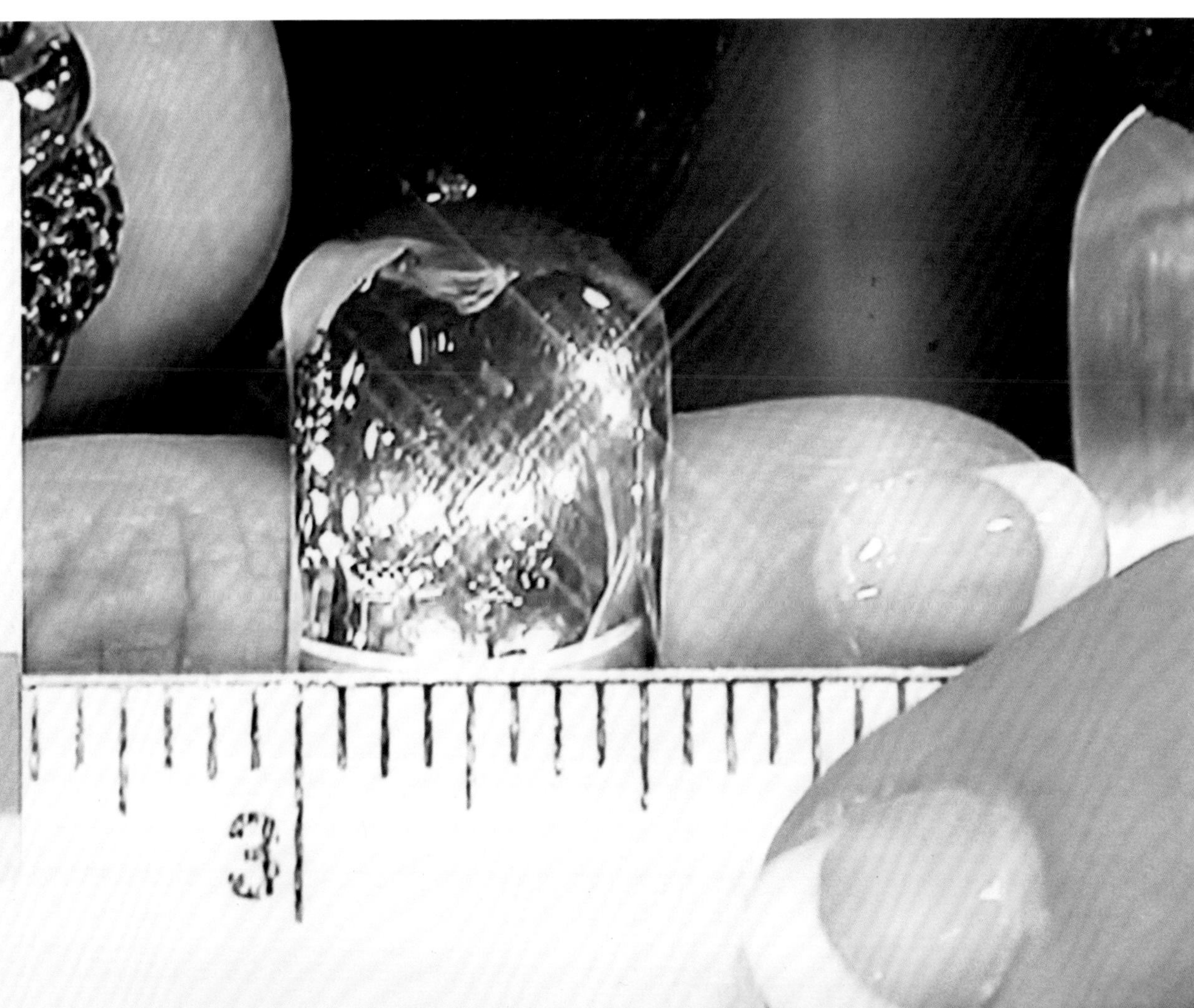
J-280339
UltraFine
Silver®
1¼" Bold
Polished
Hoop Earrings
Retail Value
$120.00
QVC Price
$75.00
Last Day at
Featured Price
$68.42
S&H $5.47 FREE
30-Day Money Back Guarantee
Order by:
iPhone® iPad® Android™ & BlackBerry® Apps
Coming Up
Quacker Factory
by Jeanne Bice
QVC

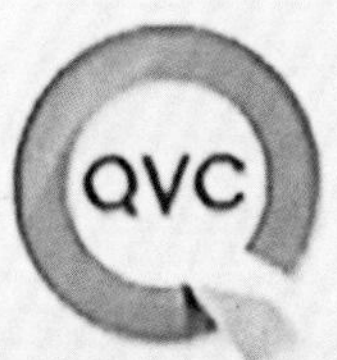

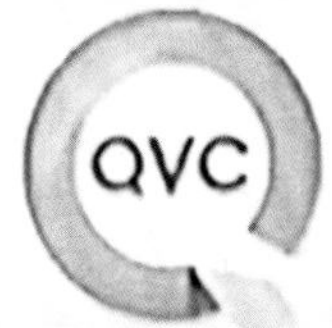
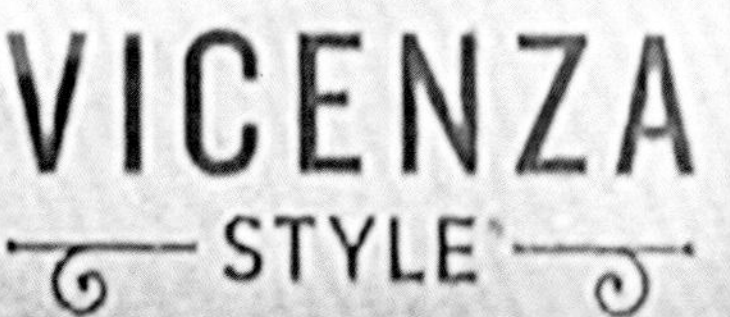

J-285554
FRESH FROM THE FAIR
Oro Nuovo™ Elongated Graduated Oval Hoop Earrings, 14K
Will Ship October 4
Featured Price $187.70
5 Easy Payments $37.54
S&H $7.72
QVC
30-Day Money Back Guarantee
800-345-1515 QVC.com
VICENZA STYLE

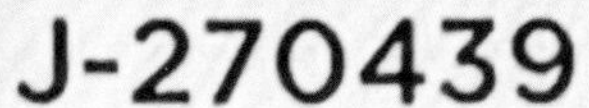

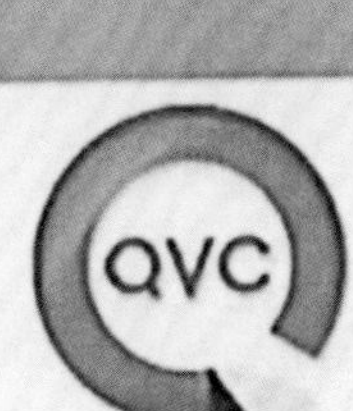

30-Day Money Back Guarantee
Order by:
iPhone® iPad® Android™ & BlackBerry® Apps

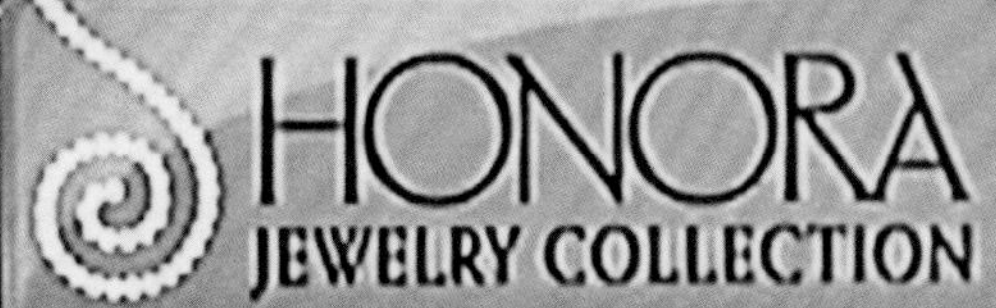

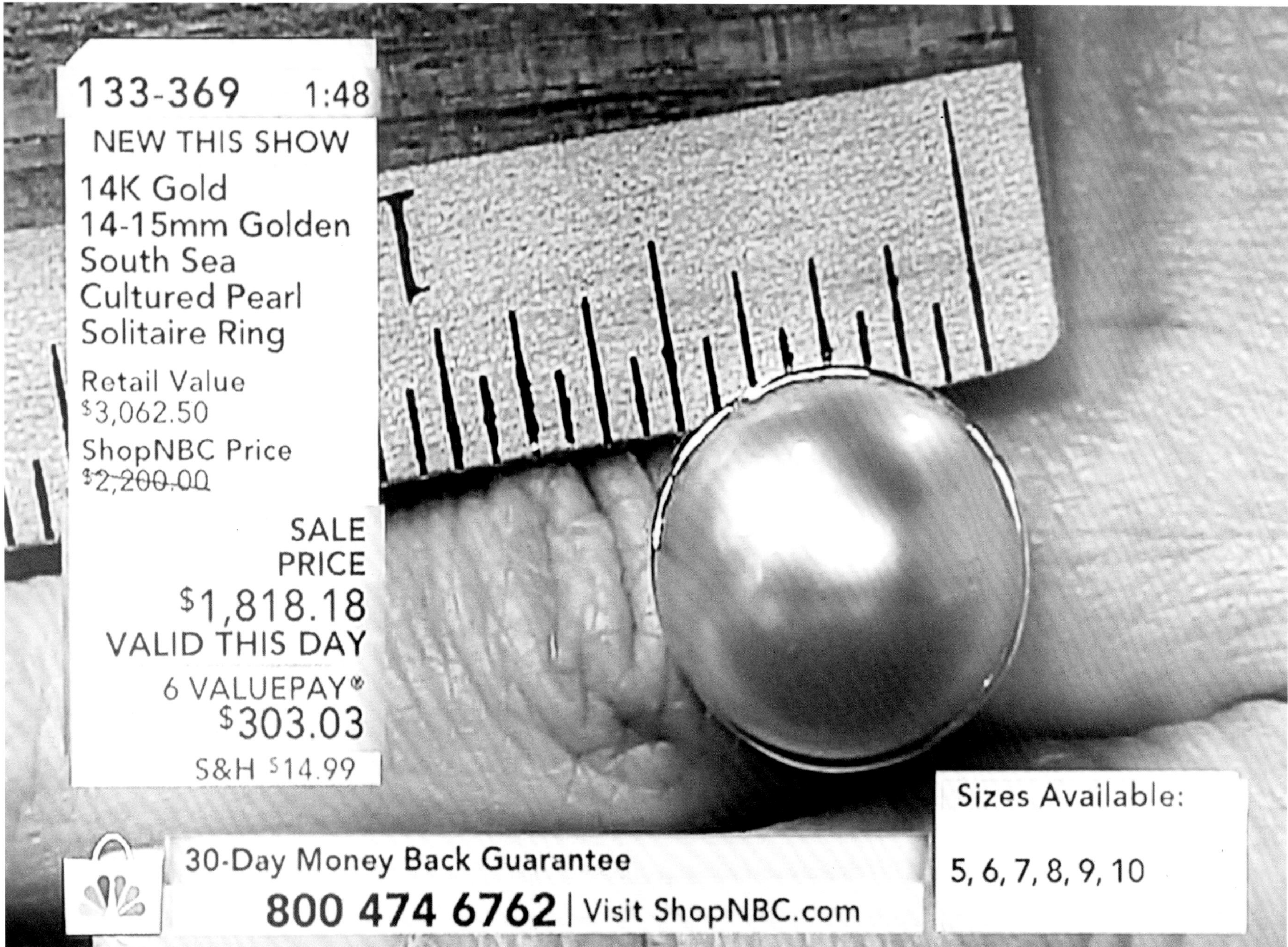
133-369   1:48
NEW THIS SHOW
14K Gold
14-15mm Golden
South Sea
Cultured Pearl
Solitaire Ring
Retail Value
$3,062.50
ShopNBC Price
$2,200.00
SALE
PRICE
$1,818.18
VALID THIS DAY
6 VALUEPAY
$303.03
S&H $14.99
30-Day Money Back Guarantee
800 474 6762 | Visit ShopNBC.com
Sizes Available:
5, 6, 7, 8, 9, 10

J-278256
NEW TODAY
VicenzaGold®
Turquoise
Cabochon
Cross Pendant
14K Gold
Retail Value
$330.00
QVC Price
$214.00
Only Day at
Featured Price
$199.00
S&H $7.97
30-Day Money Back Guarantee
800-345-1212
Automated Ordering
QVC.com
QVC
Vicenza
STYLE

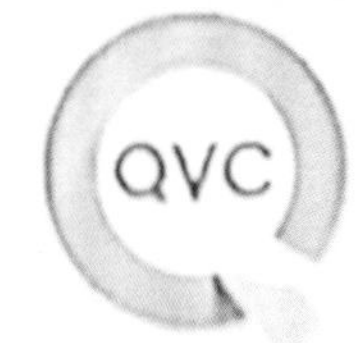
J-285539

FRESH FROM THE FAIR

Bronzo Italia
Bead Station
Multi-strand
Leather
Bracelet

Choice Of
Yellow, Rose
or White

Featured Price
$69.72

S&H $5.47

30-Day Money Back Guarantee
800-345-1212
Automated Ordering
QVC.com

VICENZA
STYLE

Before and After, 2013

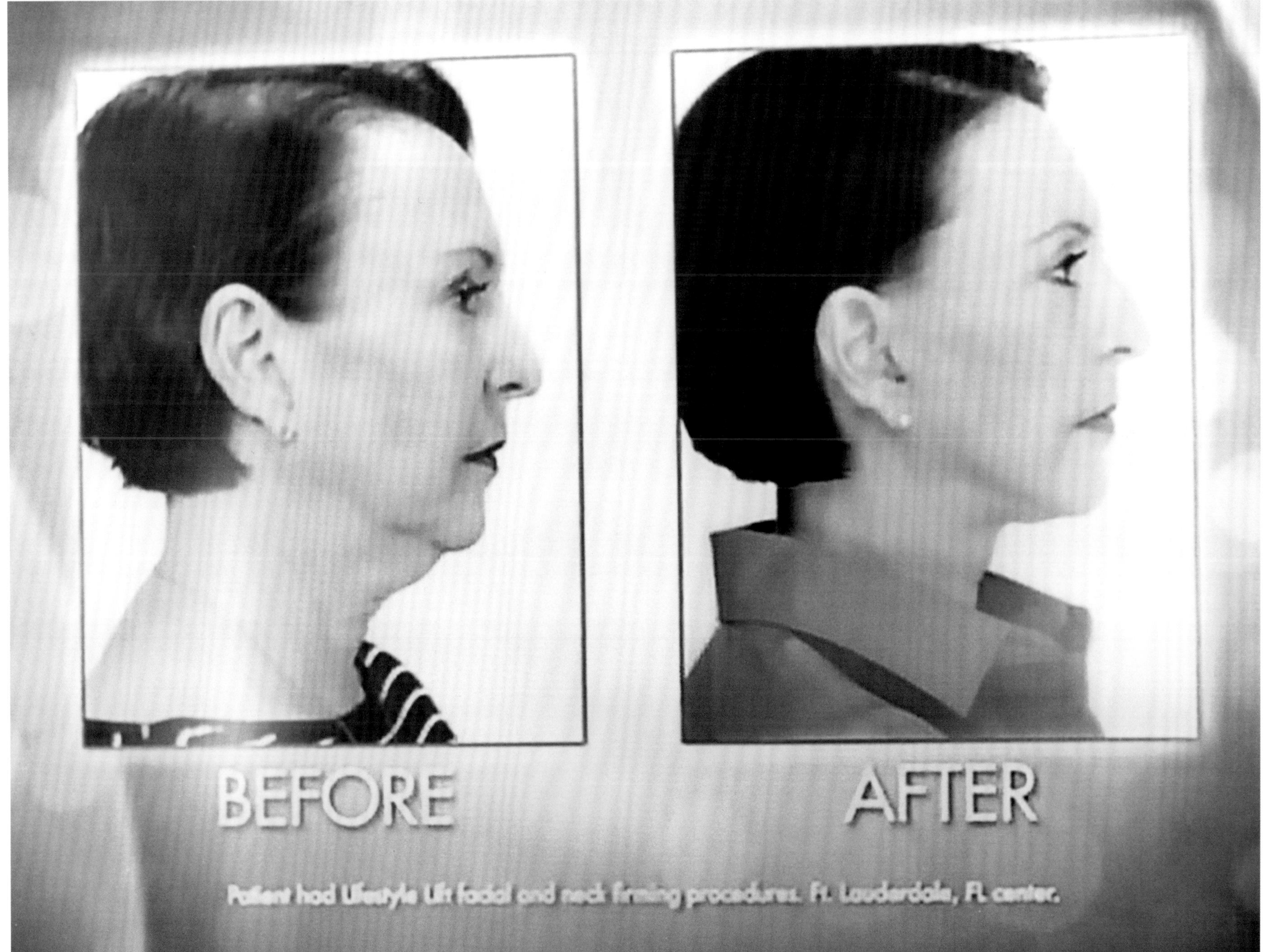

BEFORE
AFTER
Patient had Lifestyle Lift facial and neck firming procedures. Ft. Lauderdale, FL center.

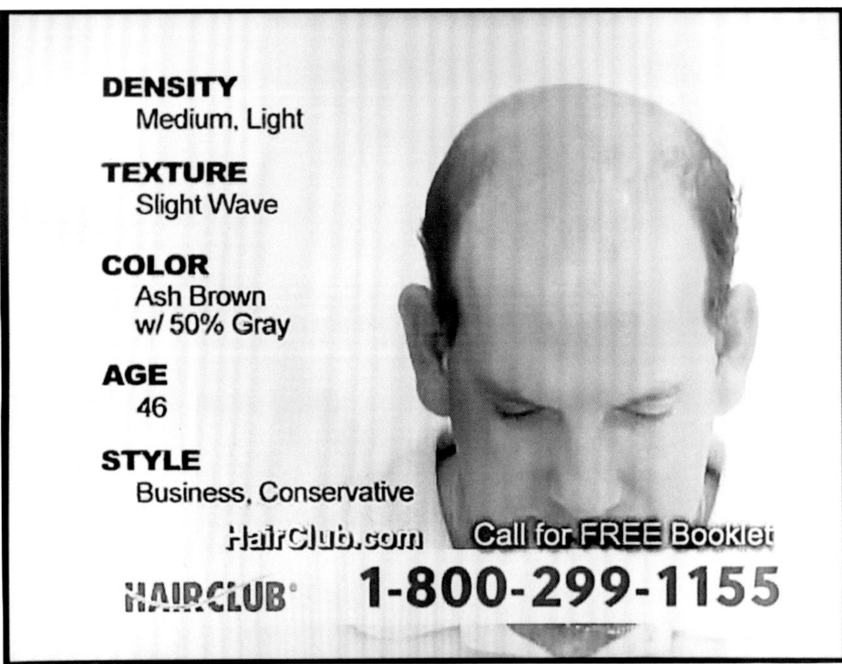

DENSITY
Medium, Light

TEXTURE
Slight Wave

COLOR
Ash Brown
w/ 50% Gray

AGE
46

STYLE
Business, Conservative

HairClub.com   Call for FREE Booklet

HAIRCLUB®   1-800-299-1155

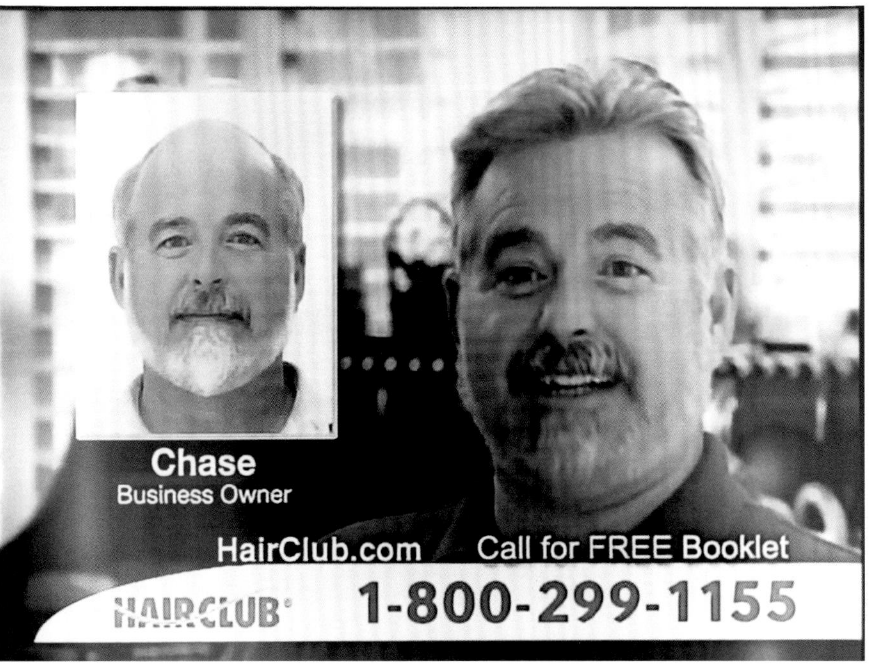

Chase
Business Owner

HairClub.com   Call for FREE Booklet

HAIRCLUB®   1-800-299-1155

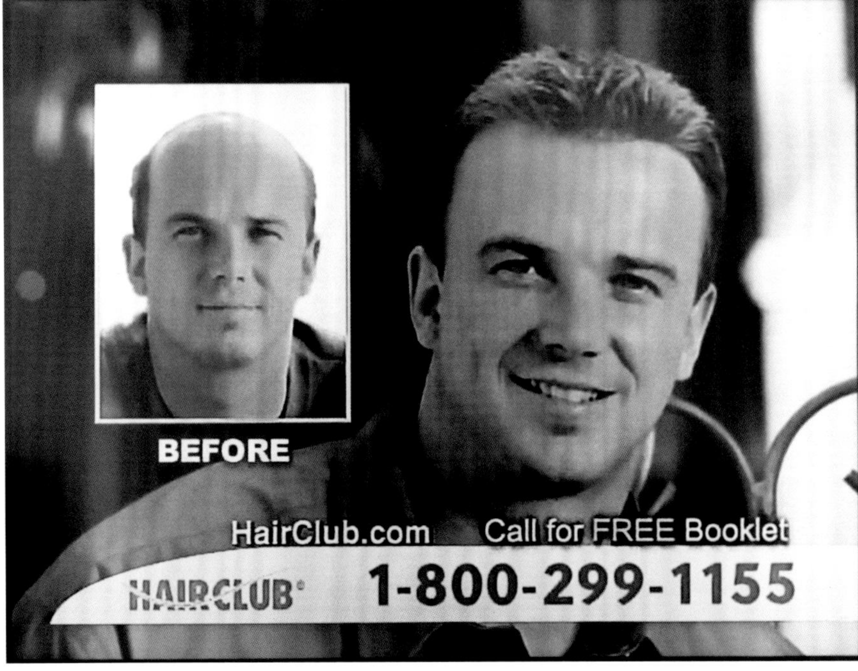

BEFORE

HairClub.com   Call for FREE Booklet

HAIRCLUB®   1-800-299-1155

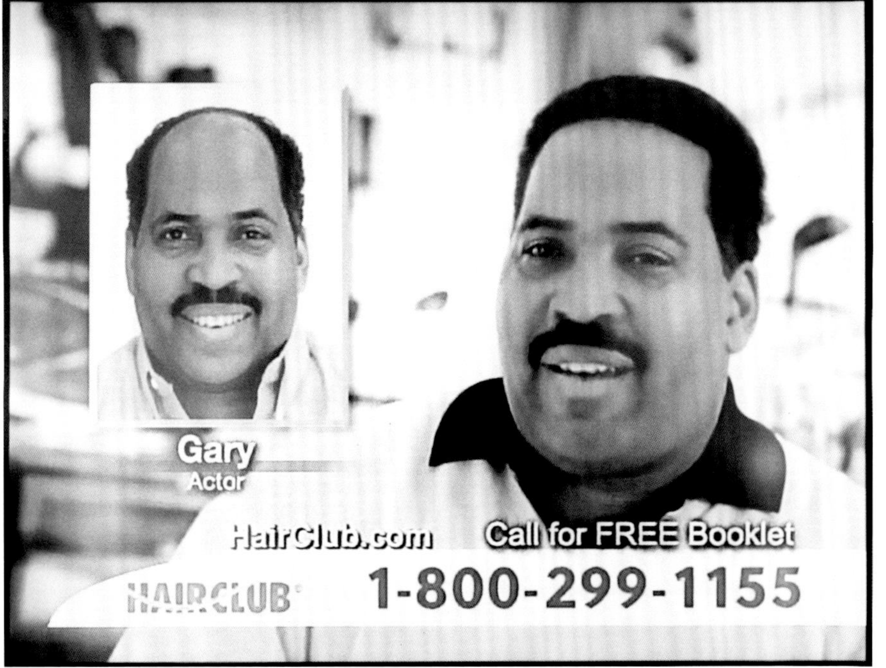

Gary
Actor

HairClub.com   Call for FREE Booklet

HAIRCLUB®   1-800-299-1155

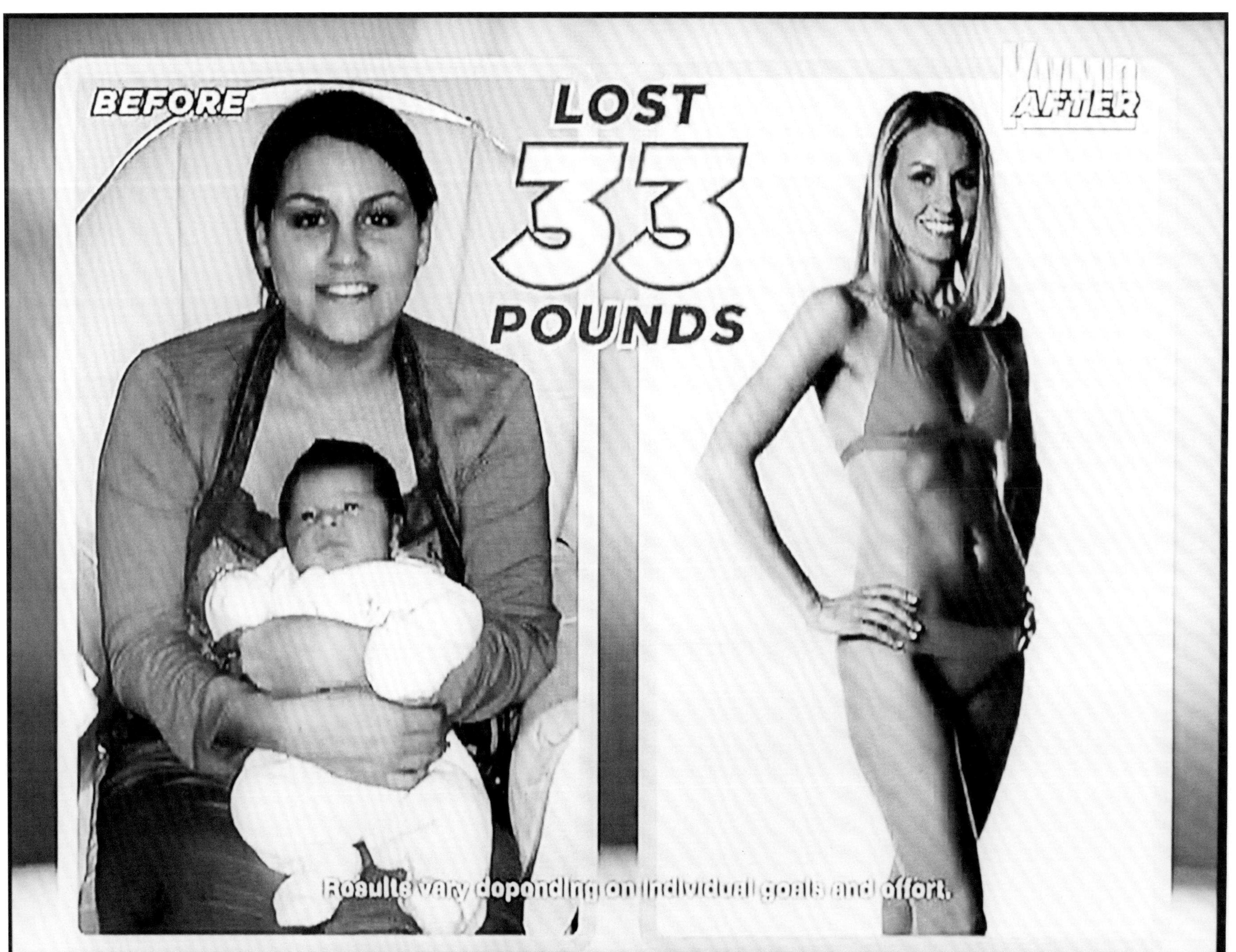

BEFORE
AFTER
LOST
33
POUNDS
Results vary depending on individual goals and effort.

UFC Fighting Television Images, 2014

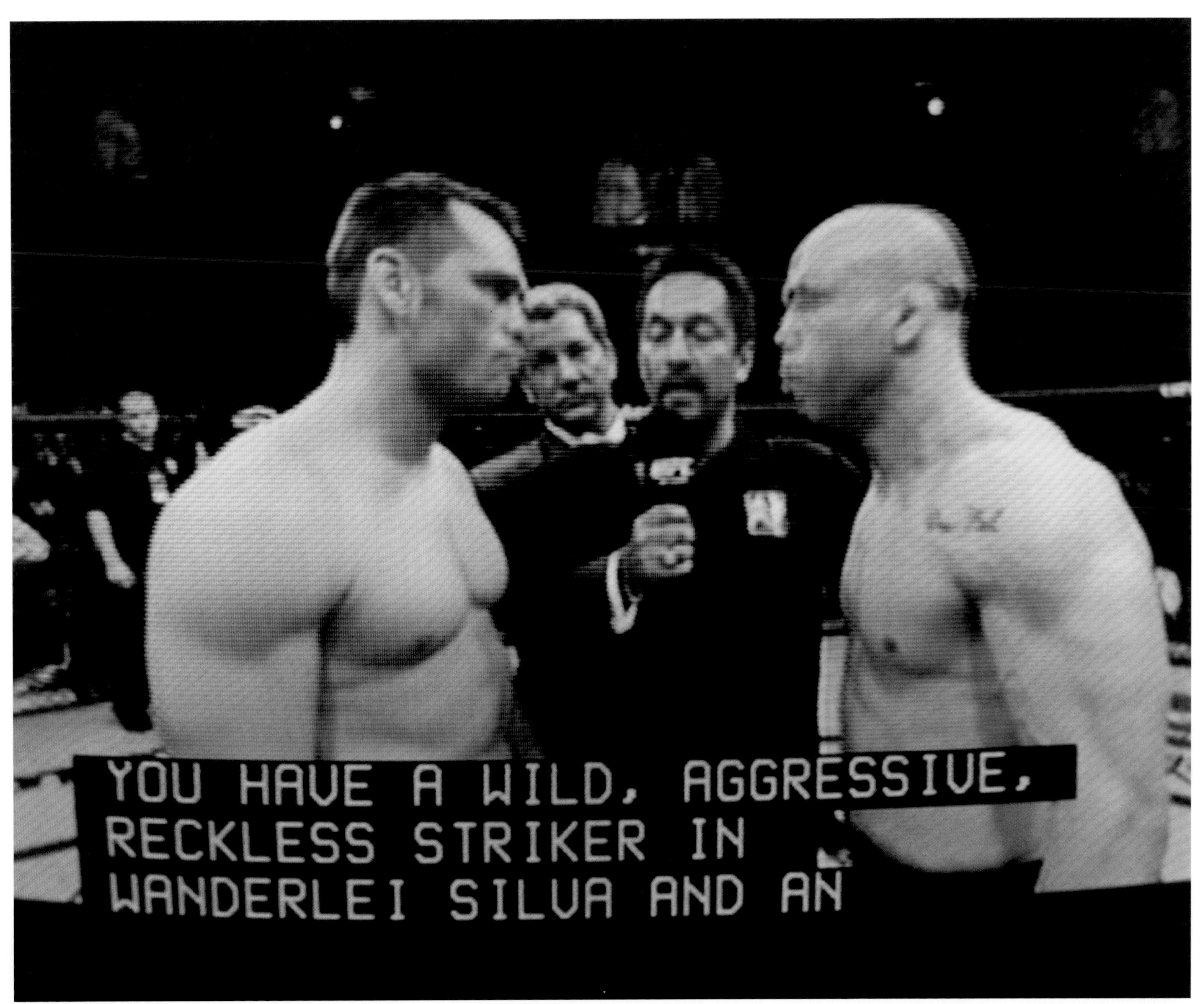
YOU HAVE A WILD, AGGRESSIVE,
RECKLESS STRIKER IN
WANDERLEI SILVA AND AN

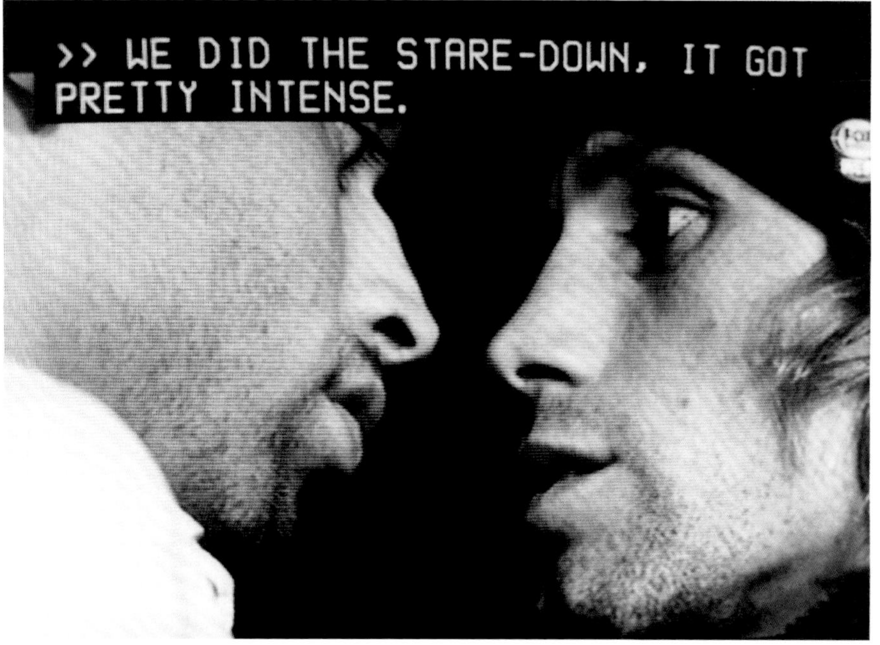

>> WE DID THE STARE-DOWN, IT GOT
PRETTY INTENSE.

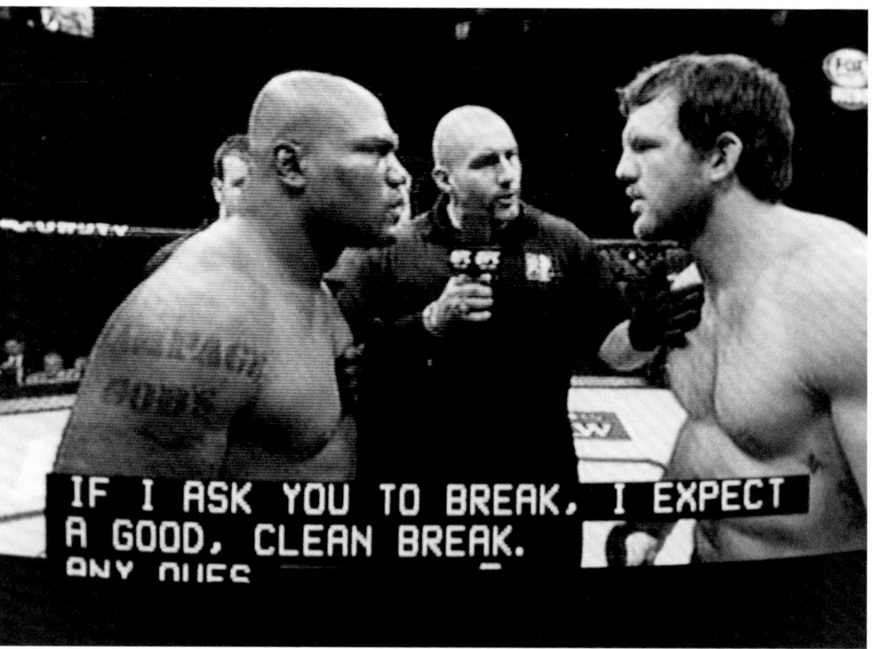

IF I ASK YOU TO BREAK, I EXPECT
A GOOD, CLEAN BREAK.
ANY QUES

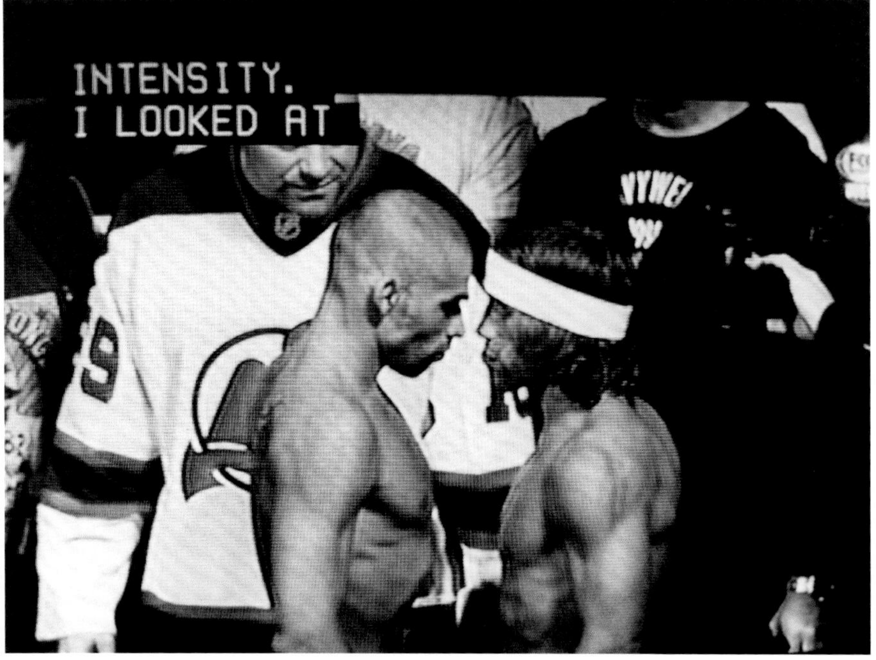

INTENSITY.
I LOOKED AT

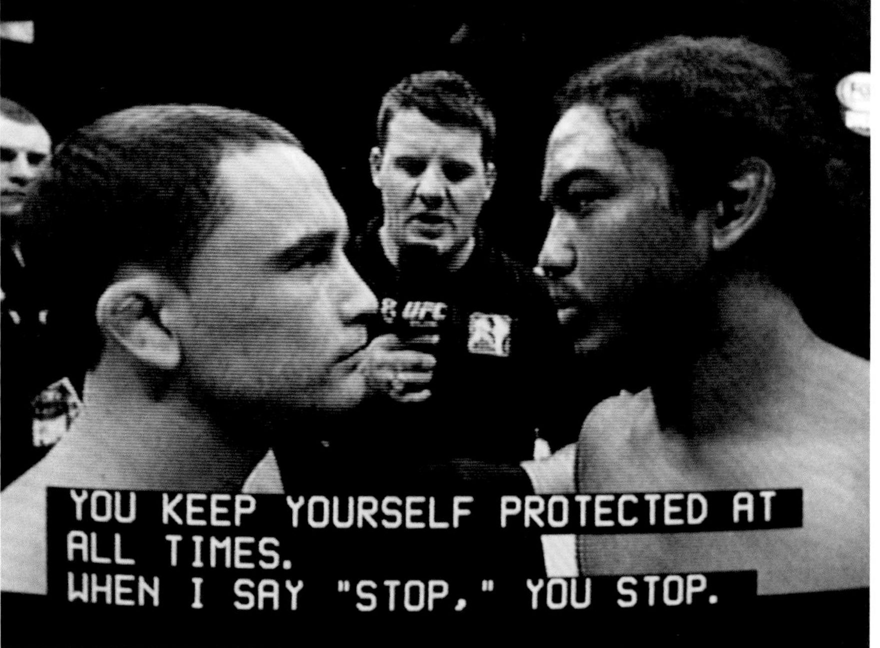

YOU KEEP YOURSELF PROTECTED AT
ALL TIMES.
WHEN I SAY "STOP," YOU STOP.

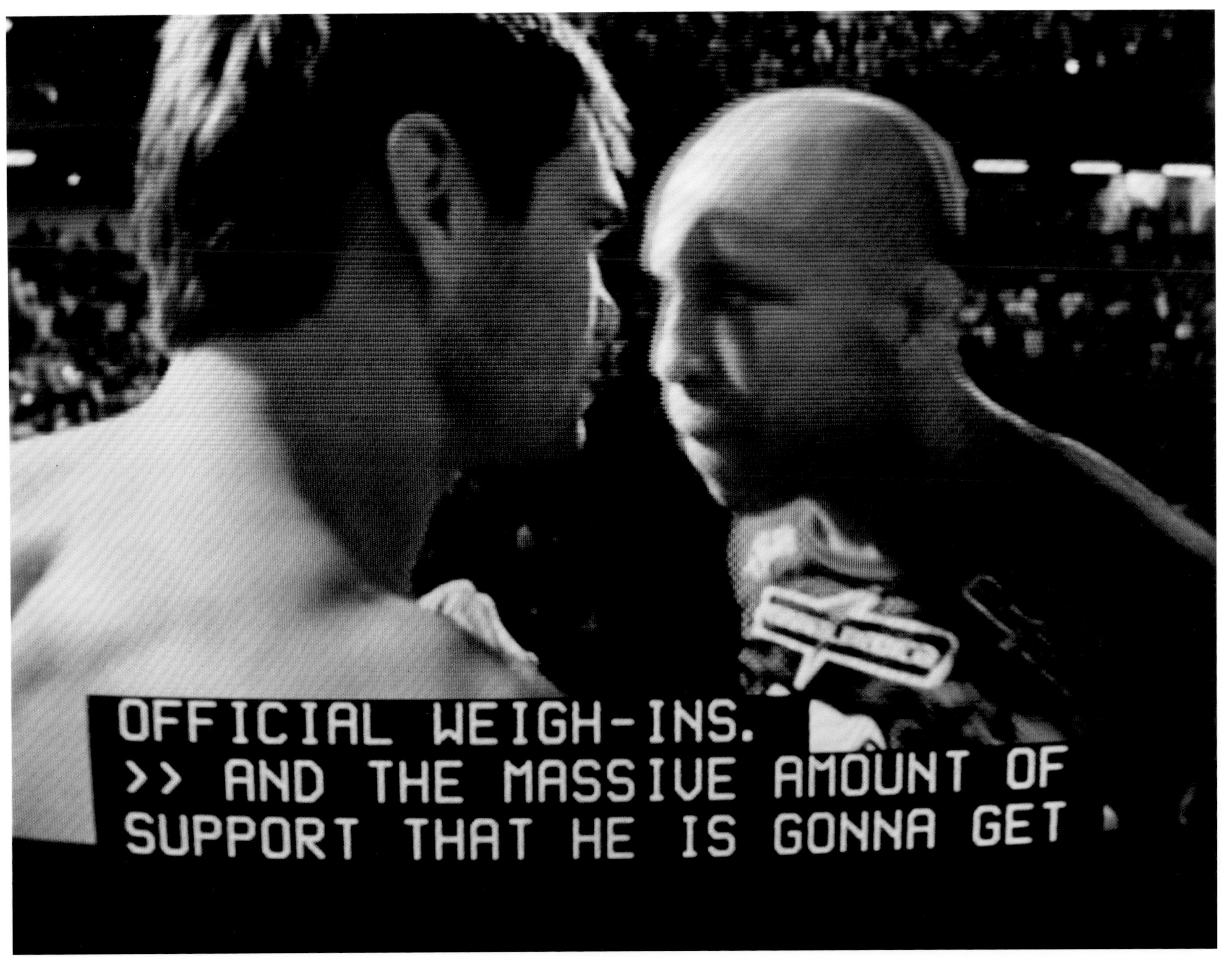

OFFICIAL WEIGH-INS.
>> AND THE MASSIVE AMOUNT OF
SUPPORT THAT HE IS GONNA GET

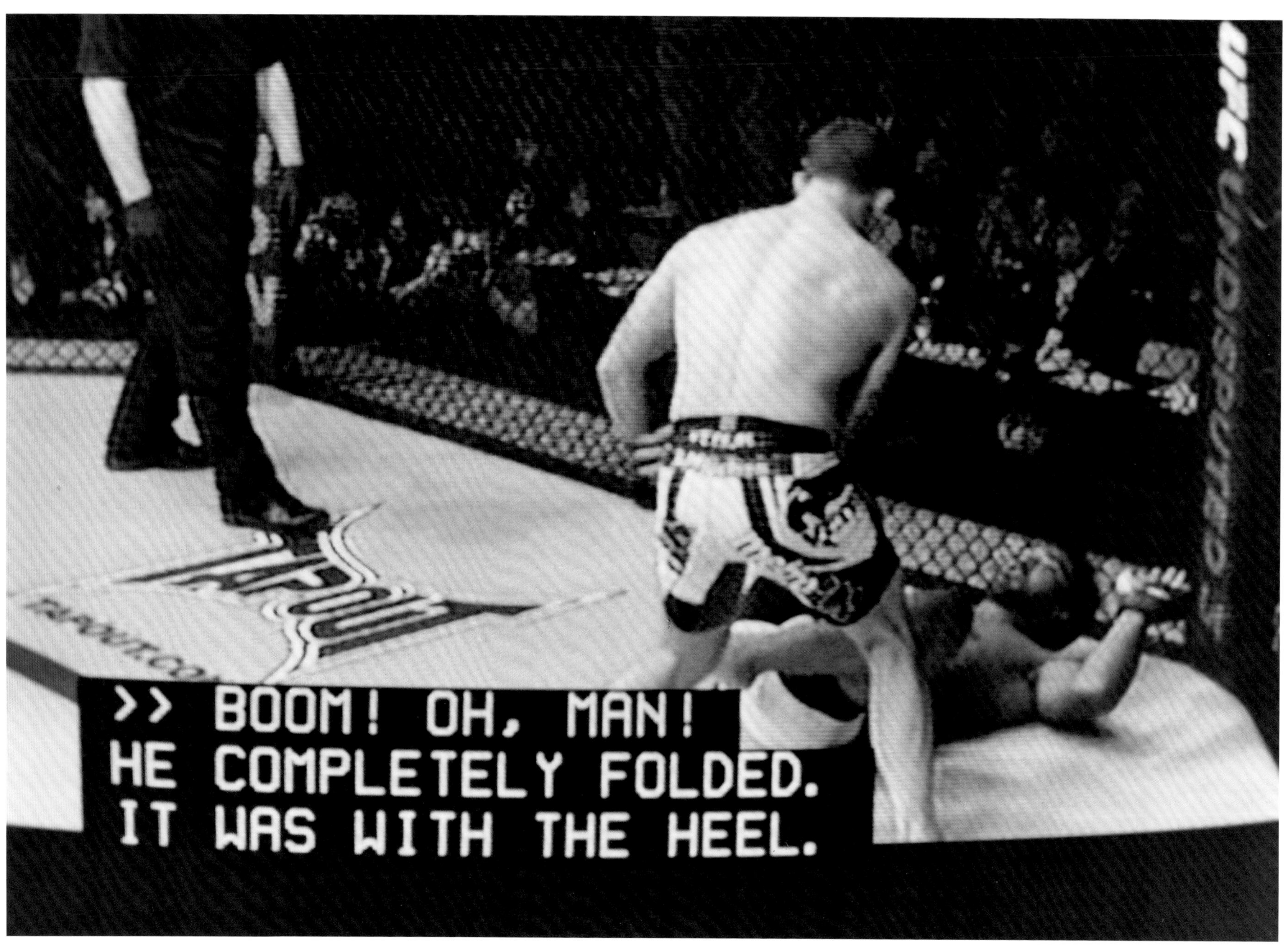

>> BOOM! OH, MAN!
HE COMPLETELY FOLDED.
IT WAS WITH THE HEEL.

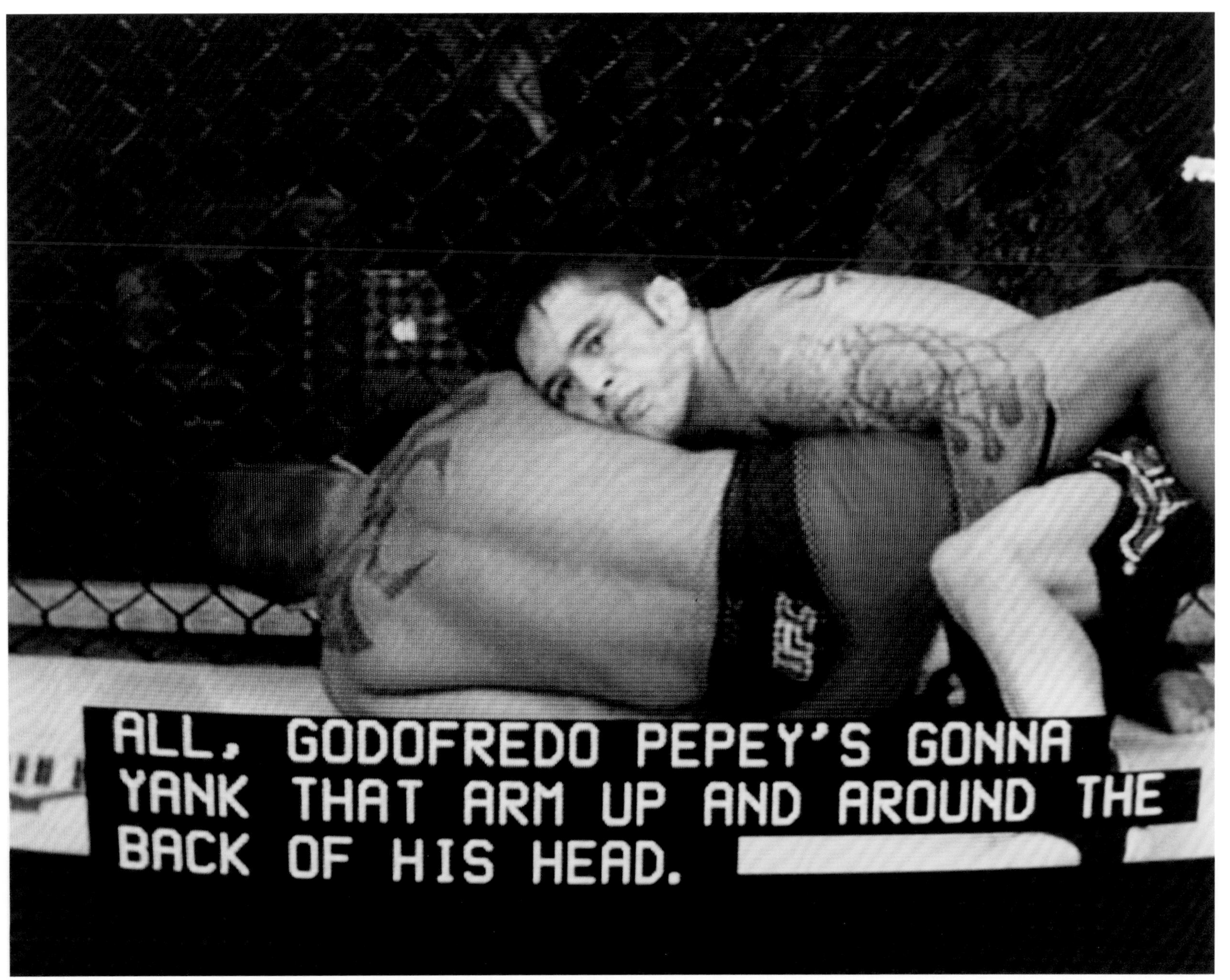
ALL, GODOFREDO PEPEY'S GONNA
YANK THAT ARM UP AND AROUND THE
BACK OF HIS HEAD.

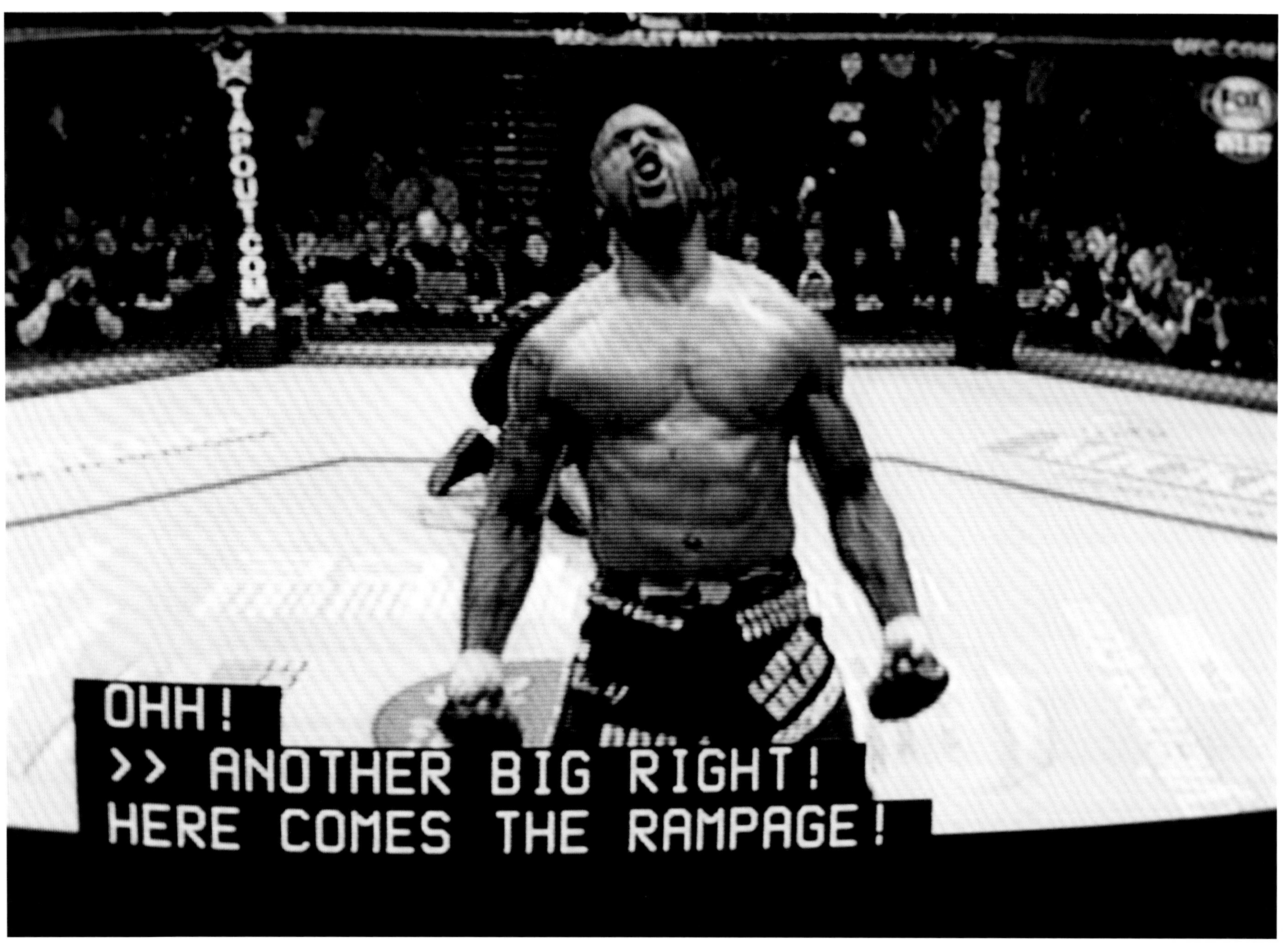
OHH!
>> ANOTHER BIG RIGHT!
HERE COMES THE RAMPAGE!

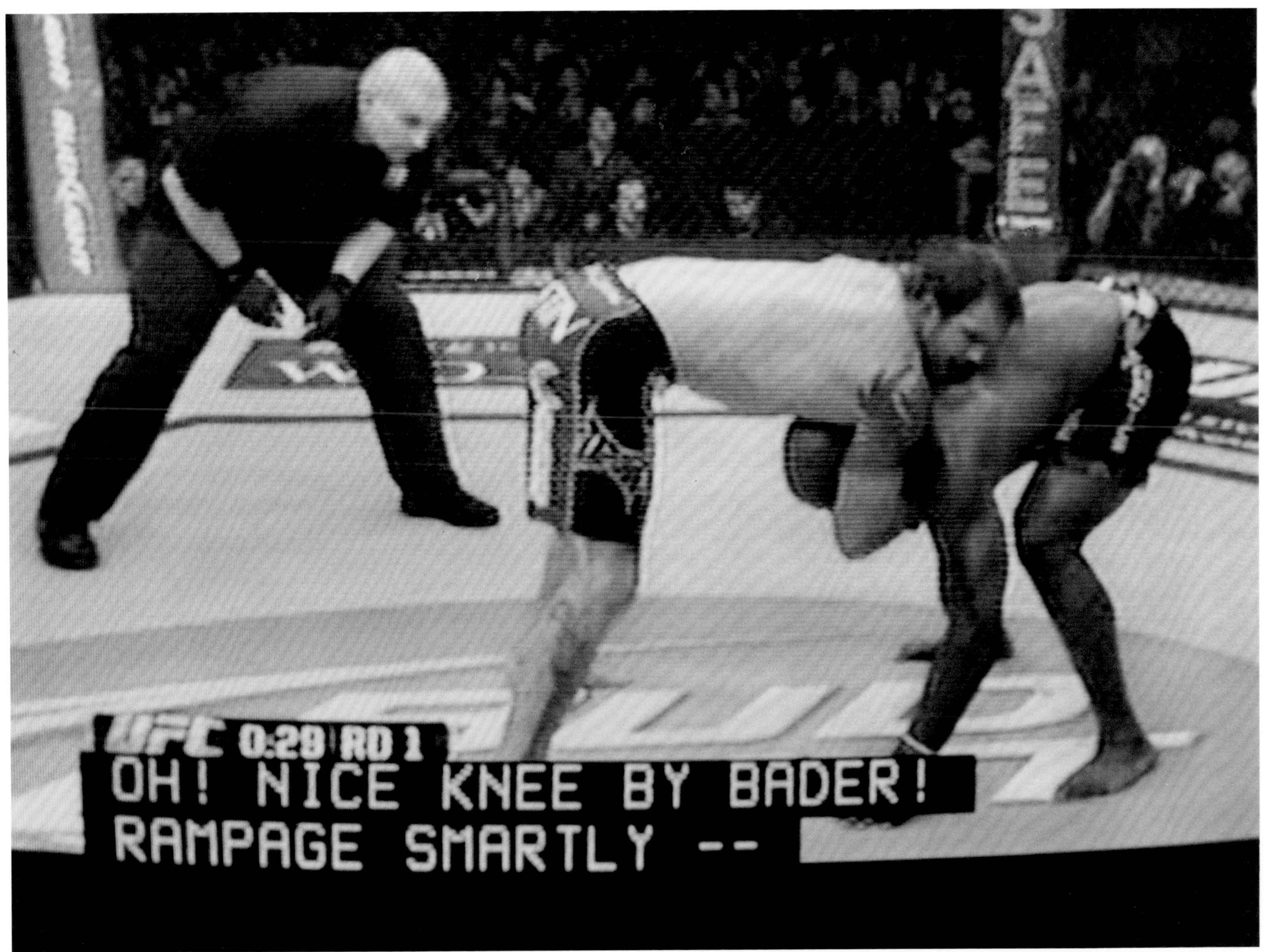

0:28 RD 1
OH! NICE KNEE BY BADER!
RAMPAGE SMARTLY --

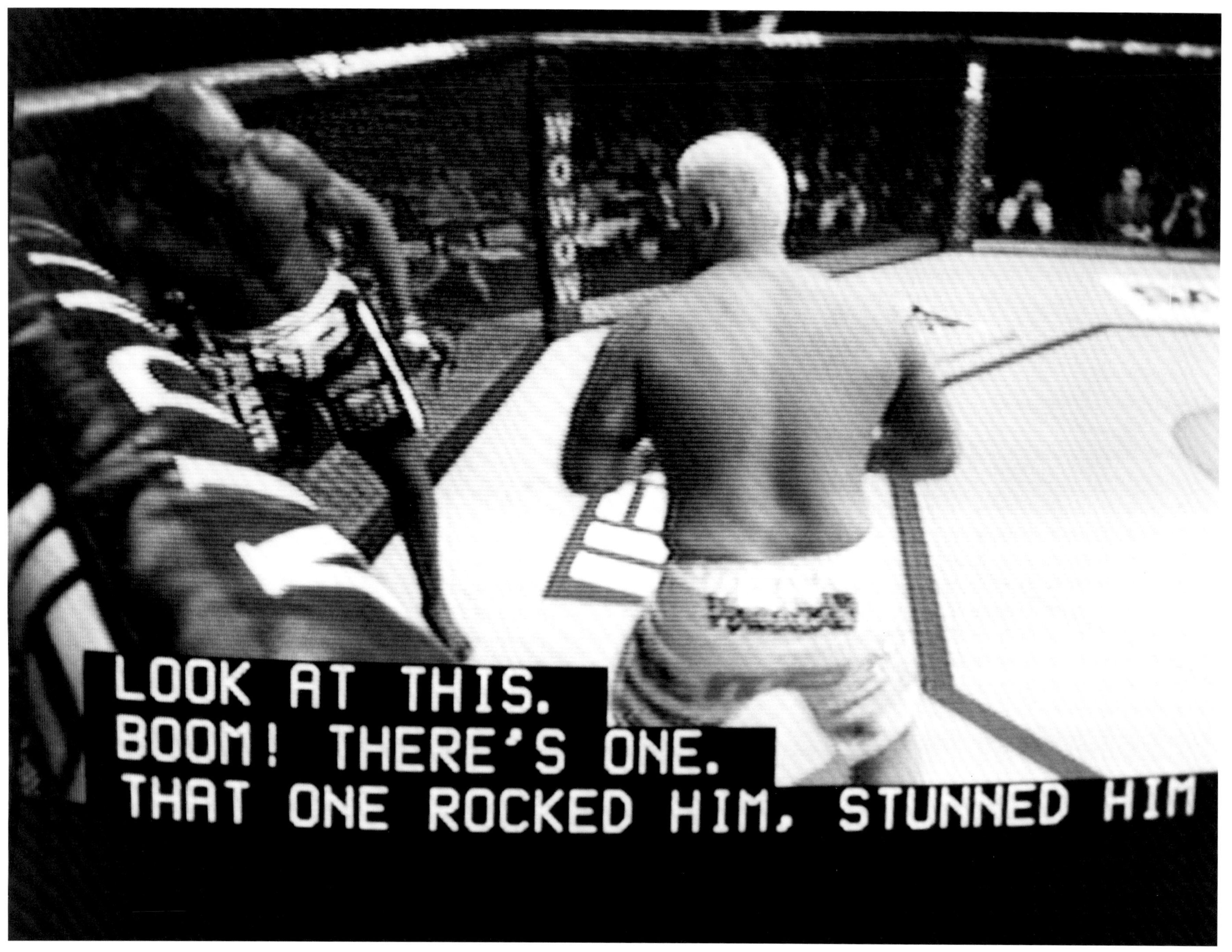

LOOK AT THIS.
BOOM! THERE'S ONE.
THAT ONE ROCKED HIM, STUNNED HIM

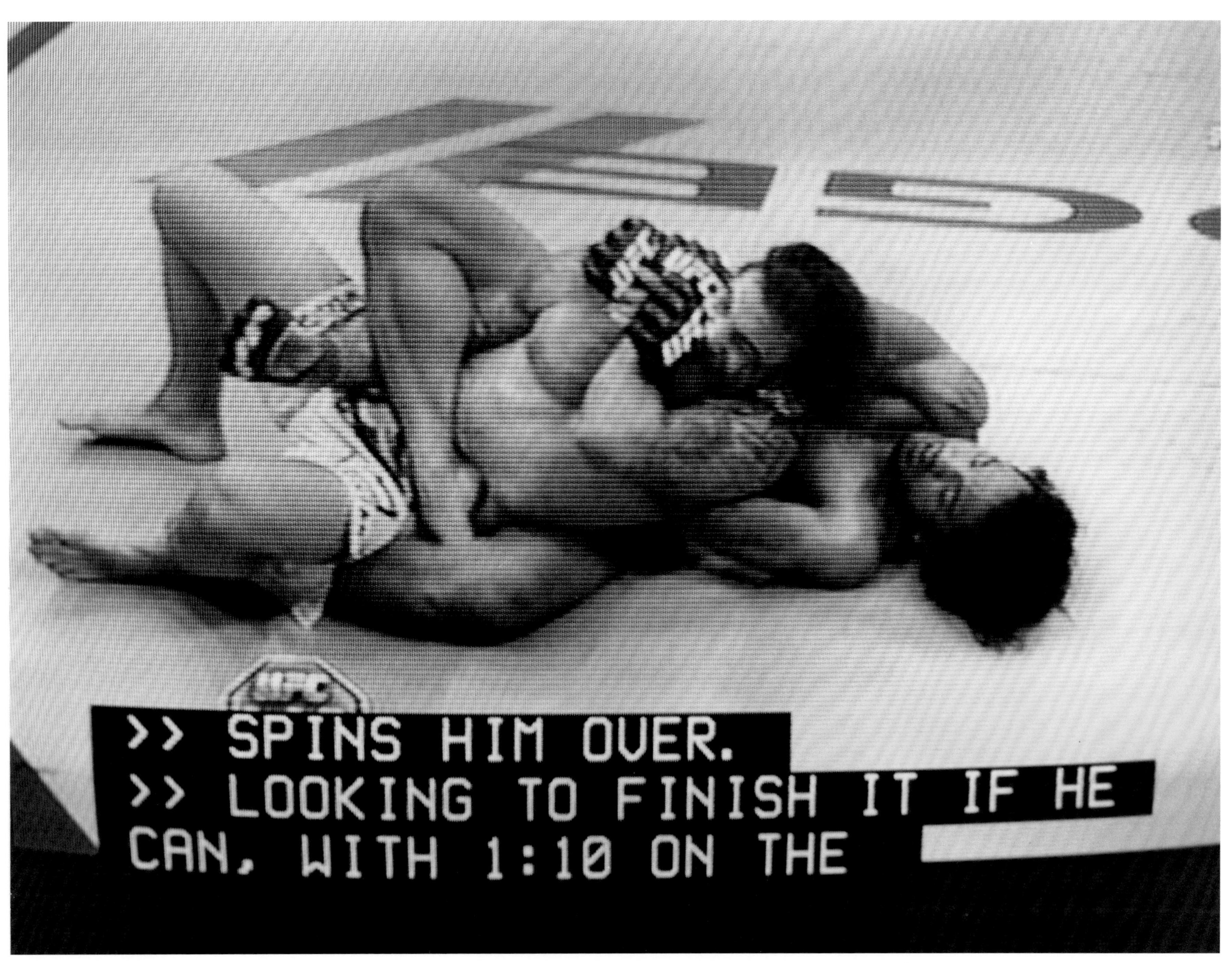

>> SPINS HIM OVER.
>> LOOKING TO FINISH IT IF HE
CAN, WITH 1:10 ON THE

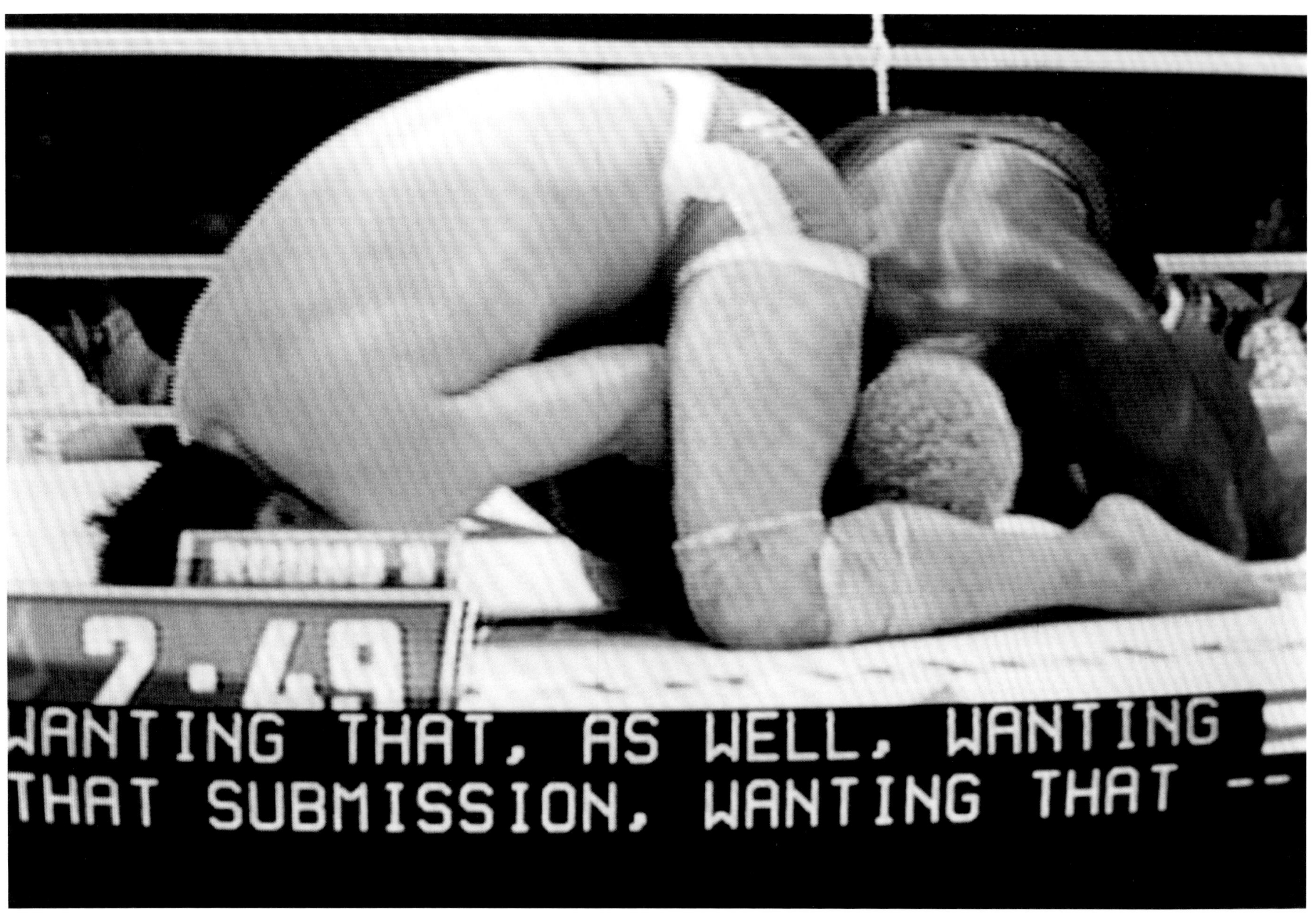
7.49
WANTING THAT, AS WELL, WANTING
THAT SUBMISSION, WANTING THAT --

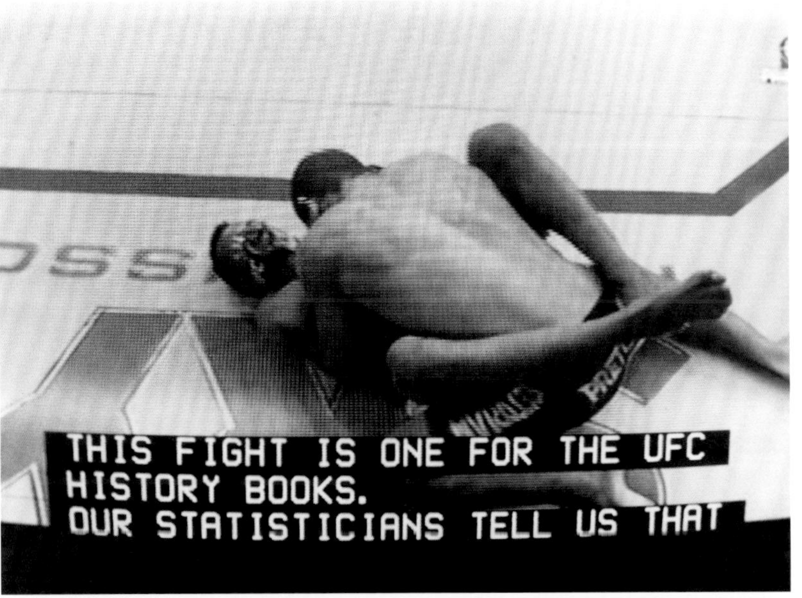

THIS FIGHT IS ONE FOR THE UFC
HISTORY BOOKS.
OUR STATISTICIANS TELL US THAT

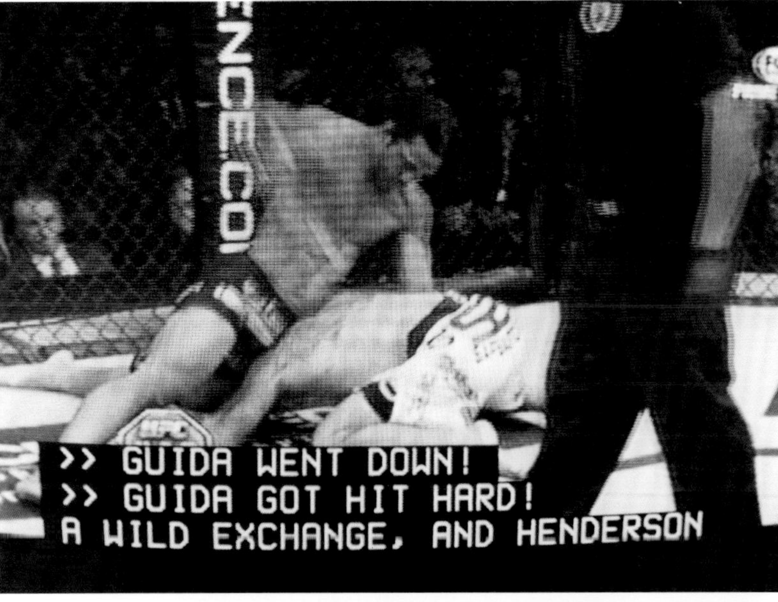

>> GUIDA WENT DOWN!
>> GUIDA GOT HIT HARD!
A WILD EXCHANGE, AND HENDERSON

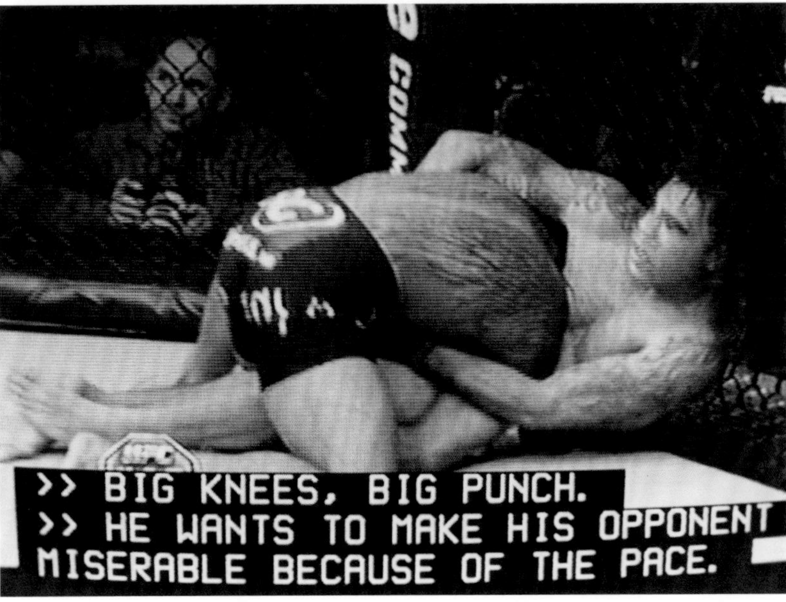

>> BIG KNEES, BIG PUNCH.
>> HE WANTS TO MAKE HIS OPPONENT
MISERABLE BECAUSE OF THE PACE.

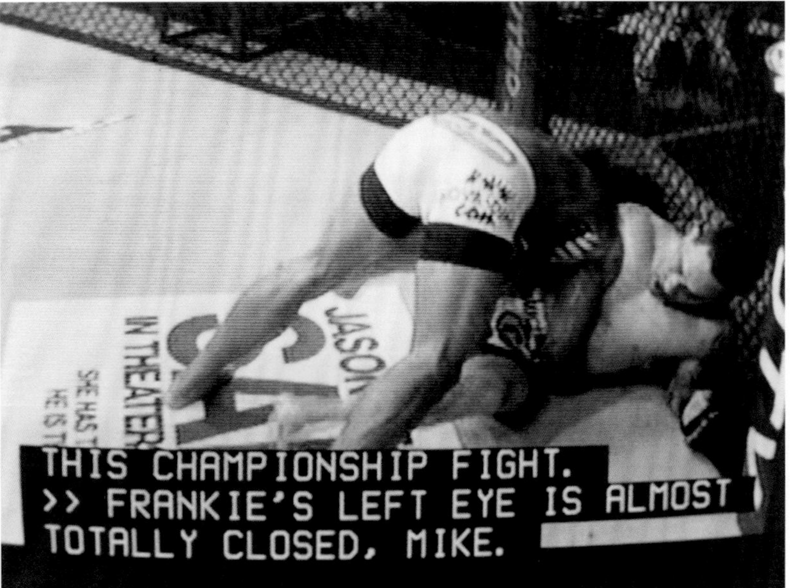

THIS CHAMPIONSHIP FIGHT.
>> FRANKIE'S LEFT EYE IS ALMOST
TOTALLY CLOSED, MIKE.

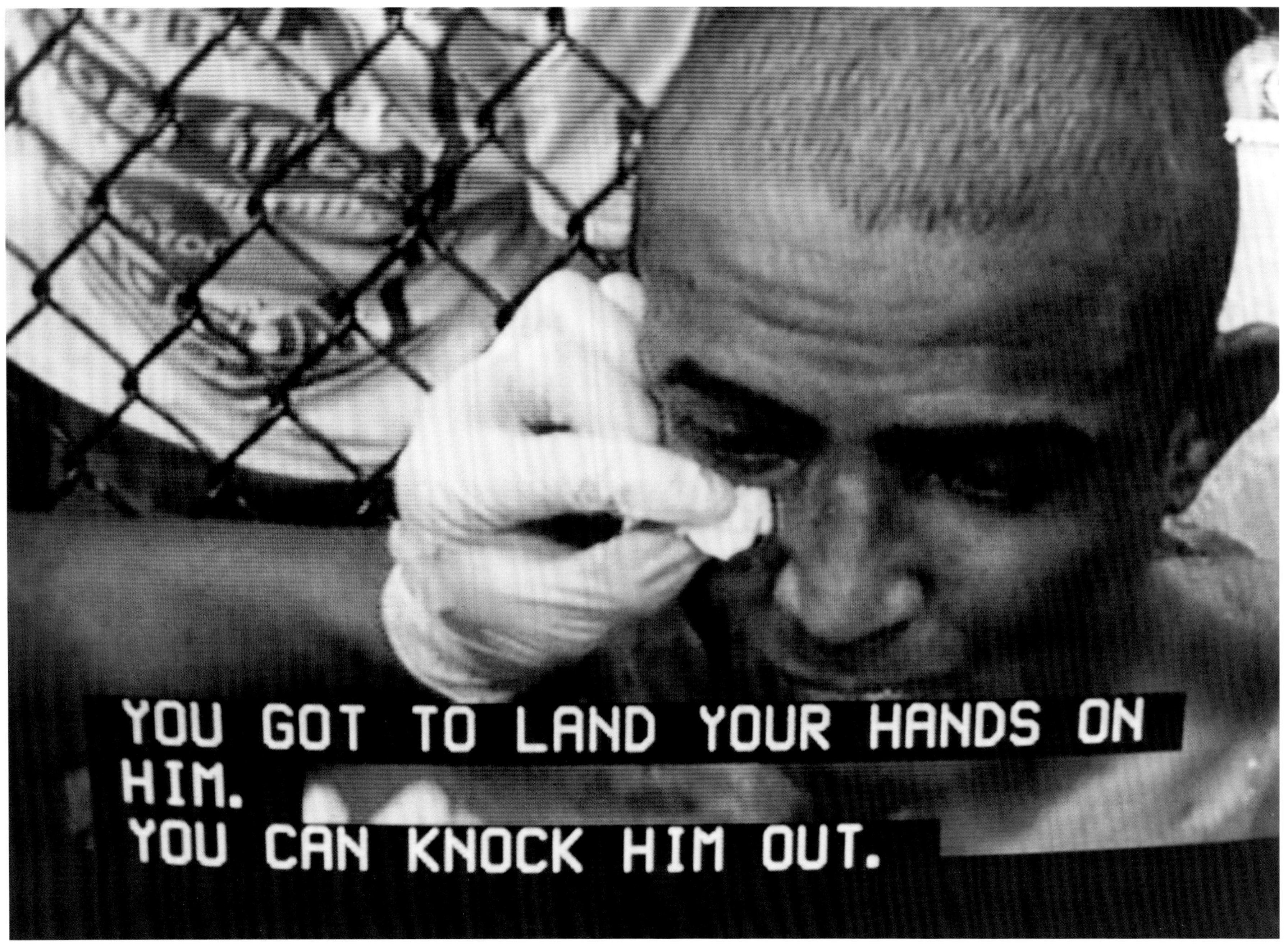

YOU GOT TO LAND YOUR HANDS ON
HIM.
YOU CAN KNOCK HIM OUT.

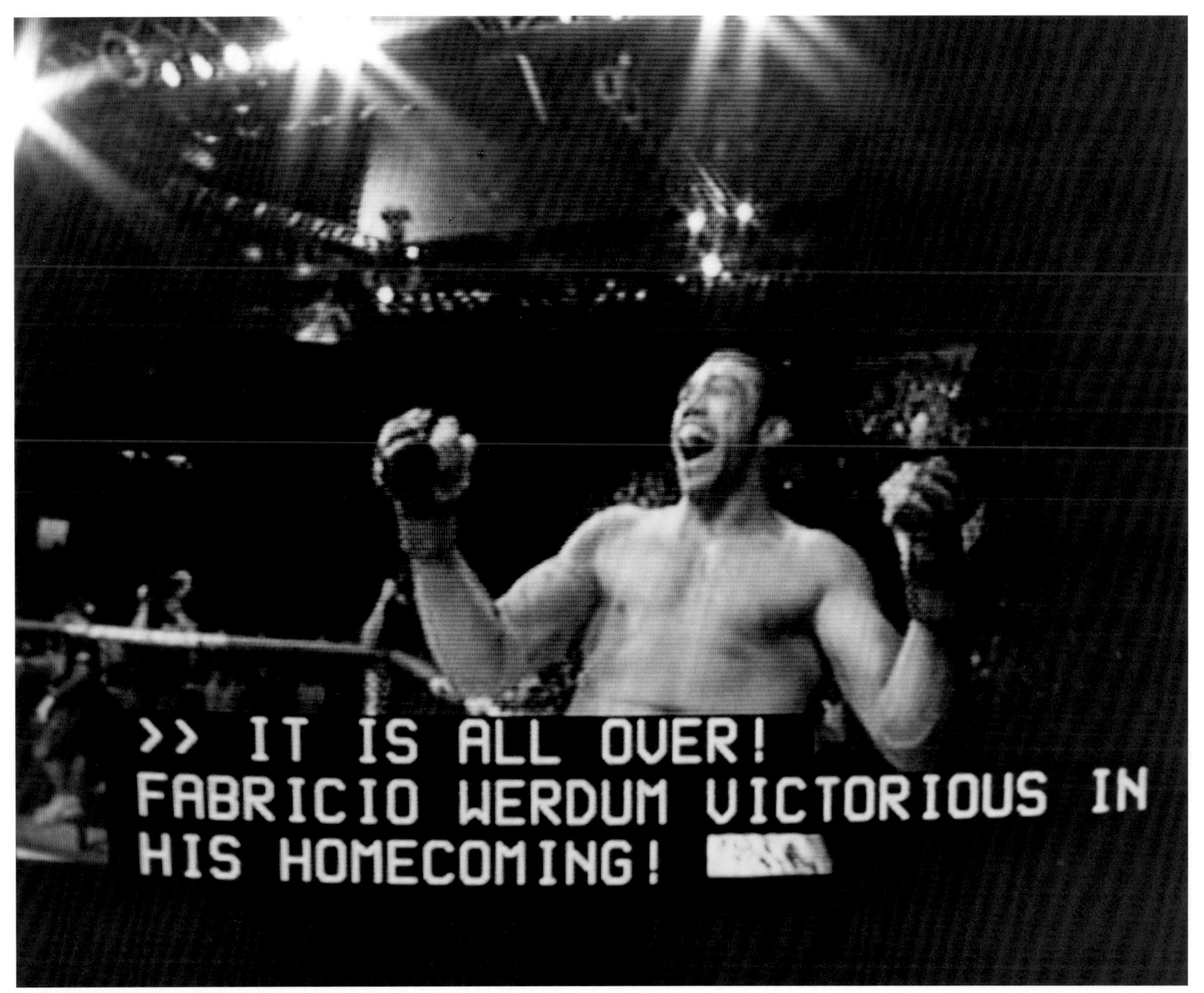

>> IT IS ALL OVER!
FABRICIO WERDUM VICTORIOUS IN
HIS HOMECOMING!

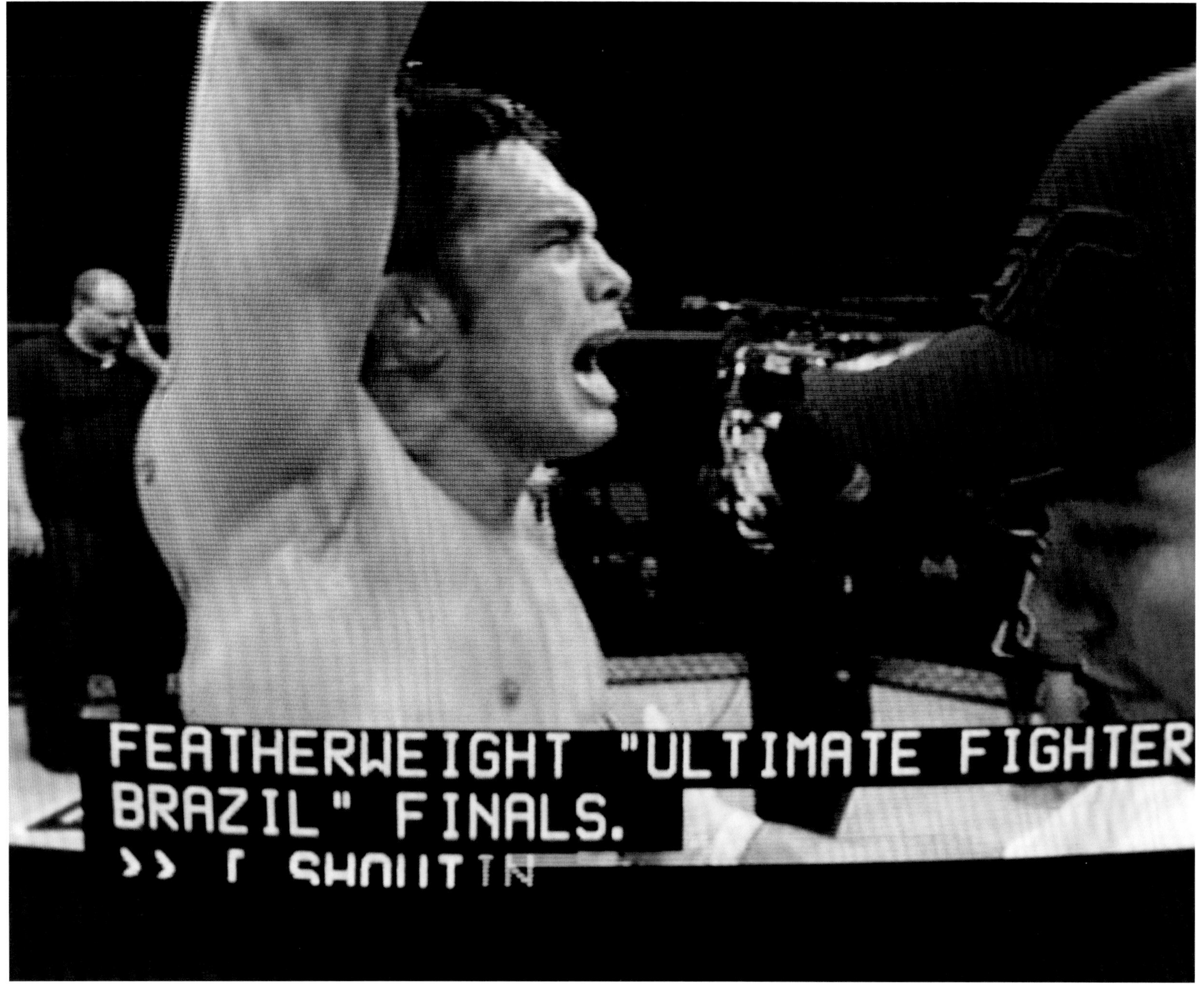
FEATHERWEIGHT "ULTIMATE FIGHTER
BRAZIL" FINALS.
>> [SHOUTIN

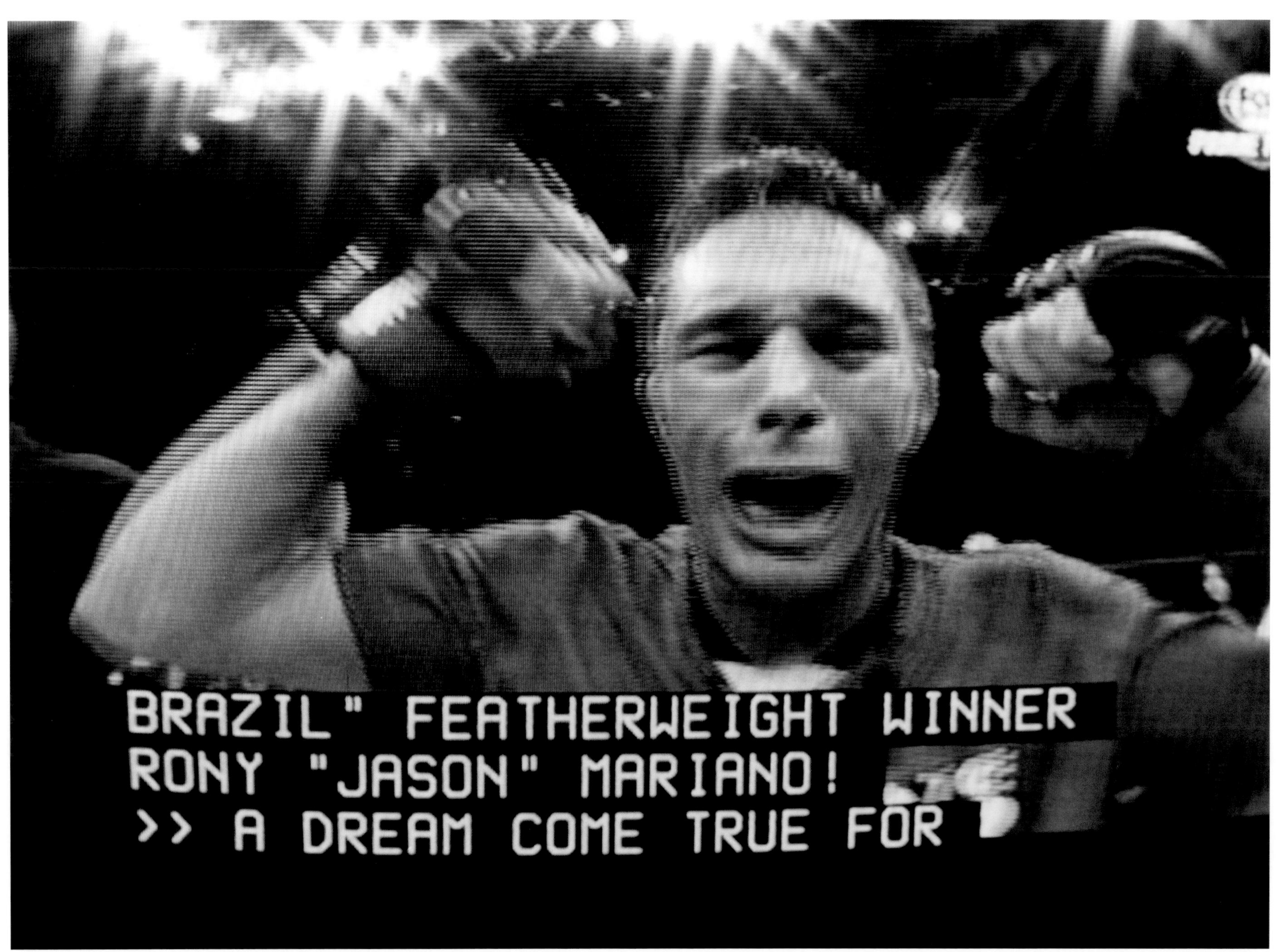
BRAZIL" FEATHERWEIGHT WINNER
RONY "JASON" MARIANO!
>> A DREAM COME TRUE FOR

Newtown School Massacre, 2012

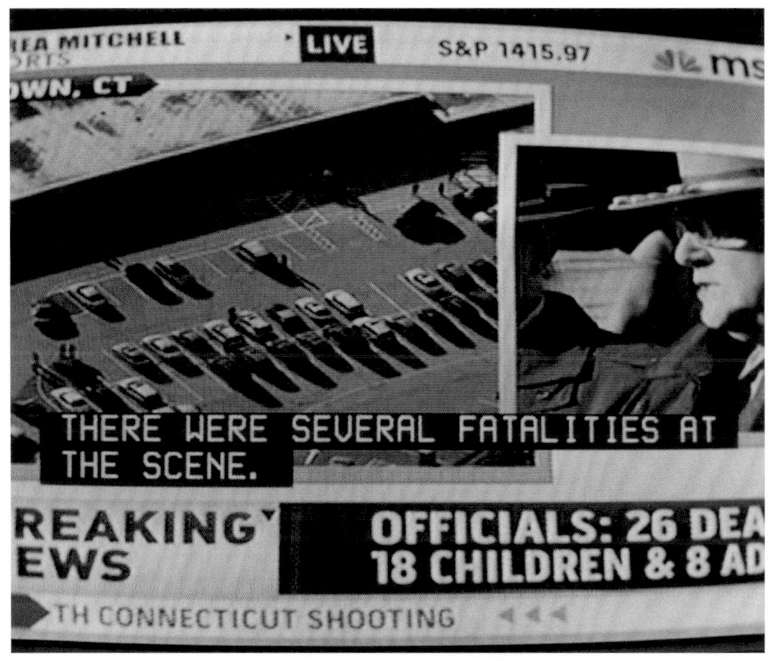
IEA MITCHELL
ORTS
OWN, CT
LIVE
S&P 1415.97
ms
THERE WERE SEVERAL FATALITIES AT THE SCENE.
REAKING
EWS
OFFICIALS: 26 DEA
18 CHILDREN & 8 AD
TH CONNECTICUT SHOOTING

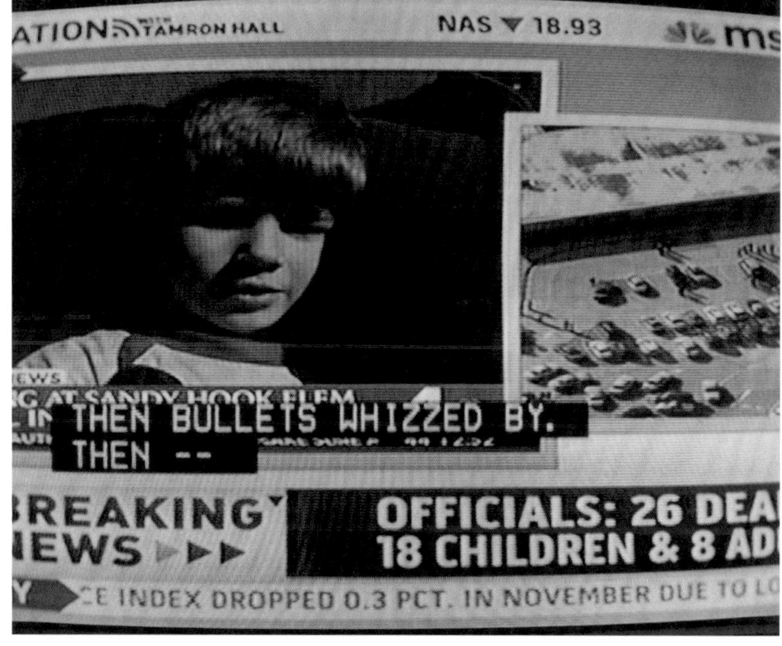
ATION TAMRON HALL
NAS 18.93
ms
G AT SANDY HOOK ELEM
THEN BULLETS WHIZZED BY.
THEN --
REAKING
EWS
OFFICIALS: 26 DEA
18 CHILDREN & 8 AD
CE INDEX DROPPED 0.3 PCT. IN NOVEMBER DUE TO LO

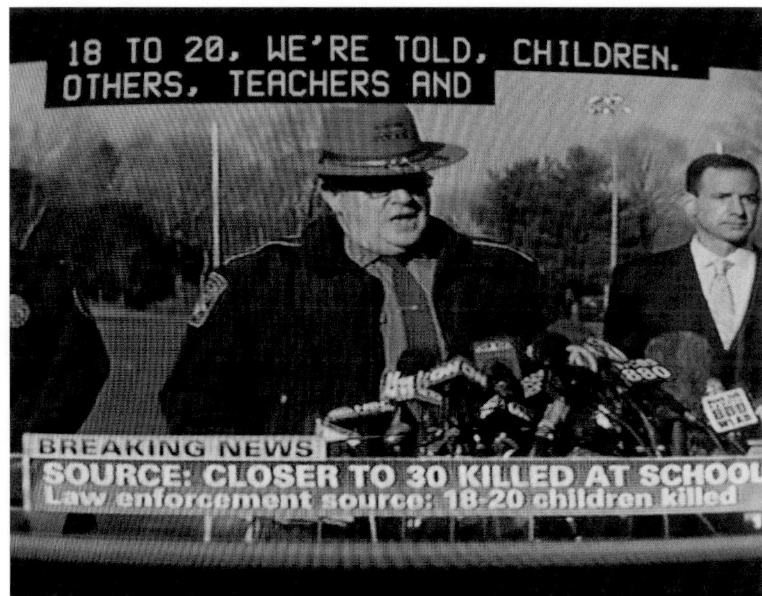
18 TO 20, WE'RE TOLD, CHILDREN.
OTHERS, TEACHERS AND
BREAKING NEWS
SOURCE: CLOSER TO 30 KILLED AT SCHOOL
Law enforcement source: 18-20 children killed

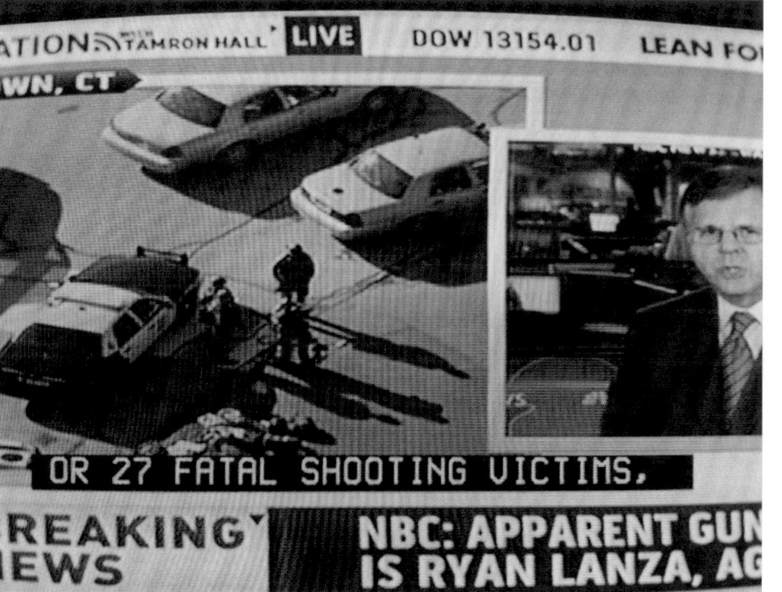
ATION TAMRON HALL LIVE
DOW 13154.01
LEAN FO
OWN, CT
OR 27 FATAL SHOOTING VICTIMS,
REAKING
EWS
NBC: APPARENT GUN
IS RYAN LANZA, AG

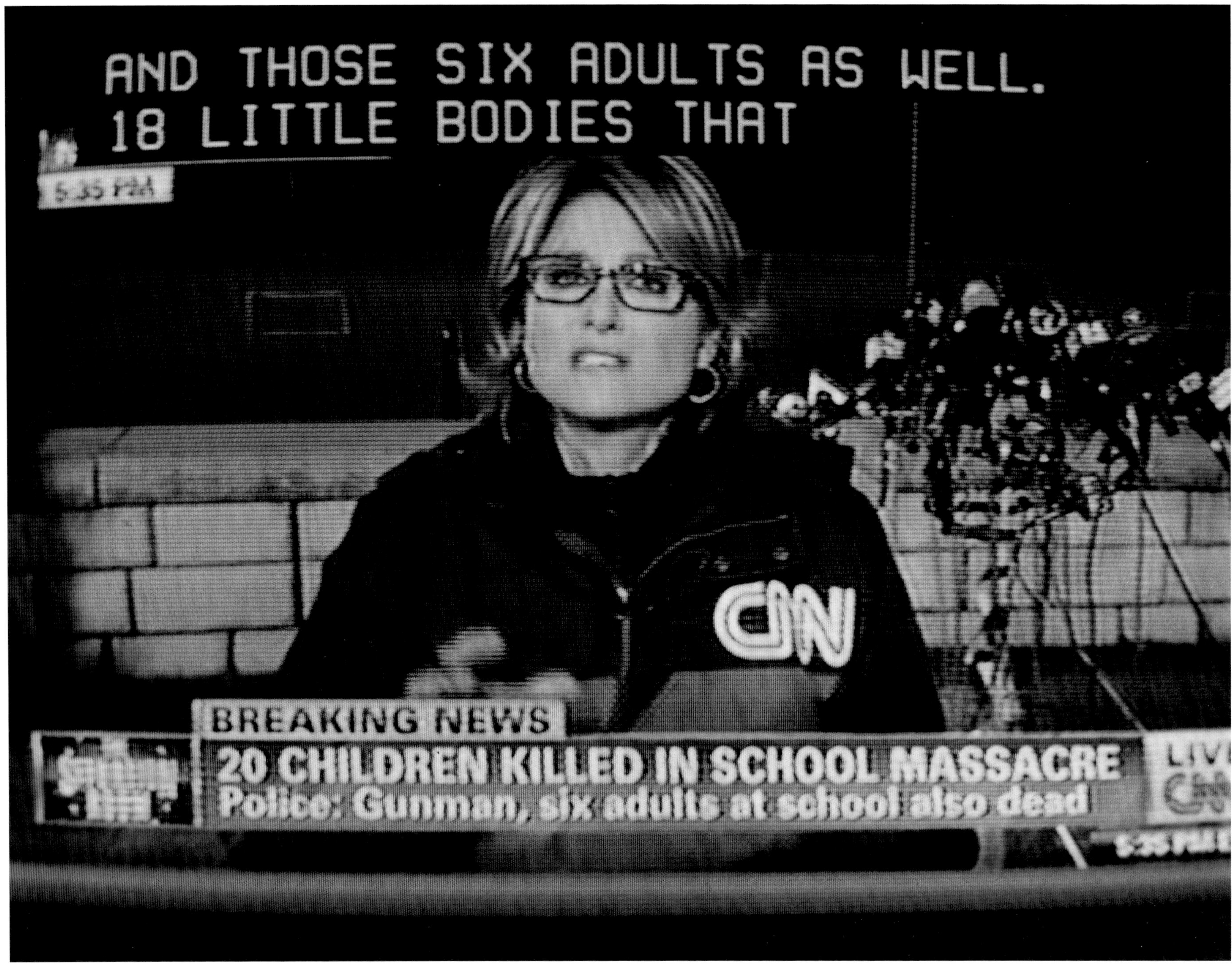
AND THOSE SIX ADULTS AS WELL.
18 LITTLE BODIES THAT
5:35 PM
BREAKING NEWS
20 CHILDREN KILLED IN SCHOOL MASSACRE
Police: Gunman, six adults at school also dead
LIVE

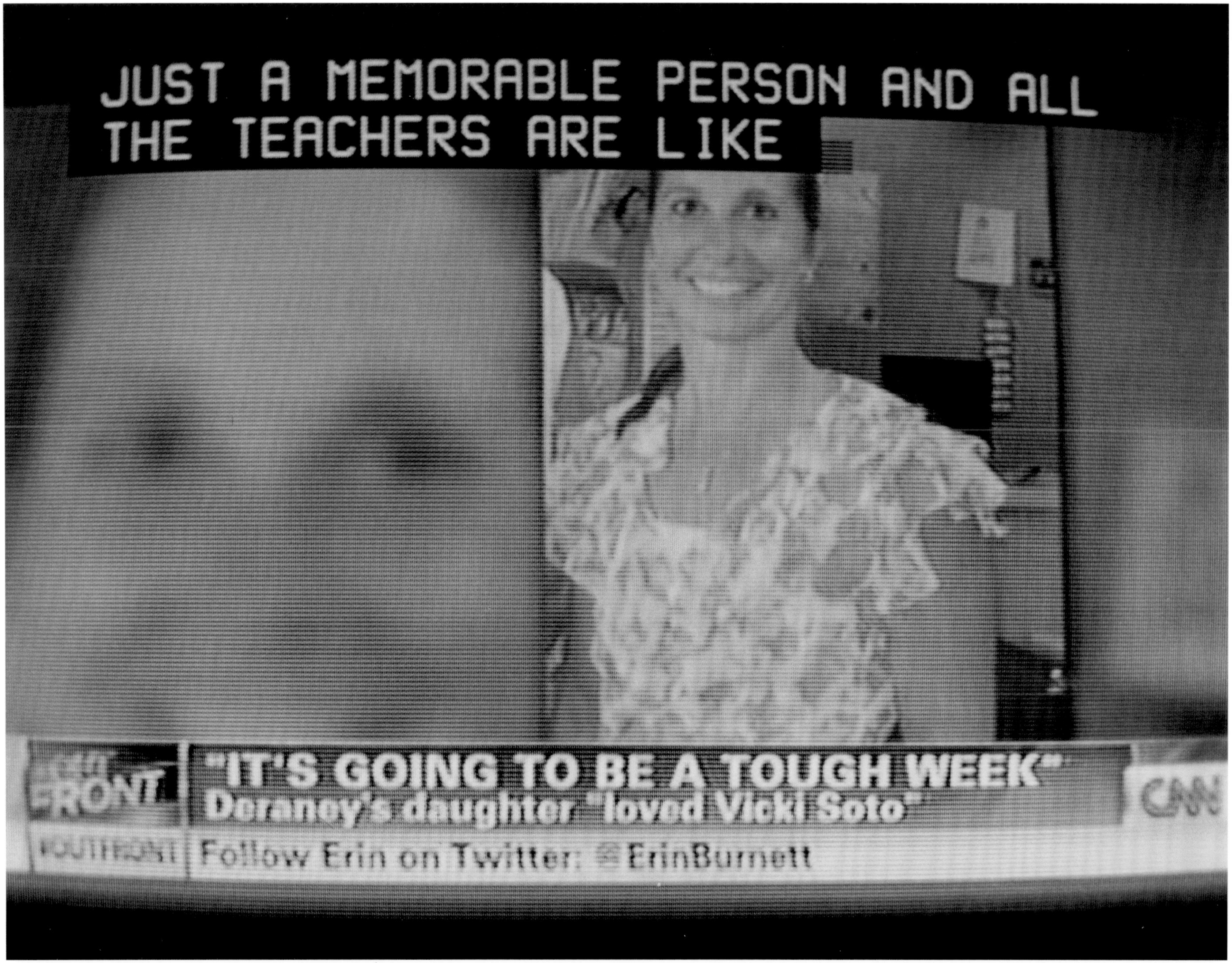

JUST A MEMORABLE PERSON AND ALL THE TEACHERS ARE LIKE
"IT'S GOING TO BE A TOUGH WEEK"
Delaney's daughter "loved Vicki Soto"
Follow Erin on Twitter: @ErinBurnett

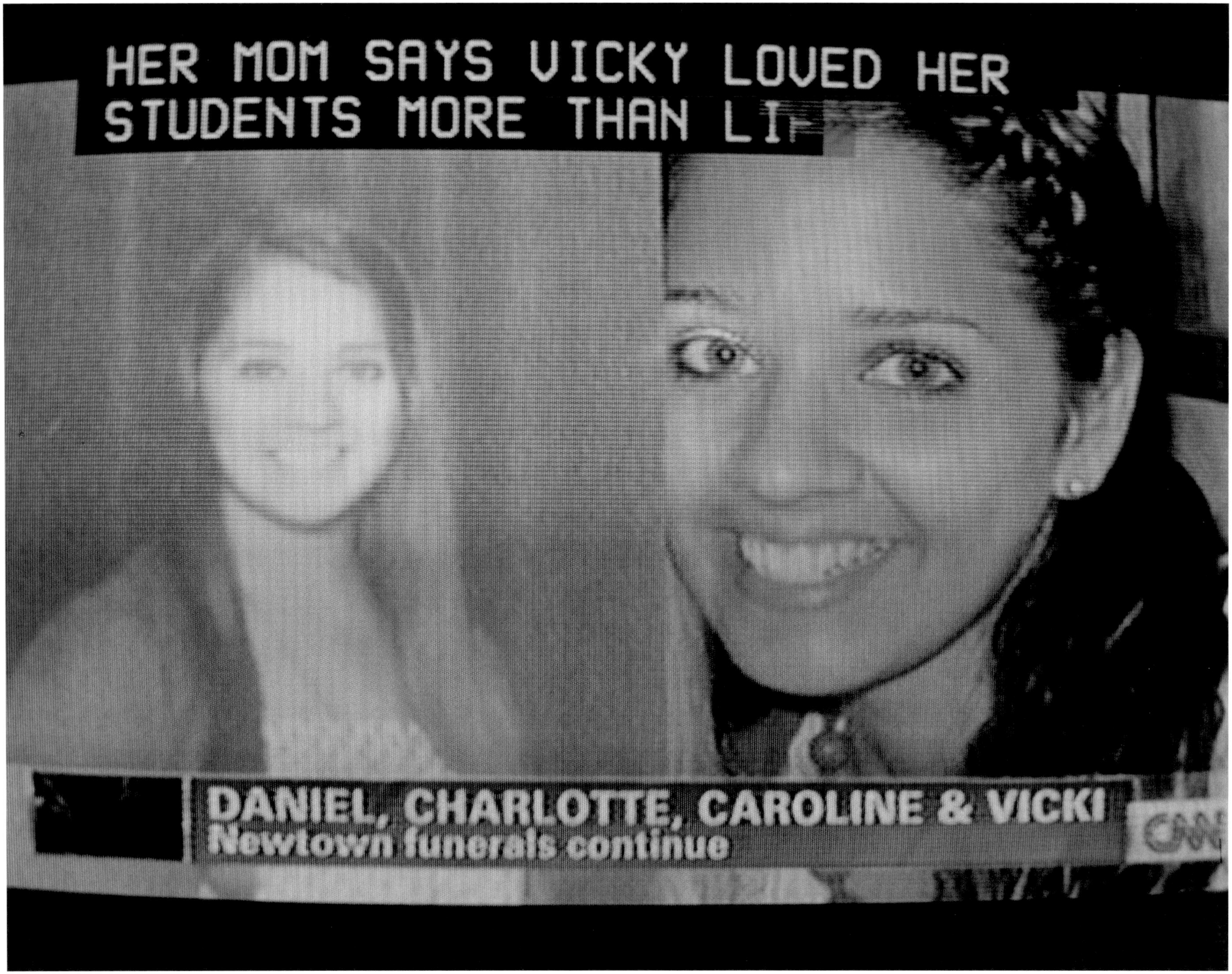

HER MOM SAYS VICKY LOVED HER
STUDENTS MORE THAN LI
DANIEL, CHARLOTTE, CAROLINE & VICKI
Newtown funerals continue
CNN

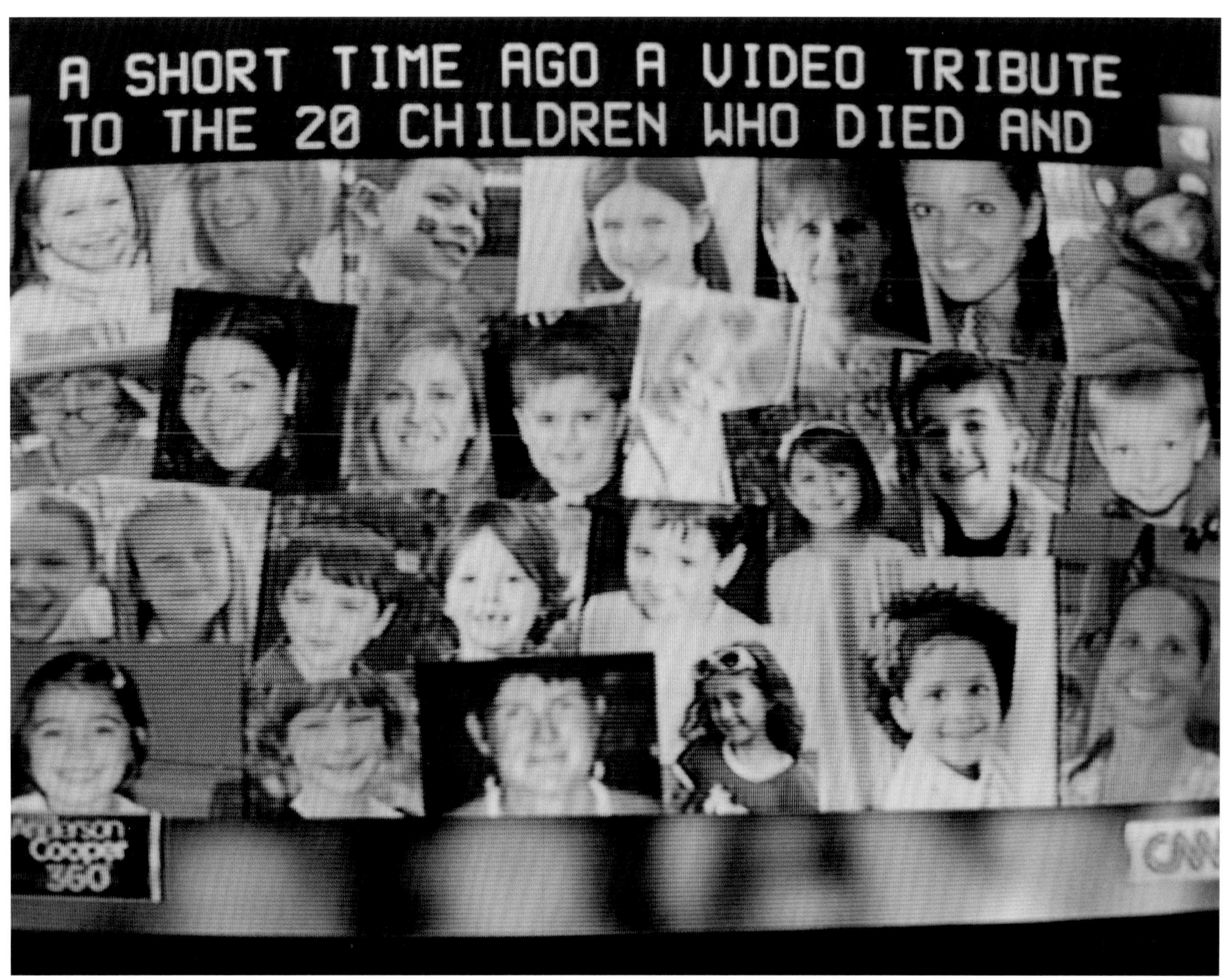

A SHORT TIME AGO A VIDEO TRIBUTE
TO THE 20 CHILDREN WHO DIED AND

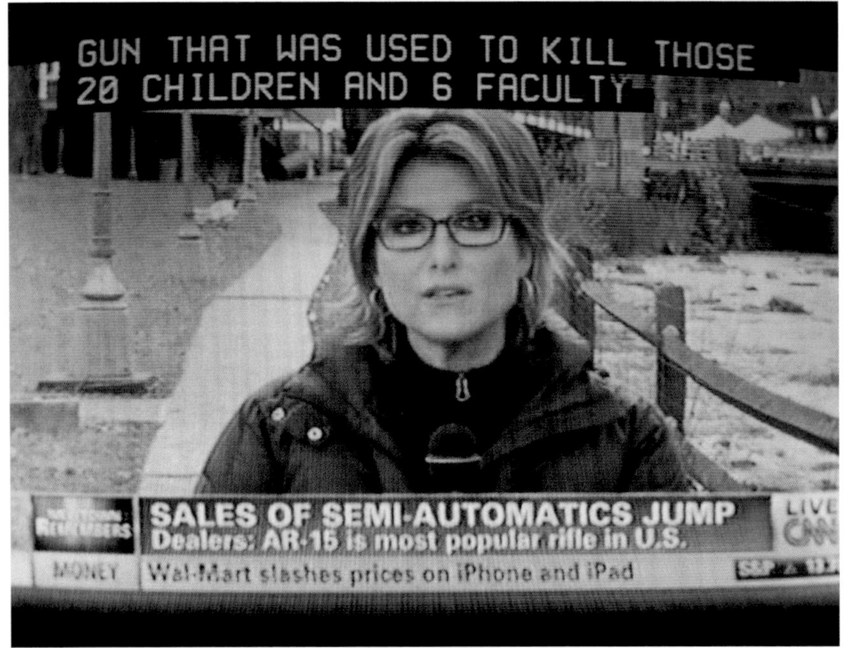

GUN THAT WAS USED TO KILL THOSE
20 CHILDREN AND 6 FACULTY
SALES OF SEMI-AUTOMATICS JUMP
Dealers: AR-15 is most popular rifle in U.S.
LIVE CNN
MONEY
Wal-Mart slashes prices on iPhone and iPad

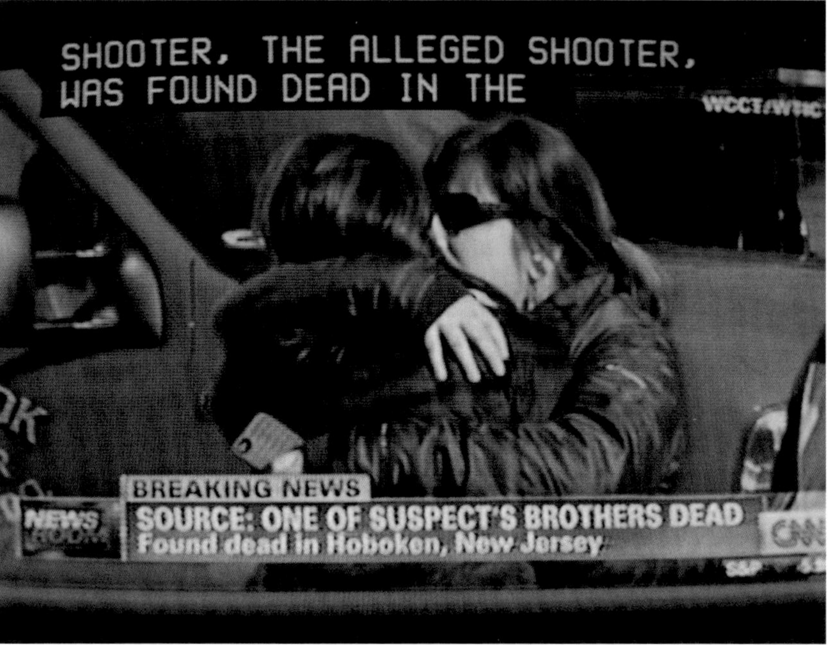

SHOOTER, THE ALLEGED SHOOTER,
WAS FOUND DEAD IN THE
WCCT/WTIC
BREAKING NEWS
NEWS ROOM
SOURCE: ONE OF SUSPECT'S BROTHERS DEAD
Found dead in Hoboken, New Jersey
CNN

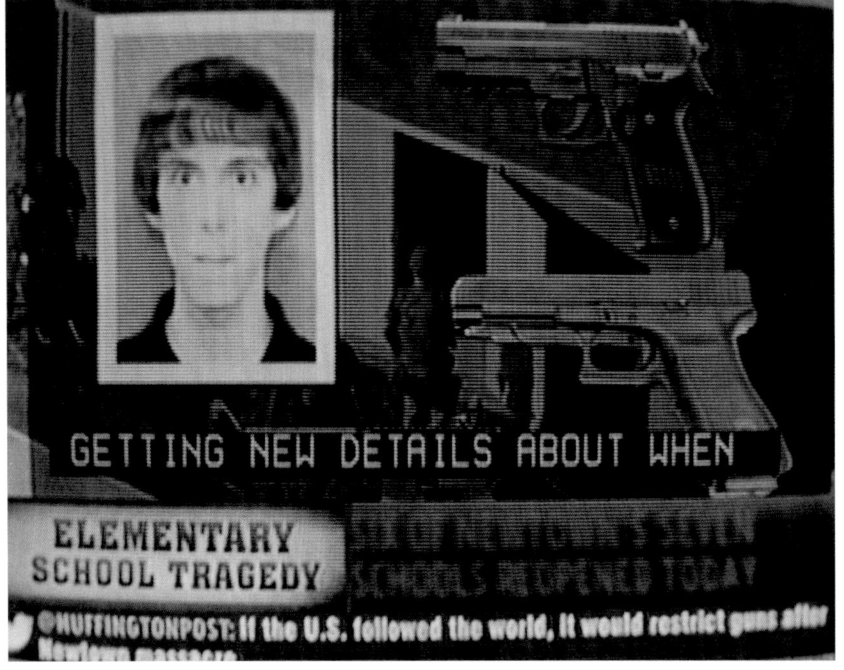

GETTING NEW DETAILS ABOUT WHEN
ELEMENTARY
SCHOOL TRAGEDY
SCHOOLS REOPENED TODAY
@HUFFINGTONPOST: If the U.S. followed the world, it would restrict guns after
Newtown massacre

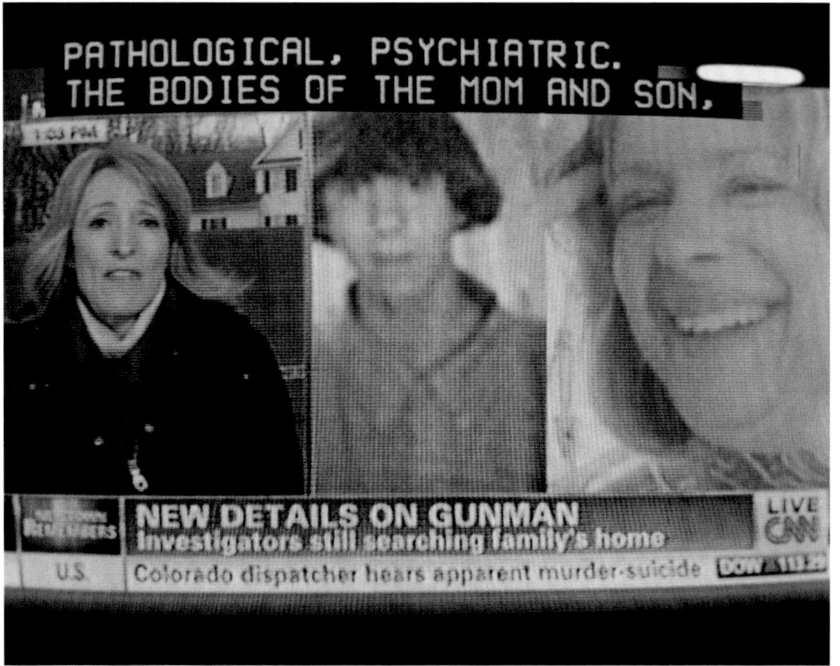

PATHOLOGICAL, PSYCHIATRIC.
THE BODIES OF THE MOM AND SON,
1:03 PM
NEW DETAILS ON GUNMAN
Investigators still searching family's home
LIVE CNN
U.S.
Colorado dispatcher hears apparent murder-suicide
DOW

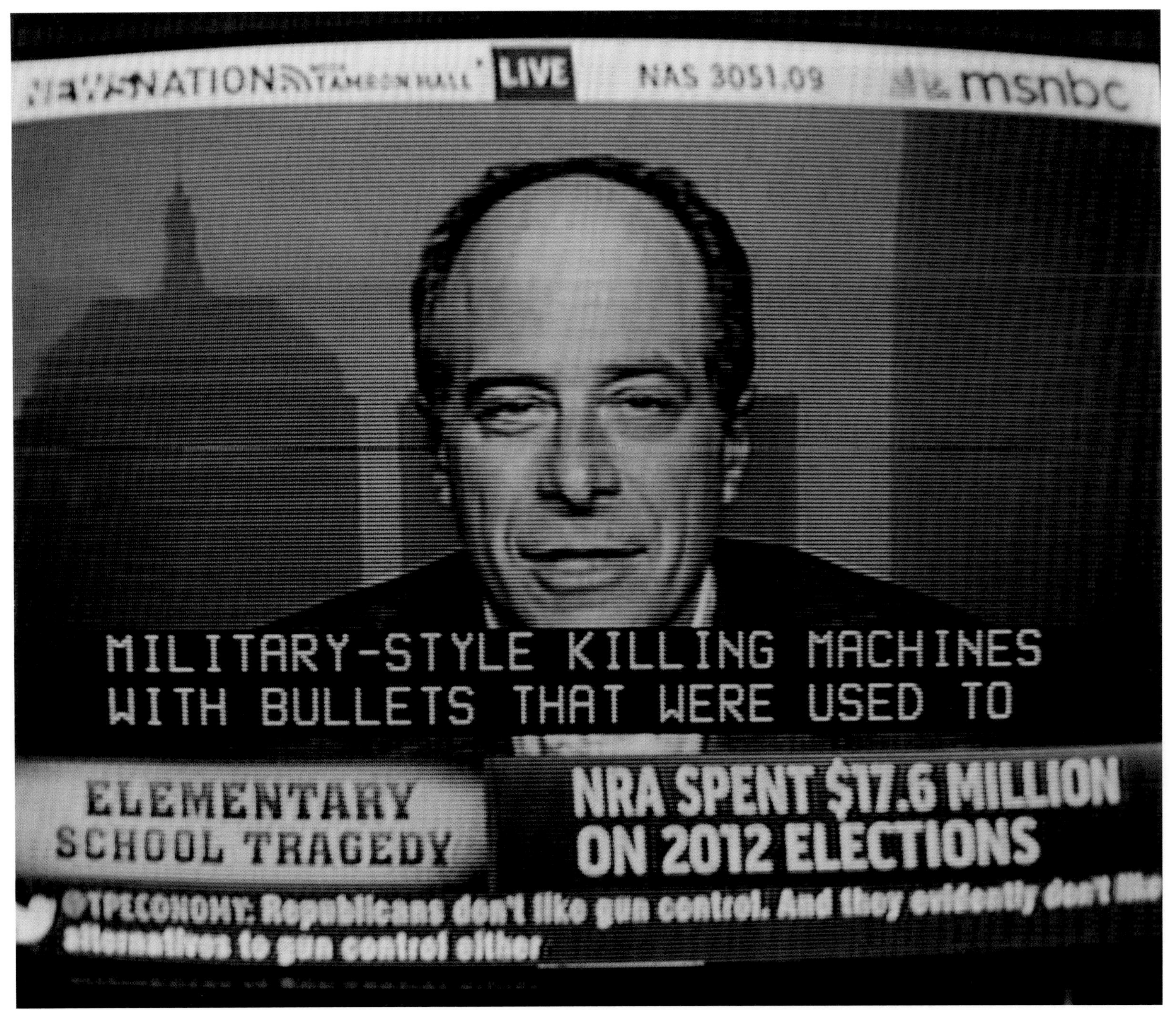
NEWS NATION TAMRON HALL LIVE   NAS 3051.09   msnbc
MILITARY-STYLE KILLING MACHINES
WITH BULLETS THAT WERE USED TO
ELEMENTARY
SCHOOL TRAGEDY
NRA SPENT $17.6 MILLION
ON 2012 ELECTIONS
@TPECONOMY: Republicans don't like gun control. And they evidently don't like
alternatives to gun control either

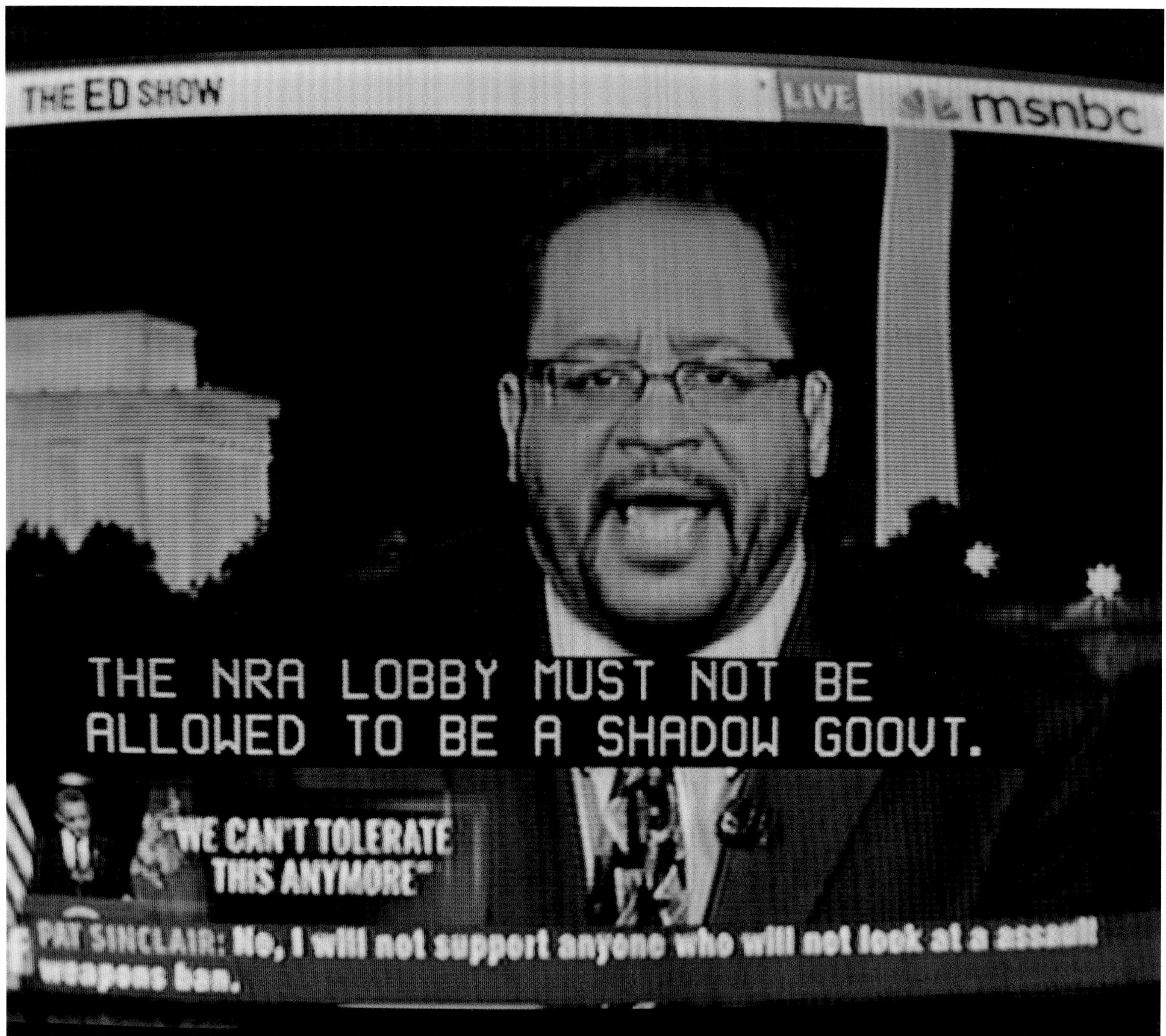

THE ED SHOW
LIVE
msnbc
THE NRA LOBBY MUST NOT BE
ALLOWED TO BE A SHADOW GOOVT.
"WE CAN'T TOLERATE
THIS ANYMORE"
PAT SINCLAIR: No, I will not support anyone who will not look at a assault weapons ban.

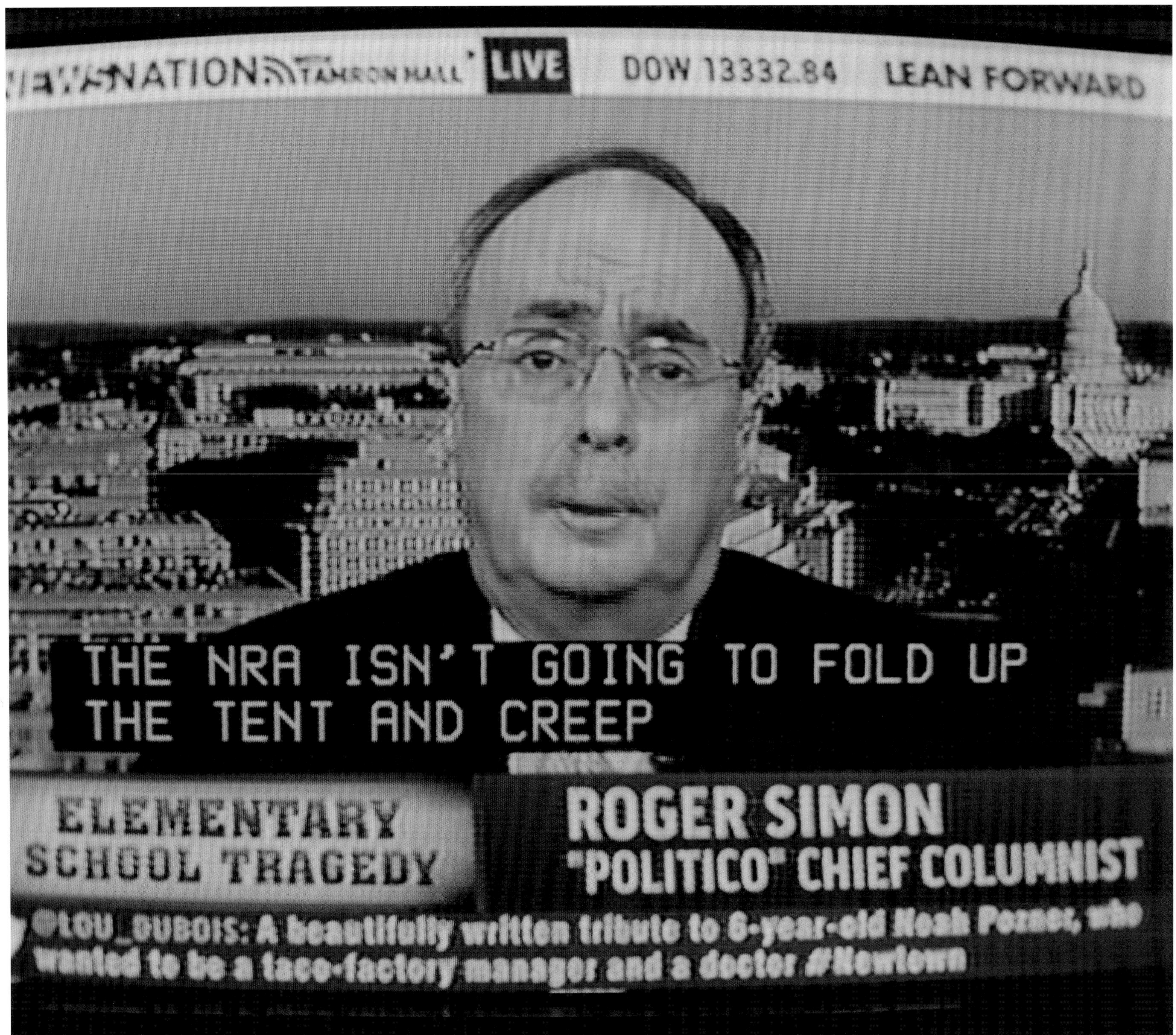
NATION TAMRON HALL LIVE   DOW 13332.84   LEAN FORWARD
THE NRA ISN'T GOING TO FOLD UP THE TENT AND CREEP
ELEMENTARY SCHOOL TRAGEDY
ROGER SIMON
"POLITICO" CHIEF COLUMNIST
@LOU_DUBOIS: A beautifully written tribute to 6-year-old Noah Pozner, who wanted to be a taco-factory manager and a doctor #Newtown

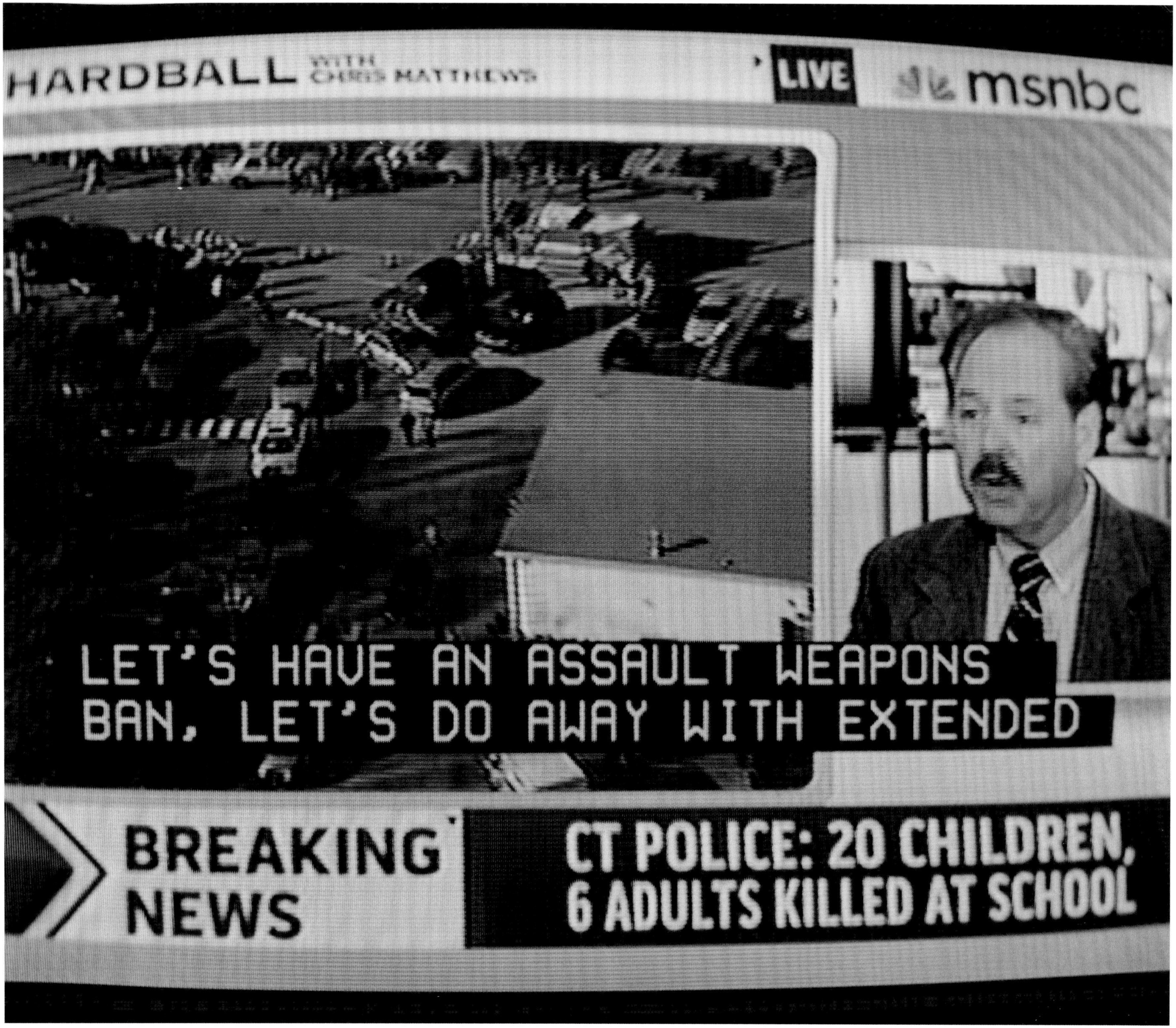

HARDBALL WITH CHRIS MATTHEWS
LIVE
msnbc
LET'S HAVE AN ASSAULT WEAPONS
BAN. LET'S DO AWAY WITH EXTENDED
BREAKING
NEWS
CT POLICE: 20 CHILDREN,
6 ADULTS KILLED AT SCHOOL

NEWSNATION TAMRON HALL LIVE   S&P ▲ 14.07   LEAN FORWARD
NRA-BACKED LAWMAKERS PROMISING
TO PUSH
ELEMENTARY SCHOOL TRAGEDY
DEMOCRATS LEADING PUSH FOR NEW GUN LAWS
DENVERPOST: Yesterday, Newtown began the sorrowful task of burying the young victims of last week's slaughter:

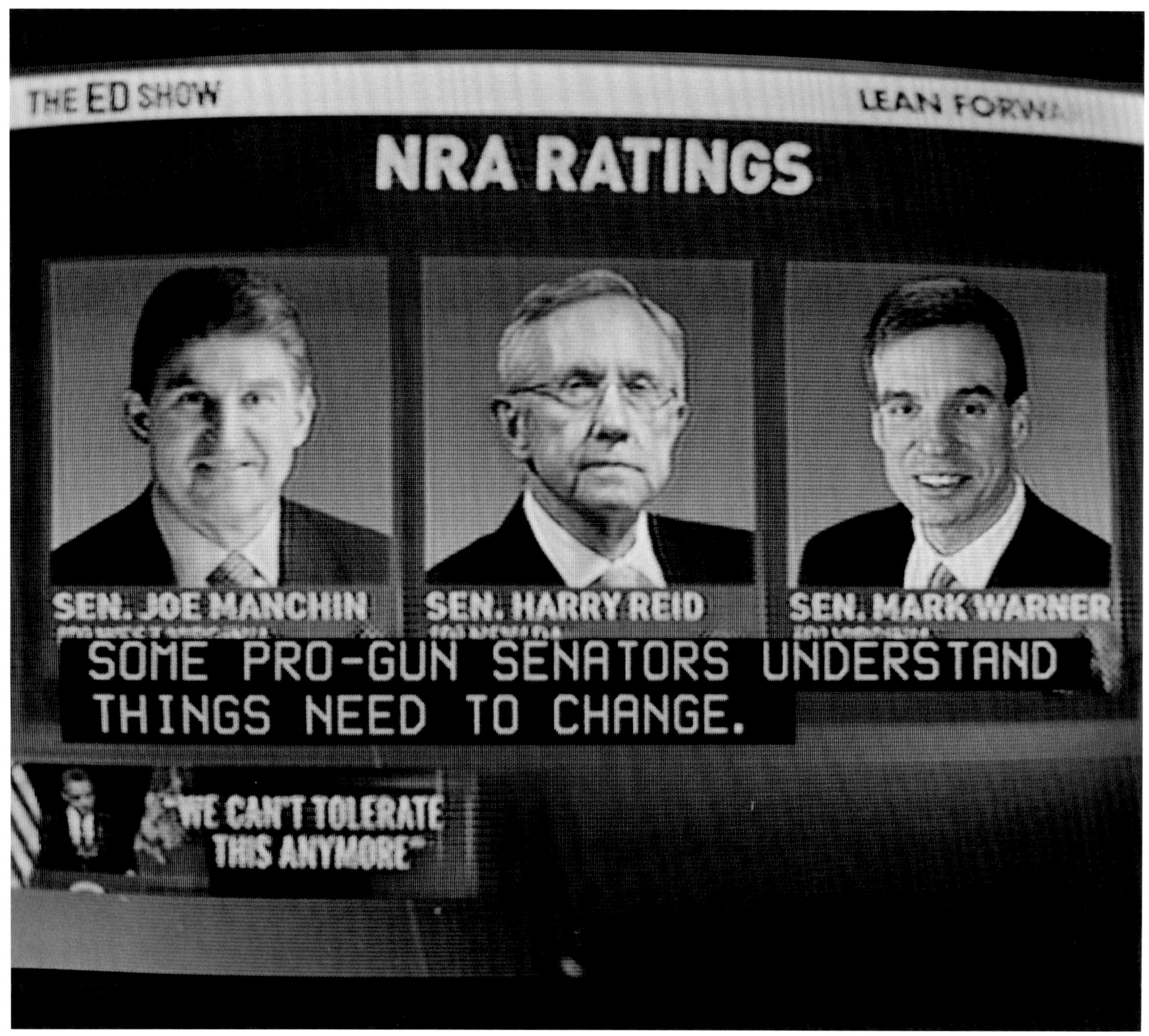
THE ED SHOW
LEAN FORWARD
NRA RATINGS
SEN. JOE MANCHIN
SEN. HARRY REID
SEN. MARK WARNER
SOME PRO-GUN SENATORS UNDERSTAND
THINGS NEED TO CHANGE.
"WE CAN'T TOLERATE
THIS ANYMORE"

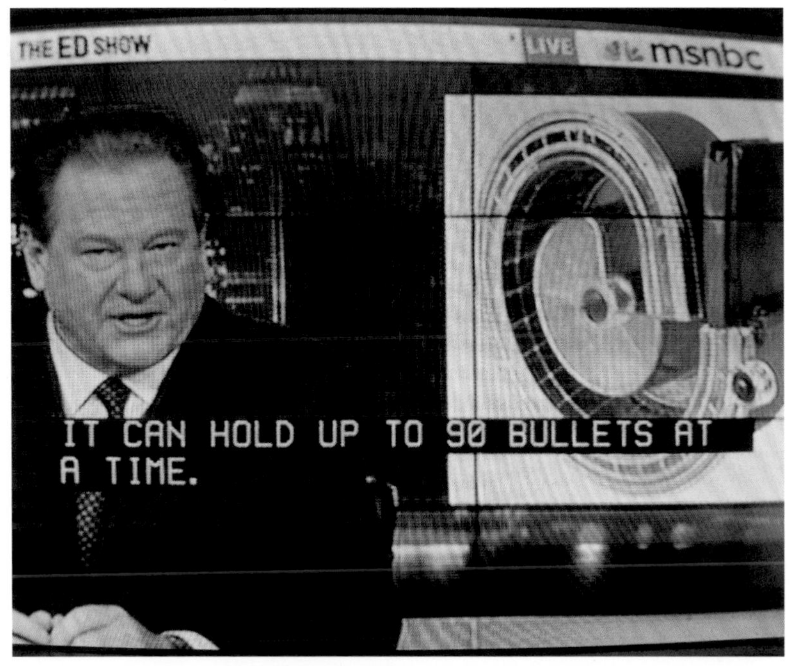
THE ED SHOW
LIVE
msnbc
IT CAN HOLD UP TO 90 BULLETS AT
A TIME.

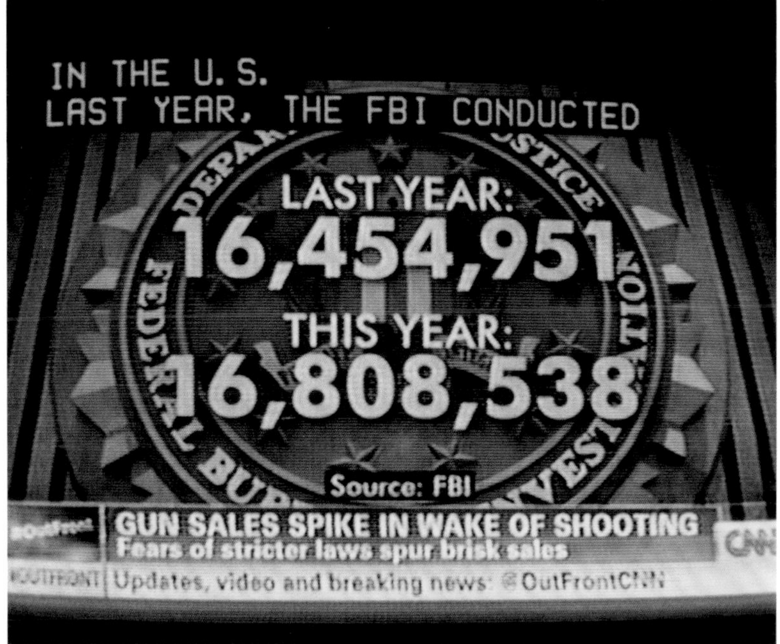
IN THE U.S.
LAST YEAR, THE FBI CONDUCTED
LAST YEAR:
16,454,951
THIS YEAR:
16,808,538
Source: FBI
GUN SALES SPIKE IN WAKE OF SHOOTING
Fears of stricter laws spur brisk sales
CNN
Updates, video and breaking news: @OutFrontCNN

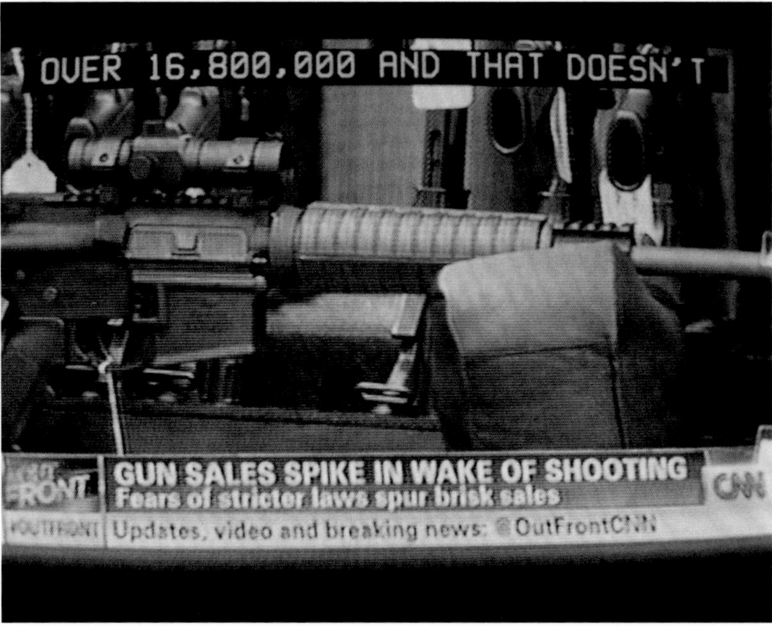
OVER 16,800,000 AND THAT DOESN'T
GUN SALES SPIKE IN WAKE OF SHOOTING
Fears of stricter laws spur brisk sales
CNN
Updates, video and breaking news: @OutFrontCNN

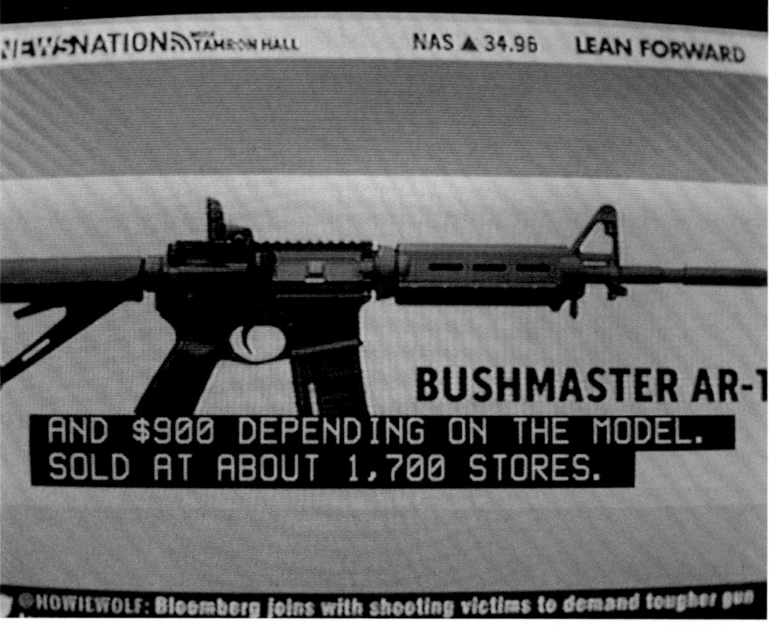
NEWSNATION TAMRON HALL
NAS 34.96
LEAN FORWARD
BUSHMASTER AR-1
AND $900 DEPENDING ON THE MODEL.
SOLD AT ABOUT 1,700 STORES.
HOWIEWOLF: Bloomberg joins with shooting victims to demand tougher gun

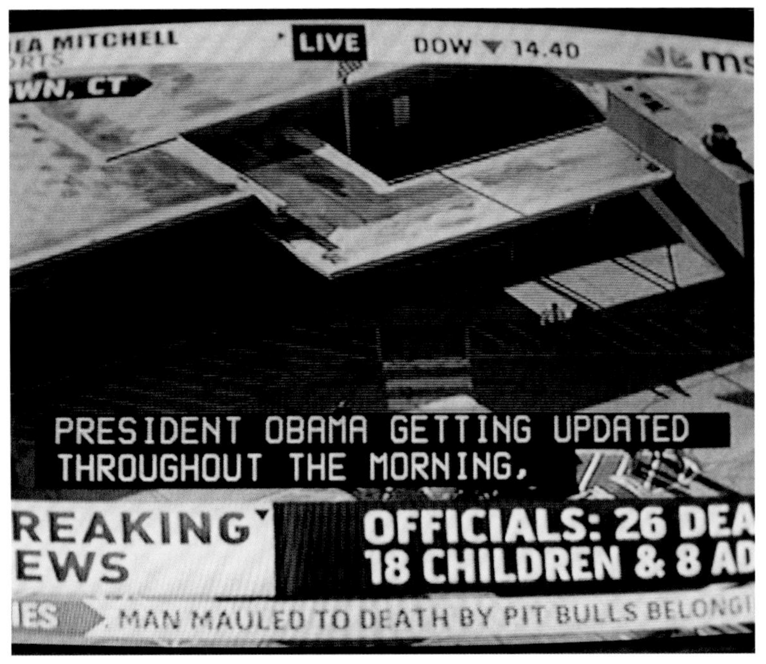
HA MITCHELL
ORTS
WN, CT
LIVE
DOW ▼ 14.40
msn
PRESIDENT OBAMA GETTING UPDATED
THROUGHOUT THE MORNING,
REAKING
EWS
OFFICIALS: 26 DEA
18 CHILDREN & 8 AD
ES
MAN MAULED TO DEATH BY PIT BULLS BELONGI

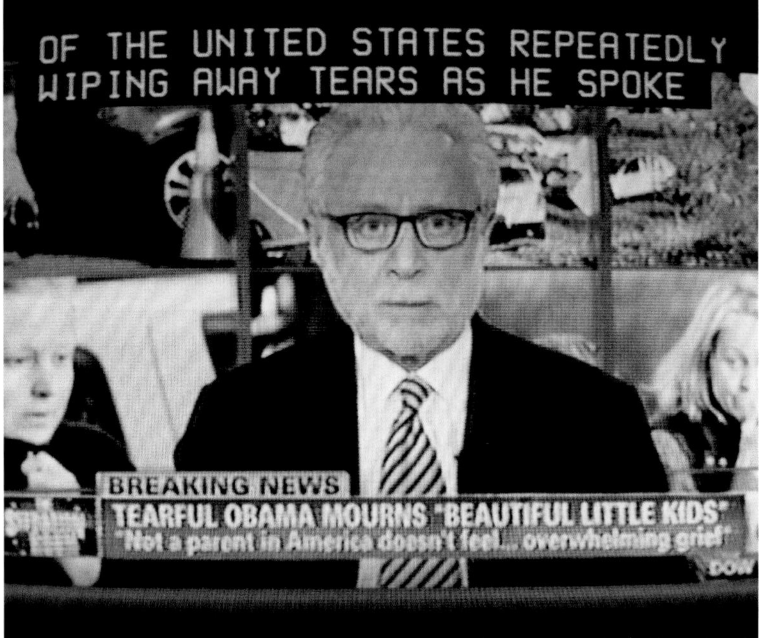
OF THE UNITED STATES REPEATEDLY
WIPING AWAY TEARS AS HE SPOKE
BREAKING NEWS
TEARFUL OBAMA MOURNS "BEAUTIFUL LITTLE KIDS"
"Not a parent in America doesn't feel... overwhelming grief"

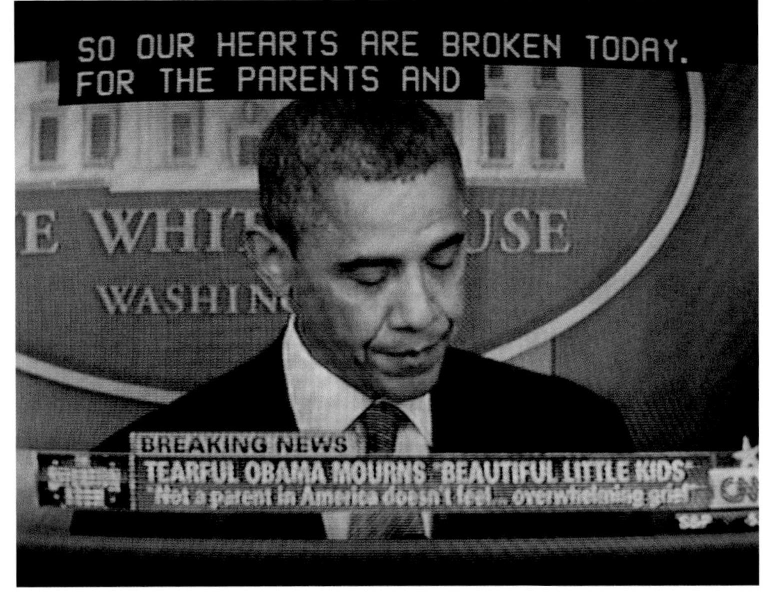
SO OUR HEARTS ARE BROKEN TODAY.
FOR THE PARENTS AND
THE WHITE HOUSE
WASHING
BREAKING NEWS
TEARFUL OBAMA MOURNS "BEAUTIFUL LITTLE KIDS"
"Not a parent in America doesn't feel... overwhelming grief"

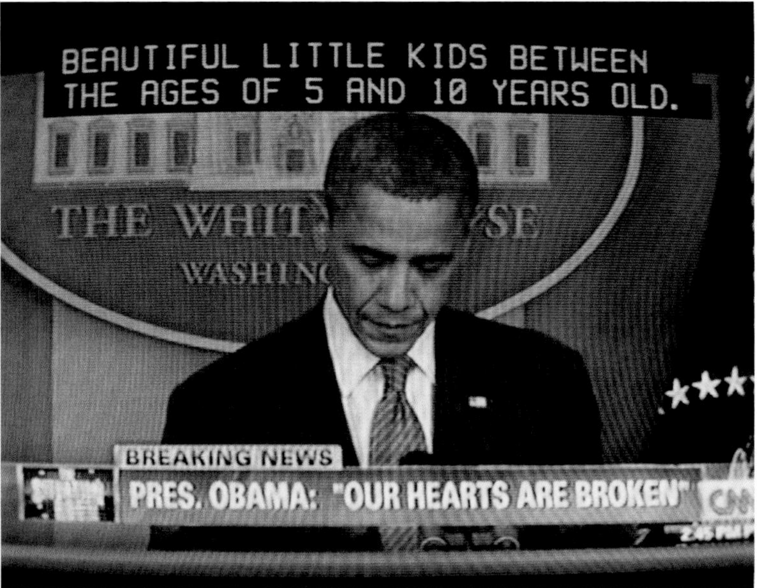
BEAUTIFUL LITTLE KIDS BETWEEN
THE AGES OF 5 AND 10 YEARS OLD.
THE WHITE HOUSE
WASHING
BREAKING NEWS
PRES. OBAMA: "OUR HEARTS ARE BROKEN"

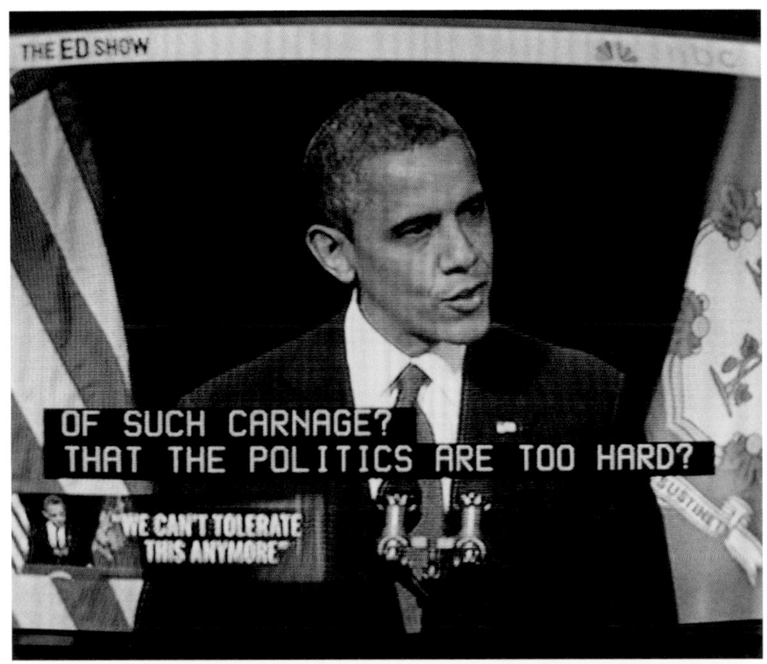

THE ED SHOW
nbc
OF SUCH CARNAGE?
THAT THE POLITICS ARE TOO HARD?
"WE CAN'T TOLERATE THIS ANYMORE"

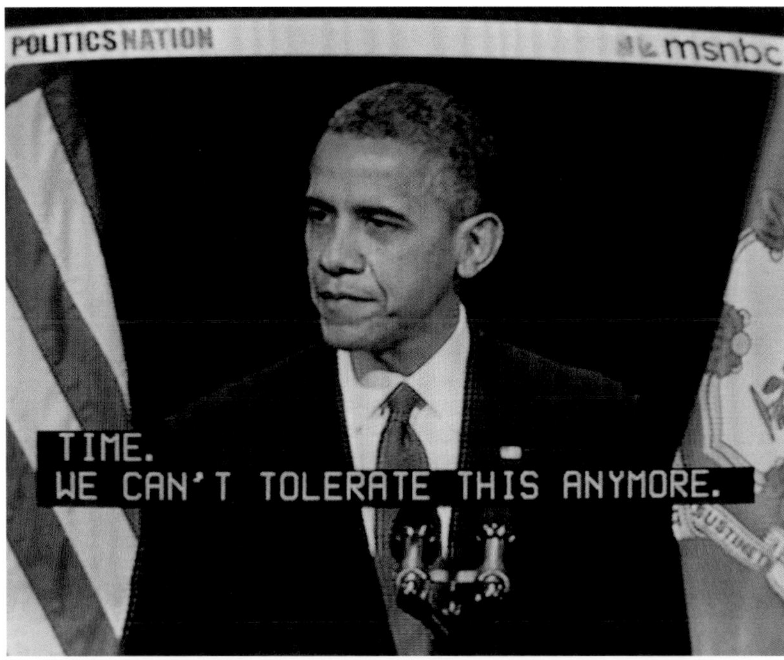

POLITICS NATION
msnbc
TIME.
WE CAN'T TOLERATE THIS ANYMORE.

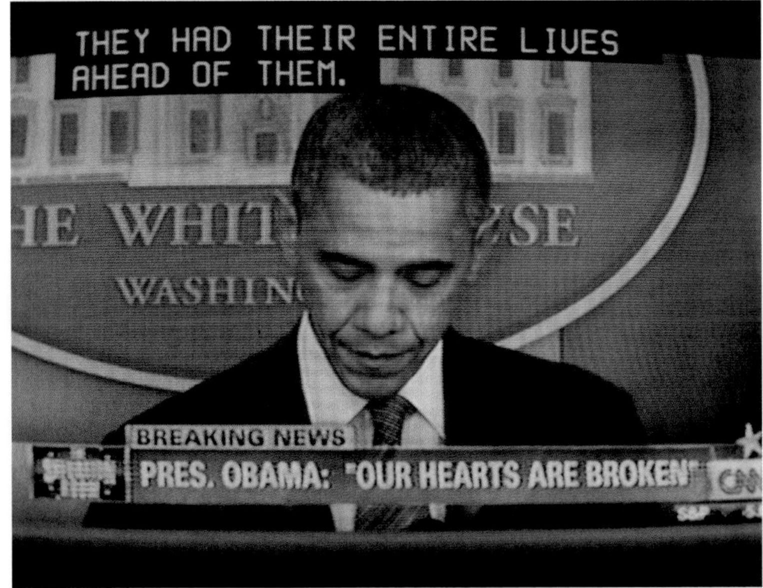

THEY HAD THEIR ENTIRE LIVES
AHEAD OF THEM.
THE WHITE HOUSE
WASHING
BREAKING NEWS
PRES. OBAMA: "OUR HEARTS ARE BROKEN"

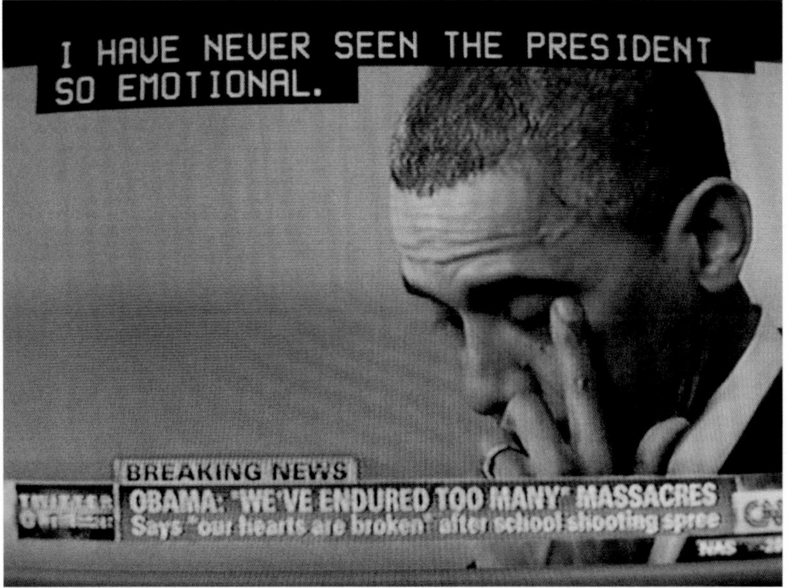

I HAVE NEVER SEEN THE PRESIDENT
SO EMOTIONAL.
BREAKING NEWS
OBAMA: "WE'VE ENDURED TOO MANY" MASSACRES
Says "our hearts are broken" after school shooting spree

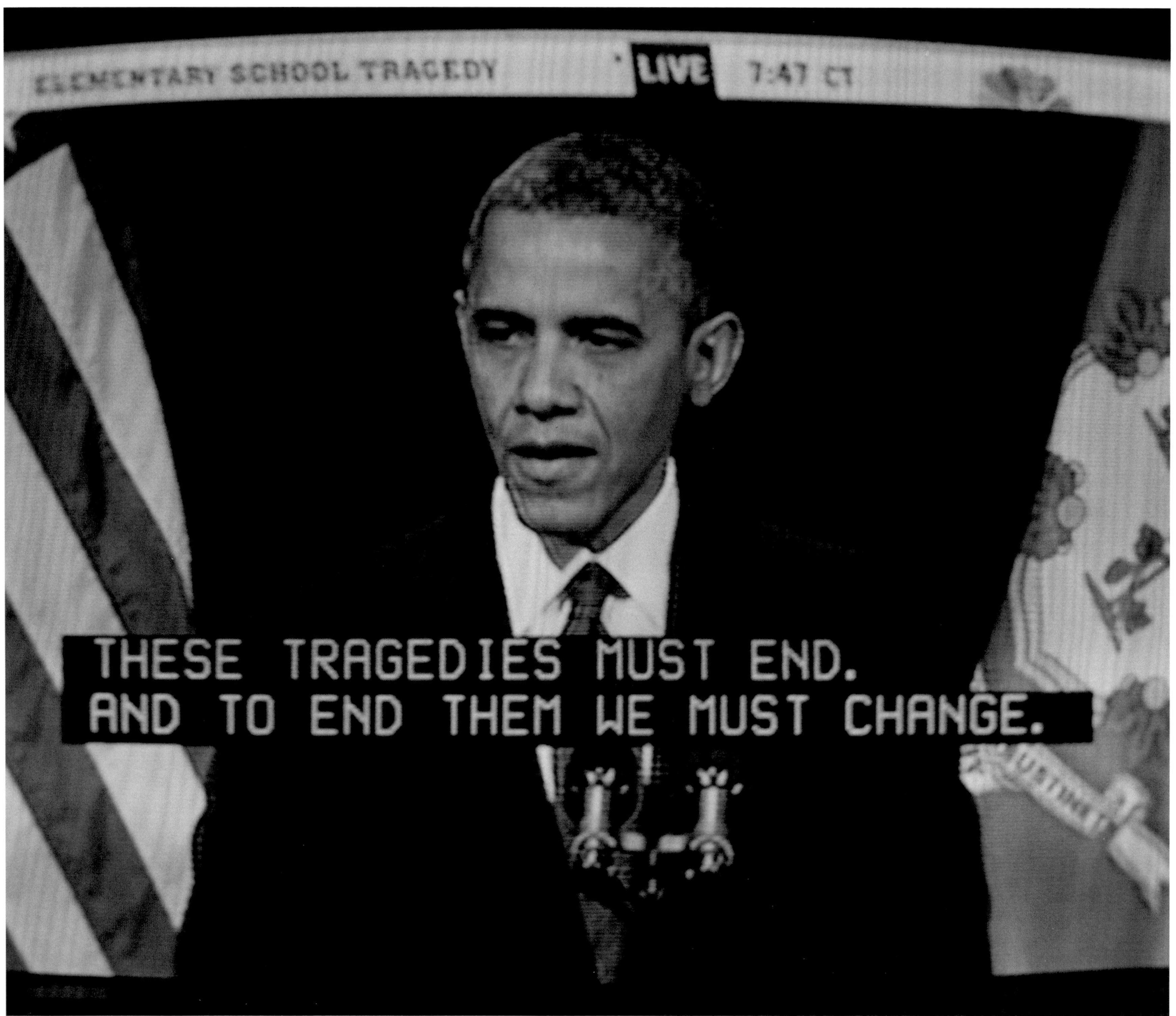

ELEMENTARY SCHOOL TRAGEDY
LIVE
7:47 CT
THESE TRAGEDIES MUST END.
AND TO END THEM WE MUST CHANGE.

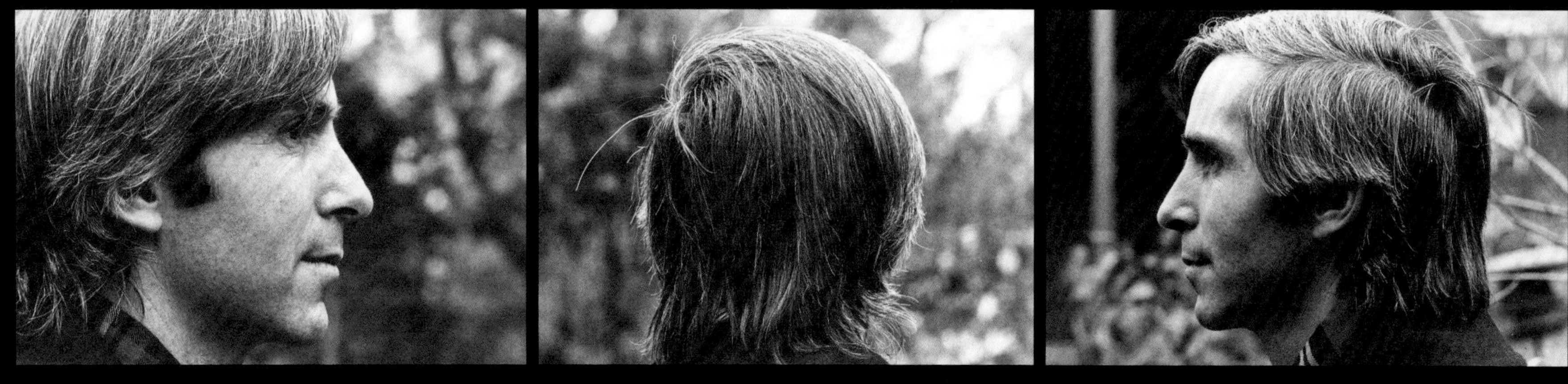

HOW I BECAME A PHOTOGRAPHER

Donald Blumberg

I flung words in fans like those the sower throws over the ploughed field when the earth is bare.
—Virginia Woolf, *The Waves*

As a photographer, I have always hoped to render photography with the same elegance and beauty as a well-turned Virginia Woolf sentence. Just a few of her laced-together words engender such sensuous, physiological pleasure. There is a mysterious process associated with the conveyance of style from one art form to another. How does a written sentence or paragraph impact the development and execution of a photographic concept? I am not talking about the direct translation of words into pictures, but rather the expression of the essence of words into the essence of a photograph.

I have never been very successful at doing anything other than making photographs. I am essentially a semirecluse and have always suffered from situational panic disorder. So working alone with a camera, and developing and printing photographs in the complete isolation of a darkroom, has very well suited me. The slow singular steps required to make a black-and-white photograph have turned my emotional deficits into assets and assisted me in developing deep powers of concentration. I have always worked from a conceptual base, formulating a project and working at it until all its parameters are resolved. One completed project has suggested the possibility of others, and so the sequence of renewed photographic ideas has been generated over the years.

I enjoy the play between negative and positive images and photography's dependence on additive and subtractive light. The process is fugal: first, the camera transmits and restricts light-fall upon the negative; then, the negative repeats the process of exposing and withholding light upon the light-sensitive photographic paper. The process is also a constant sequence of reversals. The more transmitted light, the darker the final image; the more subtracted light, the brighter the image. The intensity and richness of photographic black and white and the subtleness of grayscale tonality do not exist in any other art form. Sharpness is formed at the edges where blacks and whites collide. The frame functionally includes and excludes objects, informing the viewer of images within and implying those exterior to the picture frame.

I have photographed the horizon line where the sea meets the sky, standing on the shore in Santa Monica; in western Sicily; and high above the Adriatic from a cliffside on Italy's Gargano Promontory. To me, in my most extravagant thoughts, nature's horizon line is the progenitor of all abstract art. One can visually place the line at the center of the panorama and create two quadrants of equal dimensions. Raising or lowering the eyes divides the visual field into a series of quadrants and spaces of variable sizes. Josef Albers, Ellsworth Kelly, Richard Diebenkorn, Cy Twombly, Jules Olitski, Helen Frankenthaler, and other field painters borrowed in a variety of ways the horizon line found in nature.

My initial interest in photography came soon after World War II ended, when I bought a packet of bubble gum that also contained a sheet of photographic sun-print paper and instructions saying that if you lay a leaf or other object on the paper and place them in the sun, you could make a photograph. And somewhat to my surprise, I ended up with a sepia-toned photogram that lasted for several months and then just faded away. I eventually had a collection of several dozen such images, which over time also vanished.

In 1955 I volunteered for the draft and was stationed in Germany. A local German photographer and his wife were teaching photography at the enlisted-men's club. I bought a Rolleiflex and then a Leica IIIF and made several hundred negatives and many prints. It passed the time and was a great source of pleasure.

I was discharged from the army in January 1957. I had applied to the Cornell University School of Agriculture and was accepted as a transfer student from Hunter College, where I had earlier completed two years of undergraduate work. There was a practicum requirement, and I was placed on a twenty-acre dairy-crop farm fifteen miles north of Ithaca, New York. Eventually, though, I decided to give up the idea of becoming a farmer, majoring instead in biology with minors in ornithology and entomology. Sometime during that year, while studying on campus in a place called "the music room," I met Grace Ganz. We became friends and were married two years later when I graduated. Grace was nineteen and I was twenty-four. That was over fifty-five years ago, and we are still together.

In 1961, the summer after I received my master's degree in biology from the University of Colorado, Boulder, but before I entered the PH.D. program in entomology, Grace and I decided to travel to Europe. We flew from New York to Limerick, Ireland, and made a rough overnight crossing to England. London was the beginning of a grand museum, architectural, and cultural tour that would take us to Spain, France, and Italy. Unbeknownst to me, this was the beginning of my photographic education. In 1961 museums were essentially empty. We could spend hours wandering through a single gallery, returning time after time to a painting or group of paintings by a particular artist. I was transfixed by the rendering of light in the Turners at the Tate, Florentine portraiture, composite religious altarpieces, and the transition from Byzantine to Renaissance painting. The harmonious relationship between architecture and the religious mosaics at San Vitale and the regional monasteries in Ravenna remain significant and influential images to this day. In Paris, we wandered with art-historical continuity from cathedral to museum. Images of Notre-Dame worked their way into my photography many years later. We traveled by train to see the curvilinear Gaudí architecture in Barcelona. We moved north along the Costa del Sol to Provence, spending time at the Picasso pottery museum and the Matisse Chapel. Matisse's black strokes floated in the chapel's diffuse gray scale of Mediterranean light and taught me the elegance of minimalism.

Shortly after we returned to the States, we abandoned our graduate studies and I decided to become a photographer. We moved back to New York. Grace recalled that a high-school classmate of hers, Larry Fink, was working professionally as a freelance photographer. Larry was generous, responding positively to the work I had done in Germany. I became his student, learning darkroom technique by watching him develop and print his work. He critiqued the photographs I began to make, supervised my printing, and allowed me full access to his darkroom when he was not doing his own work. Larry recommended the single-lens reflex camera for working on composition. I bought a used Exakta and eventually two new Nikon F cameras. I still use the Nikons today, along with a variety of other through-the-lens viewing cameras. I especially enjoy the extension of the mind's eye and unimpeded framing that these cameras provide. I have found even a between-the-lens light meter unnecessarily distracting when composing an image.

I photographed almost every day. I made it a practice not to look at the work of other photographers so that what I was doing appeared to me to be new discovery. I slowly began to make images that, in retrospect, paralleled major themes in the history of photography. When I was not photographing, I was developing and printing negatives.

I decided to photographically explore Mexico. We folded down the back seat of an old Ford station wagon, fitted the space with a mattress, and drove off toward New Orleans. I photographed French colonial architecture and the marching jazz bands. We crossed Texas, entered Mexico, and slowly drove as far south as Oaxaca. I began to feel comfortable photographing people and found myself less tentative about establishing relationships between the figure, gesture, and environment. Certain compositional elements, such as people waiting for buses, market scenes, and farmers entering and leaving the fields, tended to repeat themselves and offered opportunities to rework and refine an image. The intense Mexican sun cast deep baroque shadows within the environment and on people wearing protective clothing. Figures would simultaneously project brilliant reflected light from their white garments while their faces were cast into intense blackness beneath protective hats and shawls.

Sometime during the winter of 1962, Grace and I returned to New York and moved into a four-room Lower East Side apartment, an old law tenement on the corner of Avenue C and Ninth Street. I got a part-time instructor's job teaching biology at Brooklyn College. Grace got a job at night as the manager of an art-film cinema in Queens and began to study filmmaking at the City College of New York. The idea of making intimate, low-budget 16-millimeter films particularly interested her.

I built a darkroom in the apartment and made photographs almost every day. I enjoyed following the sun as it coursed east to west around Lower Manhattan on a bright winter day. I began to be able to read reflected light in terms of how it would render photographically. I found myself making suites of photographs dealing with different light, tonal, and textural values.

We began to watch classic films at the Museum of Modern Art and experienced the explosive international film movement of the sixties. The films of Truffaut, Godard, Varda, Fellini, Antonioni, De Sica, and Kurosawa generated filmgoers who were soon to become the audiences for the New American Cinema shown in the Charles Theatre on the corner of Avenue B and Fourteenth Street, a few blocks away from our apartment. Jonas Mekas, a reporter for the *Village Voice*, became the spokesperson for the movement and one of the major underground filmmakers of the period. Robert Frank, who had recently published *The Americans*, was moving into filmmaking. Within a relatively short period of time, he made *Pull My Daisy* (1959), *O.K. End Here* (1963), and *Me and My Brother* (1965–68). Grace and I bought a 16-millimeter Bolex and basic editing equipment. We planned a trip to Denmark, Norway, and Sweden, with a detour to Hamburg, Germany, to buy some additional equipment. Grace made *Have You Been to Hamburg Lately* (1964), an impressionistic film about the city and its people. The following year, in 1963, I had my first one-man show at Camera Infinity Gallery on Second Avenue.

By the early sixties, the Lower East Side below Tompkins Square Park had changed from a turn-of-the-nineteenth-century Jewish ghetto into a mid-twentieth-century black and Puerto Rican ghetto. The streets were always busy with people going out to eat and buying *cuchifritos* take-out from storefronts with window displays of pigs' tails, knuckles, heads, and innards, all deep-fried in a brilliant yellow-orange flour batter. Music blasted from boom boxes cradled in the arms of young men, and the sweet sound of Spanish-language Pentecostal church singers accompanied by tambourines filled the streets.

In December 1963, Hospital Workers Union 1199 was on strike, demanding higher wages, improved working conditions, and greater influence over management. A block between Madison and Fifth avenues was barricaded. The workers marched in an orderly picket line and, to monitor their activities, there was an unusually large number of police on foot and mounted on horses. A speakers' platform straddled the sidewalk and a portion of the street, and demonstrators were gathering and taking their seats.

Bayard Rustin, a skilled organizer and a master planner in the civil rights movement, took the podium and described the poor working conditions, low salaries, and goals of the strikers. Rustin introduced the first speaker, Norman Thomas, a Protestant minister, founding member of the American Civil Liberties Union, and longtime leader and spokesman for the Socialist Party of America. His presentation was both gentle and forceful. Thomas introduced the next speaker, the insurgent black Muslim leader Malcolm X. This explained the large police presence. Several nights earlier, Malcolm had been interviewed on New York Public Radio and had delivered his virulent antiwhite "the chickens will come home to roost" speech, which had caused outrage in the white community and received negative coverage in the media. Malcolm was to be assassinated two years later, in 1965. A dynamic speaker, he animated his talk with body gestures, tilting his head and raising his fist to the level of his eyeglasses, with the index finger of his right hand pointing directly at the audience. I had photographed all of the day's events and was packing away my cameras when I was approached by a middle-aged man who identified himself as an organizer for District 65, the department store and retail-workers' union. He was interested in seeing the images I had made, gave me his card, and said his name was Samuel.

I developed the 35-millimeter negatives, made contact sheets, and printed a sequence of twenty 11 × 14–inch images summarizing the events of the day. I called Sammy and made an appointment to show him the work. District 65 operated out of a twenty-story building occupying the better part of a city block on the west side of Tompkins Square Park. Sammy had a large office on the top floor, with views of Greenwich Village and the Hudson River. He introduced me to Robert, a successful commercial-exhibit designer for venues such as Grand Central Station and Rockefeller Center. Robert did volunteer work for the union. His job was to produce a publication documenting all union activities, and he needed a photographer. I showed Sammy and Robert my 1199 demonstration portfolio, and they offered me the job—my first job as a commercial photographer.

I photographed the enrollment of new District 65 union members, the plight of those seeking workers' compensation or health benefits, and many social events fostering union solidarity. A constant stream of civil rights leaders visited and spoke at the union. I photographed A. Philip Randolph, longtime head of the Brotherhood of Sleeping Car Porters, the first all-black union accepted for membership in the American Federation of Labor in 1937. Randolph was the principal organizer of the 1963 March on Washington. Ralph Abernathy, head of the Southern Christian Leadership Conference and organizer of the Montgomery Boycott, arrested seventeen times with Martin Luther King, Jr., frequently visited District 65.

I also photographed Martin Luther King, Jr. Mayor Robert Wagner had organized a massive rally and demonstration in Madison Square Garden. Ruby Dee and Ossie Davis were the comasters of ceremonies. They first presented Leon Bibb, the popular black singer and political activist. Then Mayor Wagner introduced King as the keynote speaker. Union members from all over the city roared with welcoming approval. King fused the goals of the American union movement with those of his civil rights movement. His talk was similar in content to his *I Have a Dream* speech.

Through Robert at District 65, I was put in touch with John Graham, an art director for NBC, and was hired to photograph the game shows *Say When*, with Art James, and *Concentration*, with Hugh Downs, as well as the *Today Show*, also hosted by Hugh Downs. Downs's guests included actor Peter O'Toole, promoting his just-released *Lawrence of Arabia*, and Martin Luther King, Jr., explaining his goals for the civil rights movement. Johnny Carson had just been hired to host the *Tonight Show*. One of the on-set Johnny Carson photographs I took, used to advertise his new show, was published on the full back page of the *New York Times*.

Meanwhile, District 65 was seeking volunteers to join a Freedom Ride to Westminster, Maryland, followed by a sit-in at a segregated lunch counter. Sammy asked me if I would be willing to join the demonstration and photograph the event. Earlier, when Grace and I were graduate students at the University of Colorado, we walked in a picket line in front of the local Woolworth's to protest their then-segregated lunch counters in the South. I remembered feeling awkwardly self-conscious as a demonstrator, but our efforts, among those of many others, placed economic pressure on Woolworth's, and they reversed their policy. So I agreed to go on the Freedom Ride. As I was photographing the volunteers preparing to board the buses, two young men about my age arrived with cameras hanging from their necks. Bruce Davidson was a well-established reportage photographer, and Bob Adelman had been an assistant to President John F. Kennedy's personal White House photographer. When we arrived in Westminster, a large crowd had already gathered under the surveillance of local and state police. There was a lot of shouting and pushing as we left the bus, entered, and lined the back wall of the drugstore lunch counter. Each departing customer was replaced with a demonstrator until the entire lunch counter was lined with Freedom Riders. Davidson and Adelman were already making photographs, while I was paralyzed by the predicament of whether I was there as a photographer or civil rights protester. I waited my turn to sit at the counter and never took my camera out of my bag.

During this period, there was an unusual amount of activity around Avenue B and Houston Street. A six-story tenement had been renovated and turned into office space. A long-shuttered garage and gas station reopened, freshly painted white, with a Mobilization for Youth (MFY) banner flying from the corner flagpole. A luncheonette with counter, stools, and vinyl booths was now open for business, with local young people as employees. Picketers carrying signs supporting improved housing and rent strikes peacefully marched in front of slumlord-owned tenements. Two Columbia University sociology professors, Frances Fox Piven and Richard Cloward, had received a multimillion dollar grant from President Lyndon B. Johnson's War on Poverty to implement their MFY program, designed to improve the lives of low-income groups living on the Lower East Side of New York City.

I had heard that program coordinators were looking to hire local residents with certain educational backgrounds as part-time employees. I arranged to see Sarah Penn, a Columbia University master of social work graduate who was in charge of hiring. She told me that they had plans for a neighborhood youth-socialization and safe-haven program called the Coffee Shop and that teaching photography to young neighborhood gang members was part of the program design. A two-story building just off the corner of Sixth Street and Avenue C had been rented as a space for the Coffee Shop. The first floor was completely cleared for meetings and social events. The second floor had several staff rooms and a space designated as a photographic darkroom and studio.

I was given a substantial budget and purchased two 35-millimeter Pentax K1000 cameras with built-in light meters and all the equipment necessary to operate a teaching darkroom. My first group of about ten students quickly learned how to make, process, and print black-and-white photographs. They were soon out in the street photographing their friends and neighbors.

A small bandstand was built on the first floor of the Coffee Shop Program's building, and Friday night "socials" and dances were organized. The dance floor was often filled, especially with slow dancers—intimate couples and pairs having just met for the first time. The dancers were illuminated by recessed cone lighting, which cast cylinders of light on the dancers, who would dissolve into darkness as they passed from beneath the baroque light source. My students liked to photograph their friends at these events. The off-kilter hand-held camera captured heads, arms, and other body parts truncated in space, illuminated in the bright beams of light surrounded by blackness. I saw a unique photographic essence in these images and wondered if it could be reproduced and formalized in a different setting.

Mobilization for Youth was organizing the Lower East Side for the March on Washington for Jobs and Freedom in August 1963. We were to meet on Houston Street, where rented buses would take us to Pennsylvania Station for an early morning train ride to Washington, D.C. Grace and I were among hundreds of our neighbors who began to occupy railroad cars, joined by thousands of demonstrators from the five boroughs of New York City. It was an extraordinarily orderly, festive, and multiracial

event. We shared our car with a Spanish-language Pentecostal church group, which played music and sang for the entire journey.

In Washington, we exited from the railroad cars to platforms filled with demonstrators. The crowd thickened in waves of people from all over the country. We began a slow, orderly march toward the speakers' platform at the Washington Monument. As we approached the Mall reflecting pool, I could hear Peter, Paul, and Mary singing in the distance but could not see them. Likewise, Martin Luther King, Jr.'s speech rose above our heads, but the words were muffled, interrupted periodically by the approving roar of the crowed. The enormous number of participants and the scale and significance of the event were not apparent until we returned home and watched it unfold on television over and over again. The difference between what a march participant and a nonparticipant television viewer experienced was striking and verged on the surreal.

In the fall of 1965, Grace and I moved to Buffalo, where I had been appointed assistant professor of art at the State University of New York. There, I met another new faculty member, Charles Gill, a West Coast painter with a New York City gallery. Charlie and I became friends, and toward the end of the fall semester, when announcements were circulated for a campus-wide spring arts festival, we made a proposal for collaborative artwork involving

painting, drawing, collage, and photography. I was aware of Argenta Photo-Linen, pre-sensitized with a fine-grain emulsion that could take the application of acrylic paint in the same manner as artist's canvas. We were both aware of French painters who had used *cliché-verre* as a quick in-nature drawing technique executed on a glass plate, and we felt the process could bridge drawing, collage, and photography. The art department employed a young woman named Edwina as Charlie's classroom model. He told her about a "domestic nudes" idea we had discussed as part of our festival project and she agreed to be our paid model. The three of us discussed using a 4 × 5–inch view camera to make a series of black-and-white negatives in Charlie's apartment: Edwina on the velour sofa; Edwina watching television; Edwina cooking at the kitchen stove; and, at Edwina's suggestion, Edwina smoking a cigarette on the toilet.

We made all the negatives and developed them in one day. I made a set of contact prints, and Charlie and I selected the images that would be enlarged to 4 × 5 feet and printed on the recently arrived photo-linen. We bolted an enlarger onto an elevated table, taped a piece of linen on the floor, made a small test print, and then exposed our first 4 × 5–foot image. Developing a 4 × 5–foot piece of photo-linen in our largest available 16 × 20–inch tray was like doing laundry by hand in a bathroom sink. As soon as the stiff piece of linen hit the developer, it collapsed into the tray. Charlie and I massaged it until we thought it looked properly developed, then fixed it, washed it, and hung it up to dry in the studio on a clothesline, pins and all. We repeated the process until a set of eight nudes was printed. I was already working on my photographs of Saint Patrick's Cathedral; Charlie and I printed a series of five of these images from 35-millimeter negatives, enlarged to 4 × 5 feet. We also designed and executed seven 16 × 20–inch *cliché verre* prints, fusing drawing, collage, photography, paper transfers, and the written word.

The spring arts festival film screenings were scheduled at the Student Union movie theater for the same night as the opening of our exhibition. Charlie and I thought that we would leave the show open to catch the several hundred filmgoers who would pass by the gallery when they exited the theater. There had been a series of student anti–Vietnam War rallies both on and off campus in downtown Buffalo. At first, the on-campus demonstrations were monitored only by the campus police. Later, they were joined by heavily equipped Buffalo city riot police. There had always been a somewhat tense town-and-gown relationship between the originally private university and Buffalo residents. We did have a nice crowd of moviegoers visit the show and were about to close up for the evening when a large group of antiwar demonstrators began

to run down the corridor directly adjacent to the exhibit, followed by a flying wedge of riot police. The students were cornered on the stairwell, brutally beaten, clubbed with riot batons, and arrested. This was the beginning of a prolonged conflict among the police, students, faculty, and administration that eventually led to university President Martin Meyerson canceling all classes and declaring the State University of New York at Buffalo an "open campus." Informal classes replaced regularly scheduled formal for-credit classes, which were not reinstated for several months. The events radicalized me, and I soon began working on several series of photographs based on political activities and newsworthy events of the Vietnam War era, some of which are illustrated in the present publication.

I became interested in our black-and-white television set as a source of photographic subject matter. Manipulating the control dials, I was able to manufacture abstract forms and patterns. I found that I could extend the technique to include screen figures and newsworthy events. In 1968 I made a series of 4 × 5–inch negatives of the Martin Luther King, Jr., funeral. The reportorial images were abstract. I was interested in making one image that could encapsulate the entire funeral. I designed a single mosaic by ordering the 4 × 5–inch contact prints. I then conformed the twenty-five negatives to the mock-up and glued them onto a 20 × 24–inch piece of

glass. I had designed a *cliché-verre* negative plate that could simply be contact printed, as Charlie Gill and I had done in our earlier collaboration. The mosaic design was influenced by the Byzantine mosaics that I had so much admired on my trip with Grace to San Vitale in Ravenna.

I wanted to make more politically engaged photographs. I did mosaics of President Johnson's State of the Union address, President Richard Nixon introducing his cabinet, and presidential candidate George Wallace ranting. I also designed images by placing a preselected assortment of 35-millimeter negative strips in a 4 × 5–inch glass negative carrier, arranging them, often overlapping them, and projecting the image on the easel below. These, too, were images of the political characters of the day. More significantly, they dealt with the core black-and-white photographic principle of additive and subtractive light. Non-overlapping and overlapping negatives would transmit or withhold variable degrees of light, producing a full spectrum of gray scale in a single 20 × 24–inch print.

The idea of appropriating still photographs from a kinetic televised form led to my use of images from the *Buffalo Evening News*, which was delivered daily to our apartment. The newspaper was reporting on the war in Vietnam and antiwar demonstrations at home. These transient images were disturbingly powerful. I began clipping and rephotographing a selection to make 20 × 24–inch prints. I made over one hundred enlargements and edited them into a portfolio called *Twenty Daily Photographs, 1969–1970*. I also wanted *Daily Photographs* to exist in a less-precious form than fine-art photographs. So later, in 1971, I went to the university printing shop and had them print a 16 × 20–inch offset portfolio of the twenty images, in an edition of five hundred, packaged in a simple gray envelope with a single image and title printed on the outside. The plan was to distribute the offset portfolio at shopping malls and university events for cash donations to antiwar efforts. I wrote an introduction for the portfolio, which read:

These photographs were made in response to our government's genocidal acts in Vietnam and its brutality at home. It became apparent to me several years ago that as our society deteriorated, photographers as well as other visual artists would be confronted with the absurd luxury of their work. The traditional values of art, transcendent significance, beauty, the importance of basic creation and the integrity and historical continuity of the medium, collapse when reading and watching the daily news.

I wanted to make my work political, without metaphor, simile, sentimentality or heroics. I chose to transpose typography and images from daily newspapers, inherently direct political propaganda. They were small in format, visually transient. I wanted to fix them, inescapable in scale, for you to look at.

In May 1970 *Twenty Daily Photographs* was exhibited in the recently completed Visual Studies Workshop Gallery in Rochester, New York. I presented a gallery walkthrough and talk attended by students, workshop supporters, and guests. I briefly summarized how I had arrived at appropriating the newspaper images. I emphasized my interest in the antiwar nature of the pictures, the cropped and fragmented words as poetic form, and the graphic quality of the enlarged Ben Day dots and associated design forms separating paragraphs and other stories appearing on the same page. Photographer Aaron Siskind was in the audience and commented that he was impressed with the political nature of my work, but asked how I could use original newspaper images made by other photographers. This led to perhaps one of the earliest discussions, with audience participation, of the role of the appropriated image in contemporary photography. By now, after Robert Heinecken, Sherrie Levine, Andy Warhol, and Jeff Koons, this issue has long been resolved. The appropriation of images for use in fine-art photography is now aesthetically accepted and largely legally protected by the fair-use clause of federal copyright law.

In 1972 Grace returned to school, emerging with a law degree from Harvard University, and after leaving there, we again spent time living in Buffalo, where she was an assistant professor of law at SUNY, and in Los Angeles, where she was a visiting professor at the UCLA School of Law. I was offered a one-year distinguished visiting professorship in the art department at San Jose State University and, late in the summer of 1980, I interviewed for and became chairman of the fine arts department at the Otis Art Institute, in Los Angeles, where I developed a photography major.

Over the next decade, we traveled to France, Italy, Spain, England, Scotland, Wales, Ireland, Greece, and New Zealand. For the most part, I photographed cityscapes, landscapes, seascapes, and ancient monuments. I spent the winter months developing and printing material, mostly in the form of portfolios. I had my first show in Los Angeles in 1980 at the G. Ray Hawkins Gallery, and sometime later, the Jan Kesner Gallery became the West Coast representative of my work, exhibiting my photographs on a regular basis. I stopped teaching in 1990 and devoted myself to making photographs on a full-time basis.

The story of how I became a photographer was written from long-term and recent memory. It is essentially the tale of a working-class boy from Brooklyn who never expected much from life. A great deal of my life has been a surprise to me. Who would have thought that, as I approach my eightieth year, within my lifetime, the master sets of my photographs would enter the collection of the Yale University Art Gallery, where my photographic legacy may be permanently secured.